"Publica Carmina *brings together, for the first time, all of the important aspects of an interpretive and informative nature concerning this important segment of Ovid's work. The exile collection has long been that part of Ovid's poetry which has been most neglected by scholars; Evans's book is a welcome remedy.*"

Professor Karl Galinsky, University of Texas at Austin

Ovid, exiled by Augustus, spent his final years in Tomis, on the Black Sea in modern-day Romania, where he died in A.D. 17. From there he sent two major collections of poetry to Rome, the *Tristia* (five books) and *Epistulae ex Ponto* (four books), in which he presented his experiences and reactions to exile in a new genre of elegiac verse.

Publica Carmina: Ovid's Books from Exile is the first comprehensive study of this unique group of poems demonstrating how Ovid's poetic aims and image of himself changed during his last years. From beginning to end, Ovid wanted to return to Rome, to which he felt bound as artist and as man. Within that frame, however, the change in theme and tone from his first books to the last is striking and pathetic. Beginning as Rome's greatest poet, he skillfully turns the experience of his relegation into a witty presentation of himself in exile and clever pleas for the suspension of his punishment. Ultimately he comes to realize that his exile may be permanent, declares that his poetic gifts are waning, appears to adjust as an émigré among the Getes—and becomes more direct and plangent in his pleas for return.

Harry B. Evans studies the individual poems, themes, and techniques to demonstrate the structural coherence and development of Ovid's books and to elucidate the richness and variety found in them. In thorough coverage of American and European scholarship, he surveys the extant research and offers conclusions that will provoke debate and stimulate new discussions of Ovid's achievement.

Easily accessible to the nonclassicist, this book will be invaluable to students and scholars of the classics, comparative literature, and aesthetics, and to the reader interested in the art and literature of exile.

Harry B. Evans is an associate professor of classics at Fordham University and the author of articles on Ovid, Horace, and Roman topography.

University of Nebraska Press   *Lincoln and London*

PUBLICA
CARMINA

OVID'S BOOKS FROM EXILE

Harry B. Evans

W|M

Publication of this book was aided by a grant
from the Andrew W. Mellon Foundation.
Library of Congress Cataloging in Publication Data
Evans, Harry B.
Publica carmina.
Includes bibliographical references and index.
1. Ovid, 43 B.C.-17 or 18—Criticism and interpre-
tation.   I. Title.
PA6537.E9   1983   874'.01   82-10899
ISBN 0-8032-1806-0

For Brooks Otis

in memoriam

CONTENTS

ACKNOWLEDGMENTS

I WISH TO THANK the Office of Research and Sponsored Programs of Wayne State University and the American Council of Learned Societies for financial support which made possible my preliminary research and writing.

My debts to others for assistance, both scholarly and personal, are many and varied. Brooks Otis, to whom this book is dedicated, directed my doctoral dissertation on the *Tristia* and *Epistulae ex Ponto*. Others have read and commented on my work at different stages and periods. I am especially grateful to Lawrence Richardson, jr., who first suggested the exile poetry to me as a fruitful area of study, to G. Karl Galinsky, a mentor most helpful in things Ovidian, to Berthe M. Marti, George Kennedy, and B. R. Nagle for their comments and suggestions. But none of these can be blamed for whatever errors remain. To make this point more aptly, I might borrow from Ovid himself:

siqua meo fuerint, ut erunt, vitiosa libello,
   non illis, lector, culpa sed ista mihi.

ABBREVIATIONS

Am.	*Amores*
Ars	*Ars amatoria*
Fast.	*Fasti*
Her.	*Heroides*
Met.	*Metamorphoses*
P.	*Epistulae ex Ponto*
Rem. am.	*Remedia amoris*
Tr.	*Tristia*

"at mala sunt." fateor. quis te mala sumere cogit?

*"But they're bad poems." I admit it. Who is forcing
you to read bad poetry?*

INTRODUCTION

M ANY READERS HAVE accepted Ovid's condemnation of his
books from exile (*Tr.* 5.1.69); indeed, very few Latin students are
expected to read them. Except for a few famous poems, such as Ovid's
autobiography (*Tr.* 4.10), his account of his last night in Rome (*Tr.* 1.3),
and his description of winter in Tomis (*Tr.* 3.10), the elegies from exile
rarely find their way into school anthologies or reading lists. Scholarly
interest in the exile poetry has been largely concerned, not with the
poems themselves, but with the autobiographical information they
present, the chronology of their publication, and the prosopography of
Ovid's addressees.

This is unfortunate. Although the last few years have seen increased
interest in Ovid, sparked by Hermann Fränkel's Sather Lectures and
encouraged by L. P. Wilkinson's study of the poet, as well as by the
burst of bimillennial scholarship in the late 1950s, serious literary
criticism of the *Tristia* and *Epistulae ex Ponto* remains an area aptly
described as "one of the last frontiers of classical scholarship."[1] Only
quite recently have Latinists begun to read the exile poetry as poetry.

Modern classical studies have thrown new light on this much
neglected body of Augustan literature. A. G. Lee began with a sensitive

reading of one poem, *Tr.* 3.8. Yves Bouynot provided a general literary assessment of the *Tristia,* with many observations on individual passages. In an important article E. J. Kenney argued that the poems from exile should be read as "poetic experiments" in which Ovid reworks literary conventions to present in verse his own experiences in exile. In his study of Ovidian humor Jean-Marc Frécaut made many observations on the exile poetry, especially *Tr.* 4.10. Hartmut Froesch has contributed a general discussion of the poems, together with a survey of their influence on later writers. John Barsby's review of modern Ovidian scholarship includes a general discussion of this poetry. In addition, we now have a new critical edition of the *Tristia* with commentary by Georg Luck; an historical assessment of the exile poetry, particularly the *Epistulae ex Ponto,* by Sir Ronald Syme; and, most recently, an extremely valuable study of the poetics, or Ovid's rationale for his poetry from exile, by B. R. Nagle, who has also given us a thoughtful analysis of Ovid's poetic autobiography, *Tr.* 4.10. Mary Thomsen Davisson has discussed several elegies in detail, particularly *P.* 2.7, 3.1, and 4.10.[2]

In view of all this scholarly activity, why another study of the exile poetry? Previous scholarship has been mainly concerned with individual poems from exile or Ovid's use of poetic themes in particular passages. Nagle's monograph is broader in scope, focusing, not on single poems, but on Ovid's defense and justification of his writings from Tomis throughout the books. Her study, however, treats only one of Ovid's themes, and her method, as she herself acknowledges, is synchronic, not primarily concerned with how Ovid's poetics changes over time.[3] Little or no attention has yet been paid to the corpus of exile poetry as a whole.

Much work therefore remains to be done, particularly in assessing the books which Ovid published from Tomis. The main purpose of the present study is to consider the entire block of the exile poetry diachronically, as Ovid published it, as a series of individual poetic collections which appeared over the eight-year period of his relegation. Only by examining the development of Ovid's collections can we understand what effect the experience of exile had on him. By studying the composition, arrangement, and themes of his individual books from exile we can contribute evidence on several important questions: Do the later books differ at all from the earlier ones? Does the long period of his relegation demonstrate a decline in Ovid's poetic skill? Does the poet as a poet change from year to year?

This diachronic examination is in many ways an overview and is not intended to be a comprehensive study of the exile poetry. Our debts to earlier literary criticism will be evident throughout. Yet it is also not merely a synthesis of what has already been done. Because Ovid's exile collections are one important aspect of this poetry which has been neglected, study of them is essential for establishing a framework for future examination of individual elegies and literary themes. In addition to the conclusions this work itself presents, it should be regarded as a prolegomenon for more detailed study to come.

Any survey of the *Tristia* and *Epistulae ex Ponto* immediately presents the problem of monotony of theme. Ovid's books from Tomis have been criticized and largely ignored by scholars because their content is held to be generally the same throughout. Critics have recognized, however, that Ovid is concerned with the problem of *variatio*: he attempts to vary his presentation of poetic themes whenever possible through the structural plan and arrangement of his books. In 1924 Karl Herrmann examined books 1, 3, 4, and 5 of the *Tristia* and proved that their poems were arranged, not chronologically (the thesis then prevalent), but in a deliberate artistic structure.[4] His treatment of the books was, however, cursory, and paid little attention to their subject matter.

In 1967 Hartmut Froesch analyzed Ovid's arrangement of *P.* 1–3 as a unified poetic collection, comparing it to other Augustan poetic books. Yet his study was confined to this single collection and did not relate it to other books from exile. A few years later, R. J. Dickinson contributed a general survey of the *Tristia,* arguing that the books are individual entities, not a homogeneous block of poetry.[5] Although he made good observations on individual elegies, particularly *Tr.* 1.2 and 1.4, his treatment of individual books and their arrangement was limited. There remained a need for a more comprehensive examination of these poetic collections.

Our discussion of their background can be brief. There is no need to review the many hypotheses put forward during the last fifteen hundred years concerning the reason for Ovid's sudden relegation to Tomis in A.D. 8.[6] Attempts have been made to link the exile with that of the younger Julia, granddaughter of the emperor, in the same year. No better hypothesis has yet been advanced to explain Augustus's sudden demonstration of anger. The punishment which he imposed was severe—relegation to the farthest corner of the Roman world, to a frontier outpost and garrison town. Ovid had to leave Italy at once, even during the winter months (*Tr.* 1.3.5–6, 1.11.1–4). Once he had departed, however, he seems to have been under no obligation to reach Tomis immediately; his voyage to Pontus included extended stays on Samothrace and elsewhere, and he does not appear to have arrived at Tomis before autumn in A.D. 9.[7]

The poet states many times that he committed no actions prohibited by law, but only an *error* which he does not wish to discuss. The emperor too may have found the matter embarrassing and distasteful; Ovid's references to the *error* may well conceal a scandal of major proportions. Augustus never relented in his anger, nor did Tiberius reduce his sentence after he assumed the principate. The process by which Ovid was relegated is also a mystery. It may have been Augustus's exercise of a magistrate's *coercitio* resting on the *imperium* which he as *princeps* held inside the city. Or it may have been the emperor's demonstration of his displeasure toward Ovid, an act of *amicitiam renuntiare* similar to that given to Decimus Silanus in A.D. 8 for his adultery with Julia and also to Cornelius Gallus some thirty years earlier.[8] But the punishment which Ovid received appears severe in comparison with that of Gallus for what were treasonable acts, and Silanus, who was eventually permitted by Tiberius to return to Rome.

Because Ovid was never recalled, his relegation may have been, in part, a voluntary act. Augustus may have offered him this punishment in return for his life or in place of an official *exilium,* which would have meant the loss of his citizenship and property in Rome, privileges to which Ovid himself alludes several times (*Tr.* 4.9.11–12, 5.2.56, 5.4.21–22; *P.* 1.7.47–48). The poet may have accepted *relegatio* in place of a punishment much more severe. Without realizing conditions in Tomis, he may have agreed to relegation as the mildest punishment he could receive given the circumstances surrounding his offense. This may explain his reluctance to reveal his *error*; the poet's silence may have been one condition imposed by Augustus in allowing him to keep his citizenship and property.

So much for the relegation itself, a subject which has captured the attention of scholars for much too long. Despite its fascination, without more evidence we shall never learn the exact nature of Ovid's offense. What should concern us before examining his books from Tomis is, not the background and events leading to his departure—an investigation which would be fruitless—but the literary climate in Rome at the time of the relegation.

Sources for the literary scene in late-Augustan Rome are sketchy.

Standard histories of Latin literature provide us with lists of writers during the period, many of whom are little more than names. Yet their number attests to the vitality of Rome's literary society during the last years of the Augustan principate: the literary circles and interest which had flourished during the time of Virgil and Horace continued in the years which followed. Although Maecenas, center of the circle of which Horace and Virgil were members, died in 8 B.C., Messalla Corvinus, patron of Tibullus, Propertius, and Ovid, lived on until A.D. 8.[9] Messalla was not only a patron of the arts but also wrote erotic poetry and bucolics in Greek (Pliny *Epistulae* 5.3.5; Virgil *Catalepton* 9.44). His sons Messallinus and Cotta Maximus were also interested in literature; skillful orators both, Cotta also wrote poetry (*P.* 4.16.41– 44) and was a patron to poets (Juvenal 7.95). Paullus Fabius Maximus, whom Horace addressed as a young man in 13 B.C. (*Carmina* 4.1), was also a patron of letters who showed favor to Ovid (*P.* 1.2.129–36).

Other literary circles were flourishing at this time. One may have grown up around Germanicus, who had literary interests; he wrote Greek comedies (Suetonius *Gaius Caligula* 3.2, *Divus Claudius* 11.2) and composed epigrams (*Palatine Anthology* 7.542, 9.387) as well as a poem on a tomb which Augustus had constructed for a horse. Some seven hundred lines from his *Aratea*, a Latin translation of Aratus's *Phaenomena*, are extant. In addition, we know of several poets of Germanicus's staff. Albinovanus Pedo, who served as his commander of cavalry during campaigns in Germany, was an epic poet and author of a *Theseis*; Martial (2.77.5) ranked his epigrams with those of Catullus and Domitius Marsus. The poet Carus, author of an epic *Herakleis* (*P.* 4.16.7–8), also served as tutor to Germanicus's children.

Germanicus was not the only member of the imperial family with literary interests. Augustus himself wrote poetry, if only *summatim* (Suetonius *Divus Augustus* 85), including a *Sicilia* in hexameters and epigrams composed at the baths; another work, an attempt at tragedy entitled the *Ajax*, appears to have been less successful. Augustus's prose works, such as his *Rescripta Bruto de Catone* and *Hortationes ad philosophiam*, were more in the lines of a *princeps* and man of affairs. Yet by dabbling in poetry he appears to have pursued the literary interests of any cultivated Roman of his day.

In addition to our evidence concerning literary circles of this period, we have names of thirty other poets. Many are mentioned only once as part of a catalog of writers given by Ovid in *P.* 4.16; others are well known from other sources. Ovid, however, describes all of them as his

contemporaries (4.16.4) and states that he has not included the names
of others (ll. 37–38) or mentioned younger poets (l. 39). All thirty
poets listed in the elegy were therefore active when Ovid was relegated.

And a varied list they are: Domitius Marsus, the epigrammist (l. 5);
Rabirius, author of an epic on the deaths of Antony and Cleopatra
(l. 5); Macer, who served as procurator of the imperial libraries and
wrote an epic *Antehomerica* (l. 6); Montanus, an elegist and epic poet
(l. 11); Sabinus, author of an epic and unfinished *opus dierum* (ll. 15–
16); Tuscus, who treated the love of Phyllis and Demophoon (l. 20);
Cornelius Severus, author of a *carmen regale,* a *Bellum Siculum,* and
Res Romanae (l. 9); Largus, another epic writer (ll. 17–18); Grattius, a
didactic poet, whose *Cynegetica* survives in part (l. 34); Melissus, who
invented the *fabula trabeata,* a short-lived type of equestrian drama,
wrote a collection of anecdotes in 150 books and through Maecenas's
influence was appointed head of the library at the Porticus of Octavia
(l. 30). Others in Ovid's list are otherwise virtually unknown: the
Prisci and Numa (l. 10); Camarinus (l. 19); an unnamed poet described
as a "vates velivoli maris" (l. 21–22); another author of an epic on the
African war (l. 23); Marius (l. 24); Trinacrius (l. 25); Lupus (l. 26);
Rufus (l. 28); and Turranus (l. 29). Others in the list have already been
mentioned, such as Cotta Maximus, Albinovanus Pedo, and Carus.
Still other poets known to be writing in this period, including Manilius
and Germanicus himself, are omitted.

Our review of this catalog gives important evidence about the
literary world of Rome at the time Ovid was relegated. Rome was a
city in which literary interest was flourishing and poets were being
read. Yet Ovid also emphasizes in this same elegy that he was the
leading poet of his day:

dicere si fas est, claro mea nomine Musa
    atque, inter tantos quae legeretur, erat.   [*P.* 4.16.45–46]

If I may say it, my Muse was famed,
and among so many poets, she was the
one who was read.

This is not false modesty. In this final elegy of the *Ex Ponto,* as in his
poetic autobiography (*Tr.* 4.10.125–26), Ovid affirms a fact which
both he and his Roman readership knew well: even in exile, removed
from the literary circles of the capital, he was the leading poet of
Rome.

Ovid's preeminence was not something recent. Throughout his career, beginning with the publication of his *Amores* in the 20s B.C., he had demonstrated a remarkable versatility at mastering and reworking whatever literary genre he chose to treat.[10] His love elegies wittily explored in detached, intellectual terms the role of being a lover in verse. Following their success, Ovid quickly published one work, then another: a tragedy, *Medea,* now lost, but praised in antiquity (Tacitus *Dialogus de oratoribus* 12, Quintilian *Institutes* 10.1.98); the *Heroides,* elegiac love letters of mythological heroes and heroines; the *Ars amatoria,* a mock didactic poem on achieving success in the game of love; and the *Remedia amoris,* another mock didactic poem on overcoming the unhappiness of love. All of these works are marked by imagination, verbal artistry, and sophisticated humor, which endeared Ovid to his Roman readers. The humanity and psychological insight underlying his wit have secured his position among major classical writers.

After the death of Horace in 8 B.C., Ovid became the most celebrated poet in the capital. He published a second edition of *Amores* and a third book of the *Ars amatoria,* this addressed to women. Shortly before his relegation, he had written his longest and most ambitious work, the *Metamorphoses,* a mythological poem of epic proportions in fifteen books of dactylic hexameters. At the time he left Rome he was engaged in another major undertaking, the *Fasti,* a series of elegiac books on the Roman calendar. Exile had therefore interrupted a brilliant and highly successful poetic career.

Ovid himself had also been the center of a highly cultured and sophisticated world, surrounded by friends and admirers. Through references in his own works we know that he was of comfortable means, from an old equestrian family (*Am.* 1.3.8, *Tr.* 2.111–14). His wife was also well connected, with ties to the house of the Fabii (*P.* 1.2.135–42, 3.1.77–78), and Ovid was on intimate terms with such figures as Cotta Maximus, the son of his former patron Messalla Corvinus (*P.* 2.5), and Pompeius Macer, head of the imperial libraries (*P.* 2.10). He therefore knew that his writings from exile would find an audience. Whatever he sent to Rome would be read, and read eagerly, in its literary circles. There is also no reason to believe that the books were not extremely popular. Not only did Ovid keep writing them year after year, but his elegies from Tomis also influenced later writers, among them Lucan, Martial, and Seneca, who also wrote from exile some thirty-five years later.

Because of the preeminence of his position, Ovid's exile poetry, both
in form and content, was the result of deliberate choices on his part. In
writing from Tomis he was free to experiment. Although we would not
expect this of him, Ovid could have decided on a gesture of silence to
demonstrate the impact of relegation on him as a creative artist, not to
write at all, or at least not to write for publication. He could have
turned to another type of poetry, such as didactic or descriptive works
on Pontus. He could have finished the *Fasti,* despite claims that he
lacked a proper library or reference materials in Tomis (*Tr.* 3.14.37–
38). We must remember that he was able to write the elaborately
learned *Ibis* there.[12]

Why Ovid decided on the books he did is a question already
explored by others. But it can be answered fully only through the study
of his individual collections. As we shall see, Ovid's books, while at
first glance similar, are different from each other, having been published
over an eight-year period of composition. Yet they have common
characteristics, all of them written in elegiac verse. Ovid had gained
wide experience with this meter in his earlier writing but chose it for
his books from exile because of its traditional associations as a verse
form for laments and grief. Moreover, in keeping with this tradition,
Ovid could exploit a theme which by this time had become almost a
commonplace in antiquity, that of exile as a form of death. Thus he
could play on traditional ideas to express his unhappiness in a poetic
form already familiar to him.[13]

A few words should be added about our methods and emphasis.
Because this study is concerned primarily with Ovid's books from exile
as poetic books, it is not intended to be an exhaustive analysis of the
exile poetry. One specific literary question must, however, be explored
before proceeding further, that of the poet's references to Augustus
which appear throughout these books. This problem will be treated in
the first chapter. Then we shall turn to the individual collections in
chronological order.

Our examination of individual elegies will be limited. Some poems
have already received more detailed analysis by scholars, whose work
we will note; others have been neglected. But Ovid takes special care
within his books to vary his presentation of exile from poem to poem.
The content of individual elegies is therefore important and certainly of
greater value in understanding the collections than merely examining
the arrangement of poems in structural plans.

Poems which are more important in their collections must receive
closer examination, but none will be ignored completely. In addition,

our subject is a block of poetry relatively unfamiliar to students of
Latin literature. To avoid lengthy paraphrasing and to introduce
readers to the artistry which Ovid displays in these poems, the poet
himself will be quoted frequently. The translations of Latin passages,
which are taken from the Oxford Classical Text of S. G. Owen, are my
own. For full English versions of the exile poetry the reader should
consult the translation of the *Tristia* by L. R. Lind and A. L. Wheeler's
Loeb edition.[14]

I LAUS CAESARIS Augustus in the Exile Poetry

UNTIL QUITE RECENTLY it has been fashionable to regard Ovid as an "anti-Augustan" writer. In his references to the emperor and treatment of imperial themes the poet has been thought to comment on the realities of the Augustan principate; although totally nonpolitical in his personal life, he has been viewed as a voice of protest against more repressive aspects of the regime. So pervasive has been this view that a full catalog of its adherents would be tedious. But it has been reflected in influential interpretations of the *Heroides, Ars amatoria,* and, most important, the *Metamorphoses.* [1]

Now a reaction has set in. There is really no hard evidence, it is argued, for Ovid's opposition, political or otherwise, to Augustus; indeed, imperial subjects are not major themes in his earlier poetry. When Ovid does make reference to the emperor, his purpose is, not to ridicule Augustus or his programs, but rather to incorporate panegyric into his immediate literary context. His apparent playfulness in treating imperial subjects is that of a "nequitiae poeta" (*Am.* 2.1.2), really no different from his handling of any other theme. There are therefore no grounds for reading irony into Ovid's passages glorifying Augustus; in fact it is misleading to apply terms such as "Augustan" and "anti-Augustan" to him.[2]

Although such scholarly battles seem unlikely to subside, this one is fortunately outside the main focus of our study. Yet the problem of Ovid's attitude to Augustus cannot be ignored in any examination of the exile poetry. As proponents of the nonpolitical Ovid have rightly observed, the poet did not give major emphasis to imperial themes in his earlier works. The Ovidian concordance reveals that by far the largest number of his references to Augustus appear in the books for Tomis. This is not surprising when we remember the main themes of the exile poetry, Ovid's defense of his conduct and appeals for imperial mercy. Yet because of their ubiquity, these references have given rise to speculation about Ovid's attitude toward the man who sent him into exile. Why is the emperor so prominent in the exile poetry? Is the poet's flattery to be taken at face value?

Ovid's treatment of Augustus takes various forms. At times the emperor is addressed directly (*Tr.* 2, 5.2.47–78); in other places appeals are presented to other members of the imperial family, to Livia (*P.* 2.8.43–50), Tiberius (*P.* 2.8.37–42), and Germanicus (*P.* 4.8.31–88). Most frequently, however, the poet's references to the emperor are indirect, presented in letters to his wife and friends.[3] As in the *Ars amatoria* and *Metamorphoses,* his allusions at times appear playful and even frivolous, outwardly respectful but perhaps to be read on more than one level. In other places Ovid's descriptions of hardships and warfare in Tomis might even appear to subvert Augustan propaganda or ideas: his statements that he cannot enjoy the benefits of the *pax Augusta* (*P.* 2.5.17–18, 2.7.67–68) and that the punishment he has received is far too harsh for his offense have been seen to undermine the praise of imperial *clementia* which appears elsewhere. Such treatment has prompted modern readers of the exile poetry to interpret Ovid's references as attacks or criticism, both open and disguised, on the emperor who sent him to Tomis.[4]

The problem demands detailed examination. Modern readers are of course embarrassed by imperial flattery and self-abasement; it is more attractive to see in Ovid a champion of artistic and spiritual integrity standing in defiance of the emperor.[5] Yet such interpretations fail to take account of the poet's situation and dilemma. We must not apply modern notions about exile to Ovid's relegation: there is no evidence that the poet was relegated for political reasons or principles. It is indeed much more probable that his *error* involved serious personal wrongdoing to merit the punishment Augustus imposed. Political principles, or even spiritual and aesthetic questions, were unlikely to have figured in his sentence. In addition, Ovid's choices in Tomis were extremely limited: to maintain his own dignity in a distasteful place of exile, or to indulge in adulation and abasement with hopes of a pardon.[6] We must also take at face value Ovid's constant requests to friends, named and unnamed, for support in obtaining a reprieve. In seeking something which only Augustus could grant, would he jeopardize all hopes for a return to Rome or for a reduction of his sentence by public attacks on, or criticism of, the emperor who relegated him? Whatever his personal feelings about Augustus and the punishment he received, Ovid had too much at stake to undermine his position further.

In addition, Ovid's flattery, however distasteful to the modern reader, must be assessed not only within the context of his own situation but also within the literary environment of the late Augustan principate. The books from exile are an invaluable document for the last years of Augustus's reign for not only the historian but also the student of rhetoric and literature. Like book 4 of Horace's *Odes*, they are poetry written long after the firm establishment of the principate. In them we see the results of a steady development in Latin literature treating imperial themes.

Conventions of imperial flattery were not something new: the notion that an emperor was someone more than human had been current in the East since the time of Alexander the Great, whose successors used the doctrine of divine status as a support for their power. Divine honors had been voted to Roman magistrates and commanders in the East, and Julius Caesar did not oppose claims of divine status for himself before his assassination. Following his consolidation of power Augustus promoted Caesar's divinity and took the title *Divi Filius,* "Son of a God." While Augustus moved cautiously, refusing divine honors for himself unless linked with the cult of the goddess Roma (Suetonius *Divus Augustus* 52), the desire of citizens to express their loyalty to him in religious terms was too beneficial a support for the principate to be discouraged. As early as 41 B.C. we find Virgil referring to the young Octavian as a god (*Eclogues* 1.6). His *Georgics,* published in 29 B.C., opens with a divine invocation of the emperor (1.24–42). Such references became more frequent and formal throughout Augustan literature.

By A.D. 8, the year Ovid began writing from exile, there were only so many ways to refer to Augustus. A quasi-canon of imperial themes had come into being long beforehand, not imposed directly by authority, but rather dictated by political reality. The result, however, was the same: because what a writer could say about the emperor was no longer subject to his own control, the trend was to look for new, more novel, and more striking ways to praise him. In dealing with affairs of state the poet must therefore say what is obvious, but he must also say it in ways which are ever more original, more ingenious, and more skillful.[7]

So in addition to his personal situation in exile, which placed even greater restrictions on him as a poet in treating Augustus, Ovid was also faced with what had become a problem common to all writers of the period. His references to Augustus therefore repay study.

One point, generally overlooked in earlier discussions of this question, is to be noted. Ovid's treatment of imperial themes, like other topics in the exile poetry, is not constant, but varies from one collection to the next.[8] It is therefore misleading to read one elegy or book as representative of the entire corpus. A survey of references to Augustus from book to book indeed demonstrates a clear development in the poet's handling of this theme.

In *Tr.* 1, Ovid's first book from exile, references to August are most prominent in the first three poems, the prologue to the book (1.1), Ovid's description of a storm at sea en route to exile (1.2), and his account of his departure from Rome (1.3). The emperor is also mentioned, however, in six of the other eight elegies. The poet informs his readers immediately that Augustus's anger ("ira") is the cause of his relegation (1.1.33, 101–4; 1.3.5–6, 85). From the very first reference Augustus is identified as a god (1.1.20; 1.2.3–4, 12; 1.3.37–40; 1.4.22; 1.5.38, 75, 84; 1.9.4; 1.10.42). In one passage, *Tr.* 1.1.71–74, Ovid describes the Palatine as a divine abode, an idea also seen in *Met.* 1.175–76. More specifically, he equates the emperor with Jupiter (*Tr.* 1.1.81, 1.4.26, 1.5.75–78) and compares the sentence of relegation imposed on him to being struck by Jupiter's thunderbolt (1.1.72, 81–82; 1.3.11–12; 1.9.21). Yet he also presents hopes for an improvement in his fortunes: his life was spared, a benefit which he describes as a "munus dei" (1.1.19–20, 1.2.64); no one is more moderate than the *princeps* (1.9.25); Caesar's wrath was mild ("mitissima," 1.2.61); and Ovid hopes that it will be placated further (1.1.30–33). In fact it is the emperor to whom he looks for a pardon, comparing himself to Telephus: he can be cured only by the weapon which wounded him (1.1.99–100). Moreover, he declares that Augustus approves of *pietas* among loyal friends (1.5.37–40, 1.9.23–24). Within the book Ovid

also praises the empress Livia as a model of a good wife (1.6.23–28)
and proclaims his own loyalty (1.2.99–106, 1.5.41–42).

Nothing in these references is particularly startling. Ovid's association of the emperor with Jupiter is a stock feature of imperial panegyric
which can be paralleled in numerous dedications as well as earlier
Augustan poetry, including the *Metamorphoses* and *Fasti.*[9] What is
new is Ovid's emphasis on the emperor's *ira,* which he is careful to
describe as restrained ("mitissima," 1.2.61) and sure to be softened
further (1.1.33–34, 1.9.25). Linked to this is his presentation of
himself as a victim of Jupiter's thunderbolt, an image which
complements a poetic role assumed in this collection, that of Ulysses,
another victim of divine anger.[10] Ovid's treatment of Augustus in *Tr.* 1
is standard panegyric incorporated into his literary context, that of
presenting his journey into exile. Almost perfunctory in tone, it is little
different from references to Augustus in the preexilic poetry. While the
anger of the *princeps* is mentioned eleven times within *Tr.* 1, it is not
the major theme of the book.

In contrast, Augustus is prominent in the next book, *Tr.* 2. Ovid
addresses this long poem of 578 lines directly to the emperor, much
like the format of Horace's epistle to Augustus. He not only concerns
himself with literary questions treated earlier by Horace in *Epistulae*
2.1 and in the *Ars poetica* but also expands on a theme emphasized by
Horace in the opening lines of his poem to the emperor, the
responsibilities of the *princeps:*

cum tot sustineas et tanta negotia solus,
res Italas armis tuteris, moribus ornes,
legibus emendes.   [*Epistulae* 2.1.1–3]

Since you undertake so many and such
weighty tasks by yourself, you protect
Italy with arms, adorn it by your
virtues, improve it by your laws.

Here Ovid reworks Horace's theme to introduce a catalog of many
tasks which have prevented Augustus from gaining full knowledge of
his case (*Tr.* 2.221–38).[11] The book takes the form of a prose oration in
verse in which Ovid defends himself, his life, and literary career prior
to his relegation and asks for a pardon or easier place of exile.[12]

In contrast to Ovid's first collection, *Tr.* 2 shows an unusual
dichotomy in its references to Augustus, which appear throughout the

book but are most prominent in the first half (ll. 1–238). Ovid at first presents standard panegyric like that seen earlier. In equating the emperor to deity he introduces related ideas to strengthen his appeal: even gods can be soothed by poetry, the Muse which inspired the emperor's anger can also relieve it (2.19–22). In addition, he reworks topoi about divinities to support his case: because gods have no time to concern themselves with trifling matters, Augustus was not able to read the *Ars amatoria* and realize that it is harmless (ll. 215–38).[13] Although Jupiter does not hurl his thunderbolt whenever someone sins, his authority is still manifest.[14] Augustus's moderation and *clementia* likewise inspire gratitude even among those he punishes (ll. 33–50).

Ovid's praise of imperial *clementia* is supported by expressions of thanks for Augustus's leniency in sentencing him to relegation, not exile (ll. 125–38). Caesar is addressed as "mitissime" (ll. 27, 147); his edict against the poet was on the one hand "immite minaxque" but also "lene" in the penalty it imposed (ll. 135–36). Ovid's situation has also given the *princeps* an opportunity to pardon him (ll. 31–32): he has not been hostile to the emperor (ll. 51-52) who approved of his personal conduct on many occasions (ll. 89–92, 541–42). Indeed, the poet will recover from his misfortunes as soon as Augustus's anger abates (ll. 121–24, 143–44). Invoking members of the imperial family in an elaborate appeal, he prays for a pardon or another place of relegation (ll. 155–86), a request repeated at the very end of the poem (ll. 575–78).

Scholars have recently interpreted Ovid's allusions to contemporary events such as Augustan social legislation (ll. 233–34) and military operations in Pannonia, the East, and Germany (ll. 225–30) as critical of the emperor, calling attention to recent setbacks in domestic and foreign policy.[15] But there is no reason not to accept the panegyric in the first half of *Tr.* 2 at face value, as serious rhetorical adornment supporting his plea. It is only in the second half of the poem that Ovid's argument takes a different turn. After appealing for clemency Ovid moves in an elaborately developed *refutatio* to a defense not only of himself but, even more important, of the poetic freedom of the artist. The tone of his presentation also changes. Instead of a respectful address to the emperor, he now introduces objections of an imaginary interlocutor (ll. 253–54, 277) which he refutes at length and in high spirits. His role is no longer that of suppliant but rather that of confident *praeceptor.*

Ovid's argument is that no book, including the *Ars amatoria,* can be considered in itself harmful. If the *Ars* is thought to corrupt its readers, other writers such as Ennius and Lucretius should also be banned, not to mention the theatre, circuses, and even sacred temples, all of which can promote immorality (ll. 241–312). Ovid acknowledges that his own poetic calling was to love elegy, not more serious themes, but stresses that his amatory verses did not reflect his personal life or morals (ll. 313–60). Yet of all those authors who wrote on love, he alone has been punished for his writings (ll. 361–470). Other poets, he observes, have even written with impunity on such frivolous subjects as gaming (ll. 471–96);[16] indeed, the authors of indecent mimes have gained the patronage and support of the emperor himself (ll. 497–518). Ovid's own poems have been performed in the theatre, in the emperor's presence (ll. 519–20), and pictures depicting lovemaking ("concubitus varios," l. 523) are on prominent display in Roman houses (ll. 521–28). Even Virgil, Augustus's own poet, treated love themes both in his *Aeneid* and in his youthful works (ll. 531–38). Yet the emperor has punished Ovid for the *Ars amatoria,* the work of earlier years (ll. 539–46).

Ovid's *refutatio* is not really a defense of himself, but rather an incrimination of all Roman society: in dealing with love he is only like everyone else, but he alone has been punished. The emperor's position in condemning the *Ars* is therefore inconsistent, and a pardon is in order. After the stock panegyric of the first collection, *Tr.* 2 therefore presents something new. In defending his poetry and his position as poet, Ovid adopts a position of independence and confidence. As a spokesman for poetic freedom he wittily attacks the position which Augustus has taken: the *Ars* is not dangerous, has not corrupted anyone, and reflects only the sophisticated and enlightened spirit of the city for which it was written. Ovid in fact defends his earlier poem much in the style of the *Ars* itself, citing theatres, porticoes, temples, and other aspects of urban life to prove that if the work is immoral and decadent, so too is all of Augustan Rome. His repetition throughout the book of earlier lines and motifs from the *Ars* is therefore deliberate; the very format of the poem, a long elegiac composition of some five hundred lines, may be intended to recall that of the *Ars*. Ovid's defense has been well described as a reductio ad absurdum designed to amuse its readers and ridicule the emperor's decision to relegate him because of the poem.[17]

But this is the extent of Ovid's independence. He indulges his wit at Augustus's expense only as far as the *Ars amatoria* is concerned, but says nothing in defense of his *error* (ll. 207–10). Moreover, in his pleas for imperial mercy he is careful to incorporate the type of imperial panegyric found in *Tr.* 1. Ovid criticizes only Augustus's grounds for relegating him because of the *Ars amatoria,* not the position or authority of the *princeps* himself. His association of the emperor with divinity, praise of Augustan *clementia,* and catalog of imperial duties and responsibilities strengthen his appeals for a pardon. Although addressed to the emperor, *Tr.* 2 is not intended for him alone but rather for the Roman literary public which knew the *Ars,* would recognize that it merely reflected the sophisticated life of the capital, and might be moved to work for the poet's pardon.[18] Ovid assumes a role of champion of poetic freedom but also demonstrates his recognition that it is the emperor who will recall him to Rome.

This same duality of attitude is also present in the next collection, *Tr.* 3, which describes Ovid's first year in Tomis. Scholars have observed in this book a marked change of mood:[19] gloom and despondency prevail as Ovid seeks to present his place of exile as a punishment far too harsh for his offense. Over half of the book's elegies are concerned with descriptions of Tomis itself or the poet's state of mind there. References to the emperor are relatively few. The longest and most direct appeal to Augustus within the book appears in its prologue, in which Ovid's personified *libellus* during a visit to the monumental center of Rome delivers a plea for its author before the emperor's house: the *civica corona,* awarded *ob civis servatos,* prompts it to ask the *princeps* to save one more citizen, Ovid himself (3.1.33–52). As in *Tr.* 1.1.69–72, Augustus's house is again equated with that of Jupiter (3.1.35–38), and the emperor himself is invoked as "maxime dive" (3.1.78).

Jupiter's thunderbolt appears only once within the collection (3.5.7), but there are familiar references throughout to Caesar's anger (3.2.28; 3.6.23; 3.8.39; 3.11.17–18, 61–62, 72; 3.13.11). Ovid also expresses wishes for an eventual pardon, twice through an echo of a famous Virgilian line (3.1.75–76, 3.8.19–20—cf. *Aeneid* 1.203). In addition, since Augustus showed mercy in sparing his life, Ovid hopes that he will relent (3.8.41–42; 3.5.25–26, 53–54; 3.6.21–24).

Ovid describes the emperor's power as worldwide in scope ("Caesareum caput est, quod caput orbis erat," 3.5.46) and predicts a future triumph over Germany, news of which he seeks to hear from travelers from the capital (3.12.45–48). But his most striking reference to Augustus in this book extends the role which he assumed in *Tr.* 2, that of champion of artistic independence (the passage itself is part of an epistle to a poet Perilla):

singula ne referam, nil non mortale tenemus
    pectoris exceptis ingeniique bonis.
en ego, cum caream patria vobisque domoque,   45
    raptaque sint, adimi quae potuere mihi,
ingenio tamen ipse meo comitorque fruorque:
    Caesar in hoc potuit iuris habere nihil.
quilibet hanc saevo vitam mihi finiat ense,
    me tamen extincto fama superstes erit,   50
dumque suis victrix omnem de montibus orbem
    prospiciet domitum Martia Roma, legar.   [3.7.43−52]

Why go into details? We have nothing which
will not die except the blessings of our inspiration and poetic talent. Look at me: I have lost
my country, and you, and my home. Everything
has been snatched from me which could be
taken away. Yet I still have with me and enjoy
my poetic talent; over this Caesar has been able
to hold no power at all. Someone or other may
end this life of mine with the cruel sword. Yet
when I am dead, my fame will survive, and as
long as Mars's city, Rome, will look forth from
her hills at the world she conquered, I will be
read.

Ovid here is proud and confident: as a poet he enjoys a spiritual power
which cannot be taken away from him, and renown which will survive
him, in contrast to that of temporal authority. Indeed, Augustus cannot
diminish his fame.

   This passage has been described as Ovid's "most defiant" assertion
against the *princeps* who relegated him.[20] Yet its ideas are not new. The
poet had previously celebrated the immortality inherent in creative
literature in *Am.* 1.15.42 ("parsque mei multa superstes erit") and
much more fully in the epilogue to the *Metamorphoses* (15.871−79),
where he presented a boast similar to this one, that he would live as
long as Rome's authority endured.[21] Moreover, we must recognize in
Ovid's statement of artistic independence the reworking of a rhetorical
topos, the opposition between creative genius and political power. The
elder Seneca provides a parallel in one of his *Suasoriae:* should Cicero
accept Mark Antony's promise of his life if he agrees to burn his

writings?[22] In Seneca's account the rhetor Haterius Quintus, who speaks first to the question, argues:

Ne propter hoc quidem ingenium tuum amas, quod
illud Antonius plus odit quam te? Remittere
ait se tibi ut vivas, commentus quemadmodum
eripiat etiam quod vixeras. Crudelior est pactio
Antonii quam proscriptio. Ingenium erat in quod
nihil iuris haberent triumviralia arma.   [*Suasoriae* 7.1]

Does not the fact that Antony hates your *ingenium*
even more than yourself make you love it the more?
He says he gives you your life. But he has found a
way of stealing even your past life from you. His
bargain is crueler than his proscription. It was your
ingenium against which the triumvirs' weapons
had no power.

In a later section of this same *suasoria* Arellius Fuscus, whom Seneca identifies elsewhere as Ovid's teacher of rhetoric (*Controversiae* 2.2.8), also presents a similar argument:

quamdiu rei publicae nostrae aut fortuna
steterit aut memoria duraverit, admirabile
posteris vigebit ingenium.   [*Suasoriae* 7.7]

As long as either the fortune of our state
shall stand or its memory endure, *ingenium* will survive, an object of wonder
for ages to come.

The parallels in thought are striking, and we might even be tempted to see a verbal reminiscence of Ovid's phrase "iuris habere nihil" in Seneca's passage. But both poet and rhetorician appear to use a stock expression to glorify the power of the mind. From Seneca's own introduction to this *suasoria* (6.14) and comments of Quintilian (*Institutes* 3.8.46), it seems that Cicero's case was a popular exercise in the rhetorical schools; its arguments must have been familiar to the poet's readers. To suggest that Ovid "for the first time in literary history" treats the themes of "emperor and poet" and the conflict between despotism and literary genius no doubt overstates the case.[23]

But Ovid's introduction of this topos is singularly effective in this particular context. Most of *Tr.* 3 concerns itself with the hardships of

life in Tomis, the contrast between Ovid's earlier life and the grimness
of exile. Yet despite the discontinuity between his former and present
life, Ovid as a poet is still aware of the importance of his creative
power. Poetry is now his only way to present his plight to readers in
the capital. Ovid's *ingenium,* his one possession over which the
emperor's authority has no control, is also his means of gaining a
pardon.

In *Tr.* 4 Ovid's treatment of imperial themes is in some ways similar
to that in earlier books. He again refers to the emperor as a god
(4.1.46, 53–54; 4.4.88; 4.5.20; 4.8.45–52) and compares his punishment with that of being blasted by Jupiter's thunderbolt (4.3.63–70,
4.5.5–6, 4.8.46, 4.9.14). Yet in the elegies which treat the emperor
most extensively Ovid introduces several themes not seen previously. In
Tr. 4.4, a letter to an unnamed friend, he describes the emperor as a
present deity who submits to mention in his verses: Augustus cannot
refuse, since he is the state ("res est publica Caesar," l. 15) and belongs
to all. Since Jupiter as well allows his praises to be sung by all poets,
the friend should not fear association with Ovid. His situation is secure
through the examples of two divinities, one of whom is believed to be
a god, the other is deity conspicuous (4.4.11–20).

Ovid also celebrates imperial divinity manifest on earth in *Tr.* 4.2,
which predicts and describes at length Tiberius's triumph over
Germany, the successful outcome of campaigns in A.D. 10.[24] The poem,
which complements earlier references to these operations (*Fast.* 1.645–
46; *Tr.* 2.229, 3.12.45–48), begins with an elaborate glorification of
the entire imperial household (ll. 1–18). Ovid's account of the
triumphal procession (ll. 19–56) is modeled on treatments of this
theme in the *Amores* and *Ars amatoria.* But in contrast to these earlier
versions, he no longer treats the triumph playfully, but uses it to
emphasize a serious theme, his absence from the capital and inability to
participate in public life.[25] News of the event, however late, will cheer
him: such an occasion for public thanksgiving will outweigh personal
misfortunes ("causaque privata publica maior erit," l. 74), a statement
which recalls his equation of the emperor with the *res publica* noted
earlier in *Tr.* 4.4.15.[26] The elegy is therefore elaborate flattery in which
the poet proclaims his loyalty, demonstrates good intentions, and
attempts to correct what some may have thought was a frivolous
treatment of the triumph theme in his preexilic works.[27]

It is with this background in mind that we must consider Ovid's
references to Augustus in *Tr.* 4.8, a meditation on old age in exile. Here
the poet contrasts former hopes for retirement with the actual turn of

events: his relegation has destroyed what should naturally have been secure and happy years. In the final section Ovid reflects upon his situation:

iamque decem lustris omni sine labe peractis
    parte premor vitae deteriore meae;
nec procul a metis, quas paene tenere videbar   35
    curriculo gravis est facta ruina meo.
ergo illum demens in me saevire coegi
    mitius inmensus quo nihil orbis habet?
ipsa delictis victa est clementia nostris,
    nec tamen errori vita negata meo est?   40

       .   .   .   .

hoc mihi si Delphi Dodonaque diceret ipsa
    esse videretur vanus uterque locus.
nil adeo validum est, adamas licet alliget illud,   45
    ut maneat rapido firmius igne Iovis;
nil ita sublime est supraque pericula tendit,
    non sit ut inferius suppositumque deo.
nam quamquam vitio pars est contracta malorum
    plus tamen exitii numinis ira dedit.   50
at vos admoniti nostris quoque casibus este
    aequantem superos emeruisse virum.   [4.8.33–40, 43–52]

I now, having lived fifty years without a re-proach, am afflicted in my life's decline. Not far from life's goal, which I seemed almost to have reached, a terrible crash toppled my car. Did I then in madness force him to be angry at me, that one who is gentler than anything else in the world? Was his *clementia* overcome by my sins? And yet life not denied me because of *error?* ...If Delphi or Dodona itself were to predict this to me, either place would seem false. Nothing is so strong, even though adamant bind it, that it remains stronger than Jupiter's thunderbolt. Nothing is so lofty and so towers above dangers that it is not beneath and subject to divine force. For even though part of my misfortunes was brought on through my own shortcomings, the

wrath of a deity has given me greater ruin. But
you also be warned by my fate, to win the good
will of a man who equals the gods.

Although Ovid never directly names the emperor, his point is clear; it
was his offense against Augustus that brought about his wretched old
age. The poem has therefore been described as a "bitter meditation on
divine caprice, which in Ovid's case is human caprice (the point is
rammed home relentlessly in the last eight verses)" and as ironic,
deliberately undercutting the notion of Augustan *clementia*.[28] Yet
closer examination reveals that such judgments cannot be correct. Ovid
declares that his own behavior brought him to his unhappy old age,
that his crimes ("delictis," l. 39) were so great that they overcome
imperial clemency. His use of the term *delictum* (an intentional wrong)
to describe his *error* is unusual but not in itself indicative of irony;
Ovid uses it elsewhere to describe his offense without ironic overtones
(*Tr.* 2.578, *P.* 1.7.41). His next statement, that Augustus did not take
his life (l. 40), recalls a similar assertion made earlier at *Tr.* 4.4.45, "pro
quo nec lumen ademptum," again without irony, if we are to take
Ovid's appeal to his friend to work for his recall at face value (4.4.53–
54). The poet's emphasis on the unexpectedness of his relegation (ll.
43–44) is paralleled in a later lecture on the mutability of human
fortune in *P.* 4.3.49–54, again with no irony apparent.

The last eight lines rework familiar themes: we see Augustus equated
with Jupiter (ll. 45–48), the image of being blasted by his thunderbolt
(l. 46), and divine wrath which has brought ruin upon the poet (l. 50).
But their purpose is not to attack the emperor's anger as human
caprice: "aequantem superos emeruisse virum" (l. 52) is stock
panegyric which Ovid uses again without irony in a letter to Fabius
Maximus at *P.* 1.2.118 ("aequandi superis pectora flecte viri") and in
another letter to Messallinus in which he comments on the happiness
of those who can witness an imperial triumph in person, an idea seen
earlier in *Tr.* 4.2: "felices, quibus /…ducis ore deos aequiperante frui
(*P.* 2.2.91–92). This description of old age in Tomis is an elaborate
rhetorical plea: by repeatedly emphasizing his unhappiness, with
constant references to Augustus's *clementia*, Ovid in effect challenges
the emperor to demonstrate his *clementia*. If Augustus is to be
celebrated for his mercy, he should prove it to Ovid's readers now and
in the future by pardoning the poet.[29] Rather than an attack, the elegy
is an invitation to Augustus to relent. Indeed, it is the sincerest appeal
to the emperor that we have had so far in the *Tristia*.

The opening lines of *Tr.* 5 announce that it is a new book, an addition to four already published, but distinct from them (5.1.1–2). Within the new book Ovid also declares that his poetic *ingenium,* of which he had boasted in *Tr.* 3.7.47, has now been blunted by his misfortunes (5.12.31–32). He expresses regrets for having written the *Ars,* the work defended at length in *Tr.* 2 (5.12.47–48, 67–68). He announces that if he wins a pardon, he will write poems that Caesar will approve ("quod probet ipse canam," 5.1.43–45). Along with this change in his poetic role, a subject to be discussed in a later chapter, Ovid's treatment of Augustus also takes a new turn.

There are of course familiar features: the phrase "Caesaris ira" and variants of it are common enough (5.1.41; 5.2.55, 60; 5.3.13; 5.4.17; 5.11.8; 5.12.14). Jupiter's thunderbolt appears three times, at 5.2.53; 5.3.29–30, where Ovid in an address to Bacchus compares his own fate to that of the god's mother Semele; and 5.14.27. In three passages Ovid gives an almost formulaic version of what has now become a standard argument: he owes his life to the *clementia* of the emperor; since there was no crime in his wrongdoing, he has hopes for a pardon (5.4.17–22, 5.8.21–30, 5.11.15–22). Twice he presents prayers like that seen earlier in *Tr.* 2.57–58, for the long life of the emperor (5.5.61–62, 5.11.25–26–cf. 5.8.29–30).[30]

But the longest and most striking appeal to Augustus in *Tr.* 5 is an elaborate address given prominent position immediately after the prologue, like the triumph poem in *Tr.* 4. In this epistle to his wife Ovid presents hopes for an improvement in his situation (5.2.1–36), expresses frustrations that she is doing nothing to help (ll. 37–46), and ends with his own direct address to Augustus (ll. 47–78). Ovid's appeal provides substantial evidence for the development of panegyric. His flattery is concentrated and extravagant. He even takes care to anticipate some of his arguments in the earlier section of the poem to his wife; like Telephus, he seeks a cure from the hand which wounded him (ll. 15–20); because Caesar is lenient to his enemies, an appeal to him is safe. Indeed, there is nothing more gentle in the world ("Caesare nil ingens mitius orbis habet," ll. 35–38–cf. *Tr.* 4.8.38). Ovid himself will approach the sacred altar as a suppliant, if it is proper for a man to address Jupiter (ll. 45–46).

After such preparation, Ovid's prayer begins with a general appeal (ll. 47–54) and moves to praise of the emperor for having spared his life (ll. 55–62). He next reworks a theme introduced in the opening section of the poem: warfare and the constant fear of death make life in Pontus intolerable (ll. 63–72–cf. ll. 29–32). Finally comes a specific request, that he be allowed another place of exile (ll. 73–78). We see a concentration of familiar themes: Augustus is addressed as "imago patriae" (l. 49), an extension of an earlier identification of him with the "res publica" (*Tr.* 4.4.15) and is as great as the world he rules ("o vir non ipso, quem regis, orbe minor", l. 50—cf. *Tr.* 3.5.46). There are also prayers for the emperor's late decease (ll. 51–52).

This elegy is also Ovid's first direct address to the emperor since the publication of *Tr.* 2, three years earlier. The contrast between the two poems is instructive. Here there is no playfulness and no attempt to defend himself or the *Ars*. As a suppliant Ovid is now both more concise and more abject: he does not ask for a complete pardon, but only a change of exile (ll. 77–78); indeed, he states that he deserves more than the relegation he received (ll. 59–60—cf. 5.10.49–52). We no longer find in *Tr.* 5 the tension noted earlier between Ovid as poet, independent of temporal authority, and Ovid as suppliant requesting a pardon. Indeed, as he now disassociates himself as a poet from his earlier books, Ovid's references to Augustus take on a completely orthodox tone.

This change in poetic treatment becomes even more pronounced in the *Epistulae ex Ponto*. In its literary format *P.* 1–3 shows significant changes from the earlier books of the *Tristia*, which Ovid himself acknowledges in its prologue; not only is its title different, but the poet now openly names the individuals to whom he is writing (1.1.17–18). Even more significant is the size of *P.* 1–3, three poetic books published together as a unified collection, a fact which precludes detailed citation of all of Ovid's use of imperial themes within it.

But certain general observations can be made. Along with Ovid's open requests for support, his flattery now becomes ever more blatant and elaborate. The most conspicuous example is *P.* 2.8, a letter to Ovid's friend Cotta Maximus thanking him for a present of the images of Augustus, Tiberius, and Livia.[31] Ovid does not describe the objects in detail, but uses them to introduce a direct appeal to the emperor for a change of exile:

non mihi divitias dando maiora dedisses,
    caelitibus missis nostra sub ora tribus.
est aliquid spectare deos et adesse putare,
    et quasi cum vero numine posse loqui.   [2.8.7–10]

Not by giving me riches could you have
given me a greater gift than these three

gods sent to my sight. It is no small
thing to behold gods, to think that they
are present, and almost to be able to
speak with a real divinity.

Ovid's lengthy prayer to the likenesses (2.8.23–70) is an elaboration
of themes from earlier appeals, particularly that of *Tr.* 5.2. Ovid
equates the emperor's image with that of Rome itself ("patriae faciem
sustinet ille suae," l. 20—cf. *Tr.* 5.2.49; "o patriae per te florentis
imago") and also expands on a second motif, that of appealing to an
absent divinity (cf. *Tr.* 5.2.45, "alloquor en absens absentia numina
supplex"). He asks whether Augustus's image is looking at him angrily
(ll. 21–22), then describes the emperor as surpassing the world in
virtue (l. 23—cf. *Tr.* 5.2.50: "vir non ipso, quem regis, orbe minor")
and as a "saecli decus indelebile nostri" (l. 25—cf. *Tr.* 5.2.49). He
implores him to lighten his punishment ("parce, precor," l. 25; "parte
leva minima nostras et contrahe poenas," l. 35—cf. *Tr.* 5.2.53–54:
"parce, precor, minimam tuo de fulmine partem / deme"). Ovid
supports his appeal with allusions to Livia ("perque tori sociam, quae
par tibi sola reperta est," l. 29—cf. *Fast.* 1.650 and *Tr.* 2.161–64), to
Tiberius (ll. 31–32), and to Germanicus and Drusus (ll. 33–34—cf. *Tr.*
2.165–68).

Ovid next appeals to Tiberius (ll. 37–42), expressing hopes for a
future triumph over Germany (cf. *Tr.* 4.2) and long life for Augustus
and Livia ("sic pater in Pylios, Cumaeos mater in annos," l. 41). We
may compare his wish for imperial longevity at *Tr.* 5.5.62, "aequarint
Pylios cum tua fata dies." Then in an address to the empress (ll. 43–
50) he prays that her husband and grandsons keep healthy and that
Tiberius soon celebrate a triumph as avenger of his brother's death.
Finally Ovid addresses all three images (ll. 51–70), reworking two
themes seen earlier: Augustus is a present divinity (cf. *Tr.* 4.4.19–20),
and happy are those who can see gods face to face (cf. *Tr.* 4.2.65–68).
The prayer ends with a request for a change of exile: until then Ovid
will cling to the images like an altar of refuge (ll. 67–68—cf. *Tr.*
5.2.43–44). Ovid then appends an aside to his readers (ll. 71–76).
Can he be mistaken ("me fallo," l. 71, echoing "fallor an" in l. 21), or
does the emperor's image seem to nod assent ("adnuere," l. 74—cf.
"adnuite," l. 51)? He prays that the images foretell the truth, that
Augustus will now relent.[32]

This flattery far exceeds that in *Tr.* 5.2. Indeed, it seems so overdone
that a case might be made that the poet deliberately exaggerates it to

undermine its credibility. Yet there is no reason to believe that Ovid's
contemporaries would have thought his prayer grotesque, and the
appeal cannot be read as ironic. There are within it too many parallels
of expression, too many echoes of themes found in earlier poems. It is
rather that Ovid had collected and reworked all the conventional
elements of imperial flattery to construct the most elaborate panegyric
of Augustus and his family in the books from exile, and perhaps in all
Augustan literature. His prayer to a likeness allows him to invent a
clever variation on a stock subject and also a witty and challenging
request for a reprieve: Ovid will keep the images with him wherever he
is, and the emperor whom he worships will stay in Tomis as long as
Ovid himself remains (ll. 63–70). The implication is clear: if Augustus
wants to leave this barbarous place, and he surely must, he must allow
the poet to leave as well.

Ovid's most extensive treatment of Augustan *clementia* appears near
the end of *P.* 3, in an epistle to an unnamed friend:

cur tamen, hoc aliis tutum credentibus, unus
    adpellent ne te carmina nostra, rogas?
quanta sit in media clementia Caesaris ira
    si nescis, ex me certior esse potes.   [3.6.5–8]

Yet why, when others think it safe, do you
alone ask that my poems not address you
by name? How great Caesar's *clementia* is,
even in the midst of his anger, you may
learn from my case if you don't know it
yourself.

Ovid assures the friend that association with him is not dangerous,
that Augustus does not forbid correspondence (ll. 11–12), that the
emperor who recently built a temple to the goddess Justitia has long
worshiped her in his heart (ll. 23–26), and that his punishment carries
hope of a pardon (ll. 27–44). The poet even condemns his own
practice of not having named his friends in previous books and is now
ashamed of his earlier timidity (ll. 45–50). Because the friend is
unknown, indeed probably fictitious, Ovid's real subject is, not his
reluctance to be named, but Augustan *clementia*. His discourse on
imperial mercy and his assurances of safety therefore become a
challenge to the emperor to demonstrate this *clementia*.[33]

The poet's references to his fear which kept him from naming his
friends ("pavor," l. 47; "metuens," l. 49; "terrebar," l. 50) recall an

earlier explanation of his decision to preserve their anonymity in *Tr.*
3.4.63–72: there "cautus timor" had kept him from openly celebrating
their loyalty. With the publication of *P.* 1–3 Ovid now abandons his
earlier practice and rejects his earlier reason for it. He no longer feels
that association with him will embarrass his friends and has decided
that open appeals to individuals are now not only possible but indeed
might be fruitful in winning a change of exile. But he gives no reason
for his new confidence and change of attitude except Augustus's
clementia. Given the familiarity of this theme, should Ovid's explanation be taken at face value?

The date of *P.* 1–3 may be significant: the three books were for the
most part composed during a single year, A.D. 12–13. It is perhaps
possible to connect Ovid's increased confidence and literary output
with a notice in Dio for the year A.D. 12, in which Augustus is recorded
to have promulgated restrictions on the way of life and expenditures of
exiles (Cassius Dio 56.27.2–3): when the emperor found some exiles
residing outside districts to which they had been relegated or living too
luxuriously, he decided to take corrective measures. Dio's passage is
confused and may well be an amalgamation of several separate
regulations issued at different times.[34] Yet it might well point to an
imperial edict concerning exiles in A.D. 12, including restrictions to
which Ovid, officially a *relegatus* retaining his citizenship and
property, was not subject. The poet therefore may have thought that
Augustus might reconsider his case, indeed, that circumstances were
now propitious to ask influential friends to be his spokesmen.

Ovid to be sure does not mention any such edict; whether or not he
had been affected by it, he would no doubt have thought it unwise to
do so. Only once in *P.* 1–3 does he make reference to his condition as
relegatus (1.7.41–48), and throughout the collection he uses the more
general term *exilium* to describe his punishment (1.3.43, 2.7.63,
2.8.72, 2.9.66, 3.1.10, 3.3.39, 3.7.34), in contrast to distinctions
which he made between the two penalties in earlier books (*Tr.* 2.137–
38, 4.9.11–12, 5.2.57–58, 5.4.21–22, 5.11.21–22). To support his
appeals for aid Ovid instead alludes to other, more positive, contemporary events in Rome, the most conspicuous of which was the long
delayed Pannonian triumph celebrated on 23 October A.D. 12.[35] The
ceremony is given prominent place at the beginning of book 2, where
the poet, as in *Tr.* 4.2, uses the occasion to declare his participation in
the public joy (2.1.1–18), to describe the procession (ll. 19–48), and to
address Germanicus directly, predicting another future triumph for the
young prince (ll. 49–68). He returns to this theme, the triumph and

the general happiness which it represents, in the epistle to Messallinus
that immediately follows (2.2.67–84) as well as in exhortations to his
wife and Fabius Maximus to intercede in his behalf (3.1.133–38,
3.3.85–92). All these passages emphasize that the time is appropriate
to approach the emperor. Ovid also alludes to a second event, the
consecration of Justitia Augusta as an official cult on 8 January A.D.
13.[36] Ovid makes direct reference to the cult at *P.* 3.6.24–26, mentions
it in the triumph poem (2.1.33–34), and describes Augustus as
"iustissimus" at 1.2.97. The point is clear: since his relegation to Tomis
is far too harsh, the time has come for the emperor to serve Justitia
Augusta. Hence the open appeals to patrons and friends to intercede in
his behalf.

The last book of elegies from Tomis, *P.* 4, is addressed to a new
group, individuals associated with or in the circle of Germanicus.[37]
Now Ovid's flattery and use of imperial themes are designed to win the
support and good will of the young prince to whom he had promised
poetic celebration of his own future triumph in *P.* 2.1.49–68. After the
death of Augustus in A.D. 14, Ovid's flattery takes a new turn, with
fewer references to imperial *ira*; the late *princeps,* he declares, was on
the point of recalling him when he died (4.6.15–16). He also
announces that he has even composed a poem in Getic to celebrate the
emperor's apotheosis (4.6.17–18, 4.13.17–42), a literary achievement
which may be fictitious but Ovid's warrant of good intentions in
appealing for imperial favor.[38]

The most interesting appeal in the last book is *P.* 4.8, a letter
addressed to Suillius, a member of Germanicus's staff. Like an earlier
epistle to Salanus, also connected with Germanicus (*P.* 2.5), Ovid's
communication is intended for the young prince, whom he addresses
directly in the central section of the elegy (4.8.27–88). His appeal is
based on the spiritual ties between Ovid and Germanicus as fellow
poets. Ovid stresses the fame that writers can bestow on men of action
and declares that poetry can even immortalize its subjects:

di quoque carminibus, si fas est dicere, fiunt
   tantaque maiestas ore canentis eget.

      .   .   .   .

et modo, Caesar, avum, quem virtus addidit astris,
   sacrarunt aliqua carmina parte tuum.
siquid adhuc igitur vivi, Germanice, nostro
   restat in ingenio, serviet omne tibi.   [4.8.55–56, 63–66]

Gods too are created by verse (if it is right to say

so), and such great majesty needs the mouth of
the bard....And recently, Caesar, poems played
some part in the deification of your grandfather,
whose virtue exalted him to the stars. If there is
anything still alive in my poetic *ingenium*, Germanicus, it will be completely in your service.

Ovid's declaration brings to a conclusion the development we have
observed: as a poet treating imperial subjects he has changed from
what we found in the earlier books of the *Tristia*. Although he used
motifs from conventional panegyric in his references to the emperor
throughout the books, he remained in *Tr.* 3 and 4 a poet conscious of
the power of his *ingenium* and determined to maintain his artistic
independence. In later collections he has become much more a
panegyricist and uses that vehicle to support his appeals. Even in *P.* 4.8
he is still aware of his power as a poet, but his strategy has changed.
His poetic posture is no longer that of independence, but, rather,
compliance. Ovid now uses his *ingenium* for an immediate and
personal goal, to win imperial favor.

The flattery in these books may disappoint or even disgust the
modern reader. As panegyric it is expansive and, to our taste, offensive,
certainly much more extravagant than what we read in Horace's later
works. Yet because of his poetic preeminence, Ovid's flattery had far-
reaching effects. His poetic ingenuity in appealing to Augustus indeed
became the inspiration and impetus for future trends in the development of panegyric, by framing the obvious compliments about the
emperor in more novel, graceful, and ingenious ways. His exile poetry
was no doubt popular; Augustus seems to have made no move to
censor it, and Ovid's books were certainly studied by later writers,
Seneca, Martial, and Statius prominent among them. Their influence is
strongly reflected in the panegyric of later authors.

This survey of imperial themes cannot pretend to be exhaustive.
Many examples have been omitted, and some readers may remain
unconvinced that all of Ovid's flattery must be taken at face value.
Modern reactions to imperial panegyric cannot be entirely objective;[39]
it is indeed tempting to see irony behind many of Ovid's references,
and the poet's words may have had little to do with his real feelings.
But given his situation in Tomis and the orthodox tone of his appeals,
particularly in the later books, it is difficult to interpret his references
to the emperor as subversive.

Ovid went to Tomis with his poetic independence, but later
abandoned it. It is easy for us to condemn him, but we must also

remember the alternatives open to him. If his behavior seems weak or
dreary, his predicament, like that of Telephus, was difficult. But we are
not justified in dismissing the books from Tomis on this ground any
more than in attempting to read them as sly polemic against the
princeps, an interpretation that is not supported by the evidence. The
purpose of this chapter has been introductory, to demonstrate how
Ovid's attitude toward Augustus became more compliant in the years
following A.D. 8. With this background, and the understanding that
these collections are not "anti-Augustan" tracts, we can turn to the
more fruitful study of what they are and how Ovid as poet exploits his
situation and literary skills.

nec te, quod venias magnam peregrinus in urbem
  ignotum populo posse venire puta.
ut titulo careas, ipso noscere colore;
  dissimulare velis, te liquet esse meum.

Don't think, because you arrive in the capital a
foreigner, you can come incognito. Although
you lack a title, you'll be recognized by your
style and tone. You may wish to disguise
yourself, but it's clear you are mine.

II   TRISTIA 1 Journey into Exile

O VID'S FIRST BOOK from exile is characteristically his own, a fact
he acknowledges in its prologue. (*Tr.* 1.1.59–62). In the preceding
chapter we noted the confidence and high spirits displayed in his
apology to Augustus: *Tr.* 2. does not seem to be the work of a poet in
exile. The mood of *Tr.* 1. is much the same. In 1925 E. K. Rand
described the book as "not unduly lugubrious," and his comments have
been echoed by others.[1] In both *Tr.* 1 and 2 Ovid is much like the poet
of his earlier writings. He does not appear to be excessively concerned
about his relegation: as he chooses to defend the *Ars amatoria* in the
spirit of the *Ars* itself, he likewise seems to enjoy the challenge of
describing his departure from Rome and his wintry voyage to Tomis.

Because of this playfulness, in some ways *Tr.* 1 and 2 are best
considered together. Whether they appeared simultaneously in Rome
cannot be proved with certainty, but it seems quite probable. Both
books were written in A.D. 9 before Ovid reached Tomis, perhaps
during an extended stay at Samothrace en route (*Tr.* 1.10.19–22); he
gives no indication in them that he has already reached his place of
exile. Ovid does not describe Pontus in the first book, although he
alludes briefly to the warlike conditions of his future destination in

Tr. 1.11.25–34. A short description of the area appears at *Tr.* 2.187–
206, but it is general, much less vivid and direct than accounts in later
books.[2]

In addition, both books seem to be companion pieces. No mention
of one book appears in the other, but each book complements the
other. *Tr.* 1, which treats at length Ovid's journey into exile, is balanced
by his apologia. Ovid defends himself only briefly in his first collection
(1.2.97–100, 1.3.37–38, 1.5.41–42, 1.9.59–64); in *Tr.* 1 he is more
concerned with other themes: his journey, his poetic reputation, and
the loyalty of his friends. His defense of himself and his poetry appears,
not in the first book, but in the second. Ovid presents first the
experience of leaving Rome and undertaking his voyage to heighten the
effect of his apologia. *Tr.* 2 deals, not with the poet's immediate
situation, but his past life and writings, which he uses to support his
plea.

Like his address to Augustus, Ovid's first book has received greater
scholarly attention than later collections. Karl Herrmann was the first
to study its arrangement in some detail, and Ulrich von Wilamowitz-
Moellendorff went beyond its structural plan to examine Ovid's poetic
treatment of his journey. He first suggested the title "Journey into
Exile" ("Reise in der Verbannung") for the collection. More recently
R. J. Dickinson and Hartmut Froesch have also discussed the book's
elegies.[3]

Some general characteristics should be noted. *Tr.* 1 is a poetic
collection which Ovid planned according to Augustan practice. A *liber*
(1.1.1) with prologue and epilogue, its elegies are arranged, not
haphazardly or simply in chronological order, but according to a
definite artistic scheme. In format therefore the book is highly
conventional; yet its theme makes it different. We have here neither a
poetic book about love nor a literary miscellany such as the fourth
book of Propertius or Horace's *Odes,* but a collection treating Ovid's
own departure.

By being sent to Tomis Ovid was given an opportunity to present his
experiences en route to his Roman audience. The result is this book, a
demonstration of literary virtuosity in which the poet exploits
traditions connected with elegy—songs of lament and grief, narrative
verse, expressions of personal feelings, and a medium for letters in
verse—to create something new but distinctly his own, a book of exile
poetry. Ovid had already gained considerable experience with all forms
of elegiac verse in his earlier poetry, particularly the elegiac epistle in

the *Heroides*.[4] Reworking poetic models to present his situation in exile was a challenge which he could not refuse.

Our discussion of the book will begin with the prologue and will be organized around its main themes: the journey into exile, which is the most prominent and fully developed, the demands of friendship, or what we will call the good faith and loyalty theme, and Ovid's poetry and position as a poet. We shall discuss separately Ovid's treatment of each theme before turning to the epilogue and the collection as a whole.

PROLOGUE: OVID ADDRESSES HIS BOOK (*Tristia* 1.1)

Parve (nec invideo) sine me, liber, ibis in urbem:
  ei mihi, quod domino non licet ire tuo!
vade, sed incultus, qualem decet exulis esse:
  infelix habitum temporis huius habe.

Little book, you go to Rome without me (I
don't begrudge you that.) But alas, your master
cannot go, too! Make your way, but shabbily,
as befits the book of an exile, keeping the sad
appearance of my situation.

Although generally written last, just before publication of a poetic book, a program poem sets the tone for its collection. That of *Tr.* 1 is no exception. In allowing himself to speak to his personified book, Ovid follows a long literary tradition: the closest parallel, and the poet's direct model, is Horace's address to his *libellus* at *Epistulae* 1.20. Ovid's reminiscence of Horace may be an attempt to give legitimacy to his new poetic creation, an elegiac epistle dealing with his own fate in exile.[5] But the poet adds another element, a motif from love elegy which he himself used in *Am.* 3.8.6; the book as his spokesman or representative can go where its author cannot. The adaptation is appropriate—Ovid cannot return to Rome—but its ingenuity is perhaps too clever for his lament to be taken seriously.

Ovid describes his physical book (ll. 5–16): in shabby covering, lack of ivory handles, *titulus,* unsmoothed edges, and tear-stained pages, it should reflect its contents. Again we recognize play on literary conventions and are led to think of Catullus 1 and Lygdamus 1.9–14. Yet Ovid's book is exactly the opposite of its models; its appearance, while appropriate for its master's situation, is so unattractive that it is comic, and the tear-stained pages (ll. 13–14) are an elegiac motif which the poet used at *Her.* 3.3 and elsewhere. He even ends his opening description with a well-worn and familiar Ovidian play on the word *pede* (l. 16) which his readers would immediately recognize.[6]

Next the poet instructs his book about its task as his advocate in the city. Ovid supplies the defense his book should present, in effect his first apology for the exile poetry. We see arguments which will appear again and again, demonstrating the direct relationship between the quality of his poems and the circumstances of their composition (ll. 17–48), specifically the "mare," "venti," and "fera hiems" of his voyage (l. 42), as well as a disavowal of poetic fame (ll. 49–56). Ovid insists that the new book does not teach his readers how to make love (ll. 57–68), then gives it lengthy instructions about approaching Augustus (ll. 69–104). He also plays on the father / son relationship between author and book: the *libellus* will go to its new home, the bookcase, where it will meet its brothers, Ovid's other works, including the three rolls of the *Ars amatoria* hiding in shame (ll. 105–22). The final couplets (ll. 123–28) return to the messenger theme of the opening lines.

The poem raises serious subjects: Ovid admits that he owes his life to the emperor (ll. 19–20) and portrays himself in heroic terms as a man in danger (ll. 19, 53), blasted by the divine thunderbolt (ll. 71–72, 81–82). Yet these themes are only touched on here to prepare for more extended treatment in later elegies. The dominant mood of this poem is spirited. Although his book is forlorn in its appearance, Ovid himself is not. Despite his apologies for it, he appears confident that it will be successful and presents it as a worthy addition to other offspring, such as the *Metamorphoses* (ll. 117–20). Ovid's description of his personified *libellus* does not arouse sympathy; instead, his purpose is to amuse and entertain. Although this prologue gives clear indication of its literary models, it is an address to a personified book unlike any other in Latin literature, giving its readers a hint of what is to come in subsequent poems.

THE JOURNEY: THE VOYAGE (*Tristia* 1.2, 1.4)

parcite caerulei, vos parcite numina ponti,
  infestumque mihi sit satis esse Iovem.
vos animam saevae fessam subducite morti;
  si modo, qui periit, non periisse potest.

Spare, O spare me, deities of the dark blue
sea; let it be enough that Jupiter is hostile
to me. Save my weary soul from a cruel
death, if indeed it is possible to save one
already destroyed.

Both *Tr.* 1.2 and 1.4 describe the same phenomena, storms through
which the poet must sail during the winter months. *Tr.* 1.2 is set in the
Adriatic on the first leg of Ovid's journey (1.2.91–92); 1.4 extends the
voyage, describing another, later storm on the Ionian Sea (1.4.3).

The first elegy, a carefully developed poem,[7] presents Ovid at sea beset
by physical danger and death (ll. 1–36). The situation prompts him to
think about his wife (ll. 37–44); to introduce a theme important throughout the exile poetry, that exile itself is a form of death (ll. 45–90); and to
plead that any crime he committed was not intentional (ll. 91–106). Ovid
argues that he does not deserve death, either death at sea or the living
death of exile. At the end of the elegy (ll. 107–10) the winds and waves
subside, for the sea deities whom he has invoked have realized that he is
innocent. The implication in the final lines is clear: if the sea gods relent,
can Augustus continue in his anger? As a god (ll. 11–12, 103–4) the
emperor should join fellow gods in recognizing the poet's innocence.

These reflections are presented against the background of the storm
at sea. Some have read the storm as symbolic of the poet's emotional
distress,[8] but Ovid's use of this motif is paradoxical: while the storm
might reflect his mental turmoil, his description is too literary to be
taken seriously. Ovid develops his storm with full epic trappings
comparable to those of the "Compleat Storm" of Ceyx and Alcyone in
Met. 11.474–572,[9] but also plays with details of his description,
deflating its fearfulness and terror. A few examples should be noted.
He expands Virgil's famous picture of the storm at *Aeneid* 1.106–7,
"his unda dehiscens / terram inter fluctus aperit, furit aestus harenis,"
into four lines,

me miserum, quanti montes volvuntur aquarum!
 iam iam tacturos sidera summa putes,
quantae diducto subsidunt aequore valles!
 iam iam tacturas Tartara nigra putes,   [ll. 19–22]

Poor me! What mountains of water are rolled
above! At this very moment you'd think they'll
reach the highest stars. What deep valleys yawn
as the sea separates! At this very moment you'd
think they'll reach black Tartarus,

but reduces the symbolic force of his Virgilian model through deliberate repetition of "iam iam tacturos [-as]...putes" in each pentameter. He also lists the four winds in two couplets which are too neat and artistically ordered to have been written at a time of danger (ll. 27–30). We see another feature of literary storms, the tenth wave, regarded in antiquity as a sign of impending destruction (ll. 49–50). Ovid's description of it, "posterior nono est undecimoque prior" ("the one after the ninth and before the eleventh") is deliberately whimsical. The storm in this elegy has been reduced to a mock epic setting.

Ovid returns to the same theme in *Tr.* 1.4. In this twenty-eight-line poem, the shortest within the book, the poet describes the waves which threaten to overwhelm his ship (ll. 1–16), protests that he cannot be blown back to Italy (ll. 17–22), and prays that he be spared (ll. 23–28). Here everything is much more simple and straightforward, with no philosophical reflections on the poet's innocence and no displays of descriptive virtuosity. Yet this second storm, like that of 1.2, is conventional, and there is nothing in this elegy which did not appear earlier. Ovid's description of the waves (ll. 5–8) is much like that of 1.2.13–36: the despair of the helmsman (ll. 11–12, 15–16), a stock detail in literary storms, appeared also at 1.2.31–32. We see again expressions of fear at being driven back to Italy (ll. 19–20—cf. 1.2.91–94) and a plea to the gods not to destroy one who has already perished (l. 28—cf. 1.2.71–72).

In both elegies therefore we find playful use of literary convention: whether Ovid actually encountered such storms en route to exile is quite unknowable and perhaps irrelevant.[10] We do not see here Wordsworth's "powerful emotion recollected in tranquillity," but deliberate reworking of a literary motif to color the first picture we receive of Ovid and his journey: despite the mock epic elements of his storm, he himself is heroic, beset by dangers and threatened by a death he does not deserve. Ovid presents this experience as careful preparation for the role which he assumes in *Tr.* 1.3.

THE JOURNEY: DEPARTURE (*Tristia* 1.3)

quocumque aspiceres, luctus gemitusque sonabant,
    formaque non taciti funeris intus erat.

Everywhere you would look, grief and groans were
echoing. Inside my house the scene was like a
funeral, both in appearance and sound.

Ovid's account of his journey begins with the present, the storm at sea (1.2), before turning to the past, his last night in Rome. He now develops fully the image of himself introduced earlier at *Tr.* 1.1.71–82, that of a man struck by Jupiter's thunderbolt. As he himself is a victim of divine anger, so his house and family are compared to Troy on the night of its capture (ll. 25–26). He is forced to leave behind the gods and traditions of Rome. (ll. 33–34), his *penates,* and loved ones (ll. 95–96); when he departs, he leaves as one already dead. Through deliberate echoes of *Aeneid* 2 with its picture of the fall of Troy, Ovid casts himself as an epic hero forced to leave his homeland.[11] Unlike Aeneas, however, he must depart alone, leaving friends and family behind as well as his household gods and must dissolve any bond between himself and the traditions and deities of Rome. When he developed this picture of his heroic departure, Ovid may well have been thinking of Virgil's famous lines, "feror exsul in altum / cum sociis natoque penatibus et magnis dis" ("I am borne an exile onto the deep, with my comrades, my son, my *penates,* and the great gods," *Aeneid* 3.11–12). The contrast is striking: all the companions which Aeneas takes with him at the start of his journey are denied the poet.

This *color epicus* makes the poem in many ways the most artificial of all in the book. We cannot suppose that Ovid's departure happened as dramatically as he presents it, with prayers to the deities of the Capitolium, the steady movement of the stars bringing the appointed hour, and the emotional farewell of his wife. Yet such details do not give *Tr.* 1.3 an overly literary character; instead, they add resonance to his account, heightening the impact of his separation from his former life. Ovid also describes his last night in terms of his own funeral, giving a full equation of his exile with death. The details of departure (grief, loosened hair, being carried out) all lead to the final simile describing his wife's reaction: she groans as if she had seen her husband's body on the pyre (ll. 97–98).[12]

Although he gives most emphasis to this motif of death-in-exile, Ovid also introduces other elements in the poem: his disappointment at the absence of many friends (ll. 15–16, 65–66) and the devotion of his wife, who plays a leading role. Ovid presents in direct speech her final request to be allowed to accompany him (ll. 81–86), an elegiac theme familiar from Virgil's tenth *Eclogue,* Propertius, and the *Heroides;* here the poet becomes the departing lover, his wife the abandoned heroine.[13] Another elegiac echo is Ovid's attempt to cross his threshold three times and his recall, in a symbolic wavering between departure and remaining (ll. 55–56).[14] Yet Ovid does not stumble on his threshold, averting a bad omen for undertaking a journey, no doubt because he contemplates a safe return to Rome.

In this elegy we are no longer in mid-journey, but back in the capital. Ovid uses literary convention, not to entertain or give epic trappings to his voyage, as in the first storm, but to present personal feelings with greater force. Through its heroic framework we learn what leaving Rome, family, and friends has meant to him. Ovid also gives emphasis to the importance of this elegy through its position, framed by both storm poems.

THE JOURNEY: OVID'S SHIP (*Tristia* 1.10)

illa, Corinthiacis primum mihi cognita Cenchreis
    fida manet trepidae duxque comesque fugae.

                .   .   .   .

nunc quoque tuta, precor, vasti secet ostia Ponti
    quasque petit Getici litoris intret aquas.

She, whom I first met at Cenchreae near Corinth
remains the faithful escort and companion of my
exile.... May she now, I pray, also traverse the
Pontic straits and enter the Getic waters which
she seeks.

Ovid here pays tribute to the ship "*Minerva*," which has carried him from Corinth to Samothrace, and asks for continued safe voyage.[15] He opens (ll. 1–14) with a prayer which recounts her virtues and seaworthiness and requests a favorable journey to Tomis. Lines 15–32 give an account of his voyage from Cenchreae to the Hellespont, then from there to Imbros and Samothrace. Ovid explains that the ship will continue to Pontus, while he will cross Thrace by land. The elegy ends (ll. 33–50) with another prayer for a safe voyage past the Symplegades and Black Sea cities.

Written in Samothrace (ll. 19–20), perhaps while Ovid waited for the return of spring in A.D. 9, the elegy is happy and confident. Ovid makes only two short references to his exile (ll. 10, 41–42) and provides instead a catalog of geographical sites and an introduction to the world around Tomis, an area unfamiliar to readers in Rome.[16] The poem presents elements of a *propemptikon*, a literary form which not only prays for a safe return but often includes lists of places to be visited and noteworthy things to be seen. As a memorial to a ship it is also based on a well-known model, Catullus 4. Ovid may have remembered that the *phasellus* celebrated by Catullus came from the Pontus area.[17] Lines 3–4,

> sive opus est velis, minimam bene currit ad auram,
>   sive opus est remo, remige carpit iter.

> If there is need for sail, she runs well at the
> slightest breeze; if need for oars, with oars she
> makes her way.

recall Catullus 4.3–5, and the poem, like its model, ends with an address to the Dioscuri. Through this adaptation of a famous tribute to a ship, Ovid extends his role as an heroic sailor and, in contrast to earlier storms, retells the main part of his journey in cheerful terms.

GOOD FAITH AND LOYALTY (*Tristia* 1.5, 1.8, 1.9)

> scis bene, cui dicam, positis pro nomine signis,
>   officium nec te fallit, amice, tuum.
> haec mihi semper erunt imis infixa medullis,
>   perpetuusque animae debitor huius ero.

> You know well, my friend, to whom I write,
> through allusions and not by name; your loyal
> service to me does not betray you. It will
> always be fixed in my heart, and I shall
> continually be in your debt.

Three poems in the collection treat the same theme, the loyalty which Ovid expects from friends in Rome. In *Tr.* 1.5, the longest and most important elegy of this group, Ovid appears to be writing to a real person: his opening address, which extends over three couplets, and the detail that the friend was the first to console him after his sentence (ll. 3–4) suggest that he has a particular individual in mind. Yet his addressee is dropped halfway through the poem, when Ovid appeals to all his friends (ll. 35–36). The identity of the unnamed friend does not appear to be important; Ovid uses him only to introduce his poem.

In his first section (ll. 1–40) Ovid discourses on friendship: when one is in difficulty, many friends will desert him, but loyalty is applauded. This good faith lecture, the first of many in the exile poetry, is a presentation of ethical stereotypes illustrated by stock exempla (Theseus / Pirithous, Orestes / Pylades, Nisus / Euryalus) and proverbial similes (testing true friendship like gold in a fire).[18] Yet it reinforces a picture seen earlier in 1.3.15–16, that of Ovid deserted by many friends.

In a short linking passage (ll. 41–44) Ovid turns to his own situation, requesting that the friend work to soften Augustus's anger. The second half of the poem (ll. 45–84) treats a different subject, Ovid's misfortunes:[19]

non tamen idcirco complecterer omnia verbis
    materia vires exsuperante meas.
pro duce Neritio docti mala nostra poetae
    scribite: Neritio nam mala plura tuli.   [ll. 55–58]

I would not include all of them in a
description, since their extent would exhaust
my strength. Learned poets, write of my
troubles instead of Ulysses, for I have
endured more woes than he.

Ovid introduces his troubles through a standard *recusatio* (or polite disclaimer) (ll. 47–56), then turns to a much more imaginative *syncrisis,* or extended comparison, of himself with Ulysses. In couplets skillfully balanced through the repetition of "ille" and "nos," he focuses on specific points of comparison between himself and the legendary hero: the extent of space traveled (ll. 59–62); companionship during wanderings (ll. 63–64); the home countries of each wanderer (ll. 65–70); the respective strength of each and their experiences in bearing hardships (ll. 71–74); the help of the gods (ll. 75–78); and the veracity of the legend (ll. 79–80). The comparison reaches its climax in the final lines (ll. 81–84): Ulysses reached his homeland, but Ovid can never return until Augustus's anger is softened, a return to the theme of lines 43–44, "deminui siqua numinis ira potest."

Ovid's comparison sets him directly in a Ulysses role. We have already seen the poet as a Homeric hero tossed about by storms in *Tr.* 1.2 and 1.4. Both the first storm and departure served to express another point of comparison, his separation from and feeling for his wife (1.2.37–44, 1.3.79–102). His tribute to his ship also presents an account of his wanderings. Now Ovid gives full expression to the idea underlying these motifs: through forced departure from Rome and separation from family and friends he has become another Ulysses.[20]

Our discussion of the other two elegies in this group can be brief. In *Tr.* 1.8, Ovid inverts the good faith theme in a formal protest to a faithless friend. The many parallels between the laments of this elegy and those of the *Heroides* give clear indication of its models.[21] Ovid probably does not have a particular individual in mind: his remarks that the friend was not present at his departure (ll. 13–14, 23–24) recall the situation in *Tr.* 1.3, and the addressee sems to be a lay figure representing friends who deserted him.

Tr. 1.9 is addressed to a loyal friend who has known Ovid from an early age (ll. 41–42) and has been successful in his rhetorical career (ll. 39–40, 57–58). The themes and development of this third poem are parallel to those of *Tr.* 1.5. Ovid's opening lecture on friendship in time of trouble (ll. 1–22) expands the subject of 1.5.27–30. He next moves to a theme seen in 1.5.33–40: those friends who remain faithful will be praised. He illustrates his lesson with mythological exempla, most of which appeared in the earlier poem (ll. 23–36). As in 1.5, there is an abrupt shift in mid-poem to another subject, Ovid's misfortunes and his friend's success (ll. 37–66).

But the elegy is a coherent whole. Ovid first discusses friendship, then turns to his friend's *ingenium*, contrasting the misfortune which his own talent has brought him. He ends with a plea for support; in return he hopes that his friend will continue in his success.[22] Ovid's treatment of the good faith theme is also more reflective here. He compares himself, not with Ulysses, as in 1.5, but with a contemporary who has similar talents and has been successful, not ruined, because of them. Because the comparison ends on a personal note, the contrast with the stereotyped faithless friend of 1.8 is more striking.

OVID'S POETRY: TO HIS WIFE (*Tristia* 1.6)

tu si Maeonium vatem sortita fuisses,
　　Penelopes esset fama secunda tuae.

·　　·　　·　　·

prima locum sanctas heroidas inter haberes,
　　prima bonis animi conspicerere tui.

If you had been allotted Homer as your
poet, even Penelope's fame would be second
to yours.... You would have first place
among the pious heroines of legend. You

would be first of all, conspicuous for your
goodness of soul.

Ovid's departure poem ended with a prayer that his wife remain
loyal and aid him. (1.3.101–2). In this, the only address to her within
the book, the poet pays tribute to her loyalty. Ovid first compares his
wife with Lyde and Bittis, two women immortalized by their lovers in
poetry: he loves her no less than Antimachus and Philetas loved their
mistresses. Because she has supported him and prevented him from
being robbed by an enemy during his absence, he cannot give her
sufficient thanks. If his testimony carries any weight, she knows she is
justly praised (ll. 1–18).

In the second half of his elegy (ll. 19–36) Ovid returns to exempla,
this time the classical heroines Andromache, Laudamia, and Penelope:
if his wife had married Homer, she would surpass all of them in fame.
Was her character taught or acquired at birth, he asks, or does she
follow the example of Livia?[23] Ovid's poetic abilities are not equal to
what his wife deserves; yet he will give her whatever fame he can
bestow.

The enemy may be a real person, perhaps to be identified with the
detractor to whom Ovid writes in other poems.[24] But his identity is not
important. Ovid concentrates instead on his wife; while paying tribute
to her, he also announces to his readers that he is still a Roman citizen
with control over his household and property in the city.[25] The elegy
goes still further: Ovid declares that even in exile he is a poet with
power to confer immortality in his verses. This power allows him to
move from the status of a shipwrecked exile or helpless *spolium* in the
beginning lines (ll. 7–8) to that of a master poet at the end (ll. 35–36)
who can bring fame to whom he wishes.

Ovid reintroduces themes seen earlier. His indirect reference to
himself as an "extinctus vir" (l. 20) calls to mind the death-in-exile
theme of 1.2.71–72 and 1.3.89–90; we now see in his wife's actions
the aftermath of the *funus* described in the departure poem. By
comparing his wife to Penelope he also expands his own Ulysses role.
But most important is the emphasis which he gives to himself as poet.
Ovid begins on a note reminiscent of love elegy, equating his wife with
mistresses famous in literature, then adapts to his own situation a
familiar theme, the renown which a poet can bestow on his mistress; as
in elegy, the fame of the beloved and poet are totally linked.[26] The
poem therefore becomes an expression by Ovid of his poetic position
and goals. Unlike the prologue, where he treated his role as writer in a

playful way, through comic presentation of his personified book, his declaration is serious here: he is still a poet, even in exile.

OVID'S POETRY: THE *METAMORPHOSES* (*Tristia* 1.7)

grata tua est pietas: sed carmina maior imago
    sunt mea, quae mando qualiacumque legas,
carmina mutatas hominum dicentia formas
    infelix domini quod fuga rupit opus.

Your devotion is pleasing, but you have a
more faithful image of me in my verses,
which I order you to read, such as they are—
verses telling of the changed forms of men, a
work which its master's unhappy exile cut
short.

In this address to an unnamed friend, perhaps a fellow poet or member of a literary group ("sodalis," l. 10), Ovid apologizes for the "unfinished" state of the *Metamorphoses*. The elegy opens and closes with contrasting requests; the friend should remove the Dionysiac wreath, a fitting ornament for successful poets, from Ovid's bust (ll. 1–10) and should add explanatory verses to his poem, offering an apology that it is unfinished (ll. 31–40). Ovid links his requests and his identification of himself with his poetry by playing on words for "forehead" at the beginning and end of the elegy: "fronte," which describes the beginning of the *Metamorphoses* (l. 33) recalls the temples ("tempora") of the poet's bust (l. 4). The poem concludes with the explanatory verses: while he hopes the *Metamorphoses* will be successful, he asks readers to remember that the final touches are missing.

In his apology Ovid explains that he attempted to burn all copies of the *Metamorphoses* before he left Rome (ll. 15–22), but that some copies survive as if snatched from his funeral pyre ("sed quasi de domini funere rapta sui," l. 38). This is more than simply another reference to the death-in-exile theme; Ovid makes deliberate allusion to the publication of the *Aeneid* and Virgil's instructions to his literary executors, Varius and Tucca, to burn the poem after his death.[27] His description of attempts to burn the *Metamorphoses* is no doubt literary fiction; unlike the *Aeneid*, Ovid's poem gives the impression of being complete before he went into exile. Yet this is poetic fiction with a serious purpose; by playing on the legend which had by this time developed about the publication of the *Aeneid,* Ovid deliberately imitates Virgil, inventing a comparable situation concerning the *Metamorphoses* at the time of his own death, his relegation. He even presents the *Metamorphoses* as his *Aeneid,* although he states that it had been published against his will, and gives wishes for its success ("nunc precor ut vivant," l. 25).

In theme this poem is therefore remarkably similar to *Tr.* 1.6. In the preceding elegy Ovid treated his power as a poet; now he calls attention to his greatest work, which he hopes the literary public in Rome is already reading. As in the prologue (1.1.117–20), he links his new book with the most well known creations of his earlier career.

EPILOGUE (*Tristia* 1.11)

Littera quaecumque est toto tibi lecta libello
    est mihi sollicito tempore facta viae.

                    .   .   .   .

quo magis his debes ignoscere, candide lector,
    si spe sunt, ut sunt, inferiora tua.

Every letter you have read in this whole book
was composed by me in the troubled time of
my journey....You must therefore, dear
reader, be more disposed to pardon them if
they are not—and they really are not—up to
your expectations.

In this apology Ovid is still en route and not yet arrived at his place of exile. He has left behind the Greek world described in *Tr.* 1.10 and presents himself again confronted by rough seas (ll. 19–20) and surrounded by a wild and hostile landscape (ll. 25–26). We return, both in theme and verbal echoes, to the world of *Tr.* 1.2 and 1.4.[28]

Ovid first explains that his book was composed on board ship in winter storms (ll. 1–12): on the Adriatic (l. 4), on the Aegean (l. 8), and now on the final leg of his voyage. He admits that writing verses in such a situation was madness, but confesses that composition was the one way he could relieve his distress, equating the storm with his mental turmoil ("tantis animique marisque / fluctibus," ll. 9–10—cf. ll. 33–34). Next he turns to the dangers still confronting him. At sea death is before him on every side (ll. 13–24). The landscape is even

more frightening; should he arrive safely at port, he will be prey to
robbers and war (ll. 25–34).

For these reasons, he concludes (ll. 35–44), the reader must excuse
his poems, written not in leisure, like his earlier works, but under
adverse conditions. Even now the storm is indignant that Ovid is still
writing. The poet announces that he will yield: if the storm will stop,
he will stop (ll. 43–44). And since Ovid's storm is his own creation, it
does end with the conclusion of the poem. Whatever fearfulness the
poet has presented comes to an end along with his *libellus*.

Despite concern about the book's reception in Rome (ll. 35–36)
Ovid ends his epilogue and collection on a confident note: this elegy
gives forceful expression to what he feels about his power as a poet.
Although the helmsman despairs, "immemor artis" (l. 22), Ovid
announces that his own "ingenium" has not been lost (l. 10) and shows
that he is still in command of his art, both in the skillful development
of his elegy and its elaborate sound play.[29] He even seems to enjoy the
challenge of writing poetry under such conditions. The wind and
waves allow him a novel apology for his new book: his *libellus* may
not be equal to some readers' expectations, but they must remember
the circumstances of its composition. After all, not everyone could
write a poetic book in such a situation!

THE BOOK AS A WHOLE

Our survey of individual elegies now permits discussion of the entire
collection. One striking feature of Ovid's first book is its variety. He
presents his feelings and experiences en route to Tomis in poems
developed around several themes. The most prominent is that of his
journey, the subject of five elegies: 1.2, 1.3, 1.4, 1.10 and 1.11. Both 1.2
and 1.4 treat storms at sea, but the longer of the two poems appears
first, allowing Ovid greater scope in presenting his theme. Both poems
frame his account of departure to give it greater emphasis. In the
closing elegies of his book Ovid returns to the journey, paying tribute
to his ship and reminding his readers of the dangers en route. The
conditions of the voyage now provide an apology for the whole
collection.

The journey is not Ovid's only concern. Both prologue and epilogue
give a defense of the book linking it with the poet's earlier works. Ovid
also treats his position as poet in 1.6 and 1.7, two elegies placed in
juxtaposition at the center of the collection.

The last major theme is that of good faith and loyalty, treated in
three elegies. *Tr.* 1.5 and 1.9 praise friendship which remains loyal in
time of trouble, and 1.8 is a *querela* against a faithless friend. Both 1.5
and 1.9 are long, uneven poems: Ovid may have been experimenting
with this theme at the time he wrote this collection. His complaint to
the "faithless friend," based on conventions familiar from the *Heroides*,
is more successful than straightforward praise of loyalty in others. In
addition, Ovid touches on this subject in other poems. He points out
that only a few friends were on hand at his departure (1.3.15−16),
laments his separation from his *sodales* (1.3.65−66−cf. 1.5.1), and
describes his ship as a faithful companion (1.10.10). Although Ovid's
thoughts on friendship are not original and his treatment of this subject
was certainly influenced by literary models, his concerns may well have
been real; these good faith elegies are perhaps an attempt to remind his
friends of their responsibilities to a fellow friend in exile. Yet, in
contrast to later books from Tomis, friendship is not the main theme of
this collection. Ovid's journey is much more important.

By building his book around the journey, Ovid offsets poems dealing
with this subject with others concerned with subordinate themes, thus
achieving *variatio* within the collection. We can illustrate the arrangement of the book as shown.

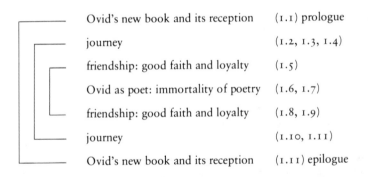

Ovid's new book and its reception	(1.1) prologue
journey	(1.2, 1.3, 1.4)
friendship: good faith and loyalty	(1.5)
Ovid as poet: immortality of poetry	(1.6, 1.7)
friendship: good faith and loyalty	(1.8, 1.9)
journey	(1.10, 1.11)
Ovid's new book and its reception	(1.11) epilogue

The poems are presented in a series of frames: elegies concerning good
faith and the journey enclose the central pieces treating Ovid's role as
poet and his poetic immortality. The prologue and epilogue, both
concerned with the new book, frame the entire collection. In addition,
the epilogue reworks motifs of the journey, presenting it as the cause of
the book's shortcomings. *Tr.* 1.11, like 1.10, is therefore linked with the

first four elegies of the book in which the journey theme is predominant.

Within this arrangement, 1.5 and 1.9, both similar in theme and development, begin and end a series of five poems addressed to individuals. Within this series 1.6 and 1.7, elegies dealing with Ovid's poetry, are juxtaposed. Ovid's address to his wife, his proudest declaration within the book that he is still in command of his poetic powers, occupies a central position within this collection of eleven poems. The poet no doubt expected his readers to understand the significance of its placement.[30]

The variety of subjects presented in individual elegies allowed Ovid a thematic rather than a more artificial or strictly symmetrical arrangement for his book.[31] But his presentation of themes within the collection is much more subtle than that which can be indicated through a simplified schematic diagram. Ovid prepares in earlier elegies for more extended treatment of motifs in later poems. The Ulysses theme is not in itself the main subject of any single elegy, but figures significantly in Ovid's journey. Although it is fully developed for the first time at only the end of *Tr.* 1.5, Ovid carefully prepares for it: he is a storm-tossed hero in 1.2 and 1.4 and expresses his separation from his wife and family in 1.3.

Likewise Ovid's wife is most prominent in 1.6; yet her role as faithful supporter is foreshadowed by references to her during the storm (1.2.37–44) and departure poems (1.3.79–102). The picture of departure with few friends on hand (1.3.15–16) prepares for later lectures on good faith. These themes, once introduced, also reappear in subsequent elegies. Ovid's comparison of his wife with Penelope (1.6.21–22) reinforces his Ulysses role. The death-in-exile theme, introduced in 1.2 and developed fully in 1.3, reappears in the two central elegies (1.6.20; 1.7.37–38). Throughout his book Ovid interweaves themes to produce a unified collection.

Also noteworthy is Ovid's treatment of time in the presentation of his journey. In beginning elegies he appears to adopt a Virgilian order, in medias res: immediately after the prologue, in *Tr.* 1.2 we see him confronted by imminent death in the storm. Then in *Tr.* 1.3 he leaves the present of his journey to return to the past, giving his account of departure as a story within a story. This time sequence may be deliberate imitation of that within the *Aeneid,* where the opening storm of *Aenid* 1.34–123 leads to the hero's account of his departure from Troy. Ovid recognizes Virgil's storm as one of his literary models (cf. *Tr.* 1.2.19–22 and *Aeneid* 1.106–7) and describes his last night in

Rome in terms of Troy's capture (1.3.25–26). Yet in *Tr.* 1.4 he returns
to another storm and at the present time, reworking Virgil's epic order
for a different effect: whatever symbolic value the first storm had is lost
when we encounter it again in *Tr.* 1.4. The time sequence in the final
elegies is also unusual. Ovid's tribute to his ship brings his own voyage
to its destination, and he announces that he will travel the remaining
distance on land (1.10.23–41). Yet the epilogue shows him still on
board beset by danger and fear. The collection begins and ends with
the present situation of Ovid's journey, the stormy sea which the poet
in the epilogue equates with his own mental distress (1.11.9–10, 33–
34); yet in *Tr.* 1.2 he describes it so playfully that it loses much, if not
all, of its fearfulness. Moreover, only in a few places does Ovid move
from immediate events of his exile to give thoughts for the future: he
hopes that his wife and friends continue in their support (1.3.101–2,
1.5.35–36, 1.9.65–66) and that his works will still be read while he is
absent (1.7.25–26).

Ovid's collection no doubt stirred great interest in the literary circles
of Rome. Its novelty and the cleverness of its presentation raise the
question of his purpose in sending it to the capital for publication.
Here the themes of the book are instructive: Ovid exploits his journey
to entertain his readers. His intentions seem more to amuse than to
persuade or present a serious subject. He hopes that friends will remain
loyal to him during his absence and even reveals concern that some
may have already deserted him. But Ovid's appeals to good faith are
general and stereotyped. He makes no specific requests for aid to the
individuals addressed in *Tr.* 1.5–1.9, and there is little emphasis in the
book on pleas for direct support. Ovid does not defend his conduct or
argue his innocence at great length. His most serious concern within
the collection is to demonstrate that his poetic career has not ended,
that he is continuing to write and expects to be read. At this point of
his relegation, as he composed this book en route to Tomis, he appears
to await a recall and an early return to Rome.

Yet even if Ovid thought his exile would be short, he decided to
present it in a poetic book. Leaving Italy gave him the opportunity to
describe his journey in strikingly novel literary terms, complete with
heroic trappings and a carefully developed Ulysses role. We can of
course interpret such motifs as Ovid's poetic expression of the effect of
exile on himself, but we must also recognize in them witty play on
traditional literary forms. Ovid's choice of Ulysses as a model also
undercuts whatever symbolic meaning can be drawn from his
presentation: his role is a confident one, that of a legendary hero who

undergoes hardships separated from family and friends but ultimately triumphs through his own resilience, trickery, and cleverness. Ovid's readers would certainly have been alert to such artistic play as his reworking of epic storms and elegiac motifs.

Tr. 1 is quite different in content from Ovid's preexilic works; the poet himself apologizes for its diverse nature in his epilogue (1.11.35–36). Yet Ovid's address to his *libellus* quoted at the beginning of this chapter acknowledges similarities between it and his other works. Indeed, in spirit and purpose *Tr.* 1 closely resembles Ovid's earlier elegiac writings; only the subject has changed. Instead of love elegy, we are given a book constructed around the experience of exile, separation from friends and loved ones, and a heroic journey.

There is an overall unity in Ovid's presentation: he relates his departure from Rome and a general outline of his journey, giving thoughts on the responsibilities of friendship and his position as poet. Yet it is difficult to reconstruct more than a bare autobiographical framework from these poems. Indeed, aside from his lectures on friendship, which are themselves highly conventional, Ovid in this book seems no more affected by relegation than he was by love in the *Amores.* As in his love elegies, the poetic role which he assumes within this book is also not uniform or consistent. Ovid moves abruptly from a mock epic description of a storm at sea to the heightened intensity of his account of departure. Within the collection he presents himself as Aeneas leaving Troy or a Ulysses figure abandoned by friends and blasted by a divine thunderbolt, but also as the author of the *Metamorphoses,* a master poet who can confer immortality in his verses. Ovid's situation, that of poet in exile, has provided an experience which he explores intellectually in a collection of elegies. We are even left with the impression that he does not take his relegation altogether seriously. Yet Ovid is still a creative artist. And he has found in the experience of his departure from Rome and journey to Tomis both the subject of a new book and a fertile outlet for his talent.

ut via finita est et opus requievit eundi,
et poenae tellus est mihi tacta meae,
nil nisi flere libet.

Now that my journey is finished and
the task of the voyage is over, and I
have reached the land of my punish-
ment, all I want to do is weep.

III   TRISTIA 3   Tomis and Rome

IN HIS SECOND collection, begun shortly after his arrival in Tomis in the late summer or early fall of A.D. 9, Ovid presents his initial reactions to his place of exile and his first testimony about life there. The book was completed and sent to Rome for publication sometime in midyear A.D. 10.[1]

In structure and format the book shows similarities to *Tr.* 1. It contains a prologue and epilogue, elegies addressed to Ovid's friends and wife, and more descriptive poems. Ovid also returns to the good faith and loyalty theme and again reflects on his position as poet. But there are also striking differences: this book is set in Tomis, not en route during the journey, and the most important subject is Ovid's present situation in contrast to his former life in the capital. Rome had figured prominently in several poems of *Tr.* 1, most notably the prologue, in which Ovid instructed his personified book about its mission, and 1.3, his account of departure. Yet as a poetic theme it was subordinate to that of the journey. Now after his arrival at his place of relegation, Ovid in poem after poem contrasts Tomis with Rome as he presents himself overcome, both physically and spiritually, by the hard climate and grim conditions there. Ovid's poetic aims have changed, and the contrast with *Tr.* 1, which he had sent to Rome one year earlier, is striking and deliberate. Ovid's place of exile and its effect on him have become the subject of his collection.

Although scholars have discussed individual elegies within the collection, the book as a whole has received less attention than the first two books of the *Tristia*. There is of course Georg Luck's commentary, as well as brief comments by Ulrich von Wilamowitz and R. J. Dickinson, a discussion of its arrangements by Karl Herrmann, and a stylistic and rhythmic analysis by Yves Bouynot.[2] Yet the collection itself, because of its change of theme and the differences between it and *Tr.* 1, merits further study, particularly its presentation of Ovid's place of exile. Our discussion will be organized like that of *Tr.* 1, beginning with a review of the major groups of elegies, letters to individuals, and more description poems, with separate treatment of the prologue and epilogue.

PROLOGUE: OVID'S BOOK IN ROME (*Tristia* 3.1)

Missus in hanc venio timide liber exulis urbem:
　　da placidam fesso, lector amice, manum.

　　　　·　　　·　　　·　　　·

dicite, lectores, si non grave, qua sit eundum
　　quasque petam sedes hospes in urbe liber.

I come trembling, the book of an exile sent to
this city. Friendly reader, I am tired; give me a
soothing hand....Tell me, readers, if it is not
too much trouble, where I should go or what
home I should seek as a guest in the city.

From the very first lines of this prologue we are invited to remember *Tr.* 1.1. In the opening section (ll. 1–20) Ovid's personified *liber* describes its contents and explains that it does not treat love (ll. 3–10), then excuses its meter and physical appearance (ll. 11–18) before asking to find a home. Although its physical description is reduced from that in *Tr.* 1.1, Ovid again plays on motifs seen earlier, such as elegiac limping (ll. 11–12) and tear-stained pages (ll. 15–16). He also makes much more explicit a theme only touched on in the earlier prologue (1.1.59): his new book is a foreigner from a savage land ("barbara terra," l. 18), a newly arrived "hospes." Unlike the book in *Tr.* 1, it has no poet to advise it and must seek the reader's assistance.

The book tours the monumental center of Rome (ll. 21–58), ending
on the Palatine Hill at the house of Augustus. Here it is prompted to
question its guide about the oak wreath on the emperor's door;
"augurium" (l. 36) is no doubt a pun on the name of Augustus himself,
connected by ancient evidence with augury.[3] Although the book
displays hesitation before the house of the emperor (ll. 55–56), it gives
a short defense of Ovid and appeals for a pardon. But the tour of
Rome is not yet over. The book now visits the city's public libraries,
seeking its *fratres* (the *Ars amatoria,* of course, excluded). All three
libraries refuse it entrance, and the *liber* becomes an exile, like its
author (ll. 59–74). Yet it prays that someday Caesar will relent and
ask that in the meantime it be accepted in private homes (ll. 75–82).

There are obvious similarities to the structure and development of
Tr. 1.1: both poems open with a description of Ovid's personified book,
which visits the Forum and Palatine and reacts to Augustus with fear.
At the end of each elegy Ovid returns to the theme of his book and its
place in libraries next to its *fratres.* As in *Tr.* 1.1, Ovid's playfulness is
evident in his *pes* puns which appear in each of the major sections: the
books' arrival (ll. 11–12), its visit to Augustus's house (ll. 55–56), and
its attempt to enter the libraries (ll. 69–70).[4] As a stranger to Rome,
the book also displays an amusing naïveté about the capital (ll. 35–36,
39–46). Yet this prologue also presents important differences. Ovid's
book, a bewildered traveler from a barbarian land, is excluded from its
natural and appropriate home, Rome's public libraries, as its author is
barred from the capital. Its exclusion gives its appeal for an eventual
pardon much greater force. All of Ovid's references to the time of this
pardon are vague ("quandocumque," ll. 57–58; "forsitan et nobis
olim," ll. 75–76; "interea," l. 79); yet he still hopes for a recall.

The prologue also exploits a literary theme which by this time had
become almost conventional, the poetic itinerary of Rome. Augustan
poets seem fascinated by the contrast between the legendary past and
monumental present of their city; we need only cite Virgil's description
of Rome in *Aeneid* 8.337–61, Tibullus 2.5, and Propertius 4.1. Ovid
himself played with the narrative technique of the walk around Rome
in his *Fasti,*[5] and *Tr.* 3.1 is itself one of our most detailed descriptions
of Rome's monumental center in Augustan times. Yet like other poetic
itineraries, it is highly selective, linking Augustus and Augustan
buildings with the oldest shrines of republican Rome to heighten the
impact of Ovid's plea for a pardon.[6]

The location of Augustus's house allows the book to visit the nearby

temple of Apollo Palatinus (ll. 59–64). In describing this temple Ovid
treats a monument celebrated by other Augustan poets. Lines 61–62,

signa peregrinis ubi sunt alterna columnis
  Belides et stricto barbarus ense pater,[7]

where there are statues of imported
marble between the columns, the
Danaids and their father, savage with
drawn sword,

directly recall Propertius's poem on the dedication of the complex:

tantam erat in speciem Poenis digesta columnis
  inter quas Danai femina turba senis.   [Prop. 2.31.3–4]

laid out in so great a display with Phoenician
columns, between which stood the many
daughters of father Danaus.

This temple complex also serves as a focal point for Tibullus's poetic
itinerary (2.5.1–18), Propertius's tour of the forum (4.1), as well as
Virgil's and Propertius's celebration of Actium (*Aeneid* 8.720–77,
Propertius 4.6.11–12).

    Yet Ovid's emphasis is different; what he describes in most detail is,
not the temple, but its library, as a natural and appropriate home for
his newly arrived book. The *liber* seeks admission at two other
libraries within the Porticus of Octavia (ll. 69–70) and the Atrium of
Libertas (ll. 71–72).[8] Both complexes were among the most magnifi-
cent in Rome at this time, but again Ovid focuses only on their
libraries. His bibliothecal tour, appropriate for the personified book, is
a novel variation on the standard Augustan itinerary.

    The book's exclusion from public libraries may indicate that Ovid's
writings incurred official displeasure after his relegation. The poet
returns to this same theme in *P.* 1.1.3–10, where he asks Brutus to
accept his new collection privately. Admittance into or exclusion from
Rome's public libraries, which were under the emperor's patronage,
could no doubt work as an indirect form of censorship. Some scholars
have read this elegy as evidence that Ovid's writings, or a portion of
them, were banned. But we must be wary of accepting what may be
literary fiction as historical fact; there is little evidence of such
censorship during the Augustan principate.[9] In stressing his book's

exclusion, Ovid no doubt indulges his poetic imagination to gain greater sympathy. Since his *liber* represents the poet himself, it is not difficult to see how its situation reflects on Ovid's own plea: won't the emperor change his mind—at least someday?

The poetic itinerary serves another, even more important purpose. Through his description of Rome Ovid emphasizes his distance from it; his book, a child of Tomis, comes from the end of the world (ll. 26, 50) and is a complete stranger to the capital. He therefore introduces the contrast between Rome and Tomis directly in the book's prologue. Ovid's initial picture of the capital becomes a poetic backdrop for later complaints.

LETTERS TO INDIVIDUALS

A Deathbed Letter to His Wife (Tristia 3.3)

tam procul ignotis igitur moriemur in oris,
    et fient ipso tristia fata loco;
nec mea consueto languescent corpora lecto
    depositum nec me qui fleat, ullus erit;
nec dominae lacrimis in nostra cadentibus ora
    accedent animae tempora parva meae.

I shall die then so far away in unknown
regions, and the very place will make my fate
bitter. My body will not waste away on my
accustomed couch, nor will there be anyone
to weep for me at my burial. Nor shall I gain
a few moments added to my life as my
mistress's tears fall on my face.

In this elegy, the most important of this group of individual letters, Ovid's use of an epistolary format is careful and deliberate: the poem is called an "epistula" (l. 1), written, he explains, by another, because he is too sick to write himself (ll. 1–4, 85–86). He also begins with the epistolary imperfect tense ("eram," ll. 2, 4) and ends with "vale" as his last word (l. 88). After his introduction (ll. 1–4), Ovid presents a deathbed scene, describing his reactions to external conditions in Tomis, the climate, water, physical surroundings, and lack of friends. Yet most of all he thinks of his wife and is even more distressed by her absence (ll. 5–28).

He next reflects on his death away from her, asks for burial in Italy
(ll. 29–64), but also explains that he will not be dying for the first
time: exile is already a living death. Then Ovid gives instructions
about his funeral rites (ll. 65–84). He requests a simple urn and
dictates an epitaph for his monument. The elegy ends with two
couplets (ll. 85–88) corresponding to the opening lines: Ovid cannot
continue but sends his "vale," perhaps the last his wife will receive
from him.

As in *Tr.* 1.3, his account of departure, and 1.6, an earlier poem to his
wife, Ovid reworks elegiac motifs; we may compare in particular
Tibullus 1.3, another sickbed poem. Ovid describes his wife as his
"domina" (l. 23), addresses her as "carissima" (l. 27) and "lux mea"
(l. 52), instructs her not to tear her hair or wound her cheeks (ll. 51–
52), states that she is constantly on his mind (ll. 17–18), and laments
that loved ones will not be on hand to perform the customary funeral
rites (ll. 41–46)[10] Yet the poet's tone in addressing his wife is quite
different from that of his elegiac model: Tibullus sick on Phaeacia casts
Delia in a Penelope role, that of a faithful wife awaiting her lover's
return (1.3.83–90); Ovid directly questions his wife's fidelity in Rome
while he is "dubius vitae" (ll. 25–28) and wonders what her reaction
will be to his death (ll. 47–50). Unlike Tibullus, who wants to recover
from his illness (1.3.3–6), Ovid would prefer to have died long ago,
before he left Italy for exile (ll. 33–36). In contrast to Tibullus, who
ends his poem with a reverie on his reunion with Delia (1.3.89–94),
Ovid does not treat his death in vague terms but, as a man already
dead when he went into exile (ll. 53–54), gives specific instructions for
his burial and epitaph: we may note the imperatives "facito" (l. 65),
"misce" (l. 69), "pone" (l. 70), "caede" (l. 72), and "dato" (l. 82). After
he dies, he will not, like Tibullus, be led by Venus into the Elysian
fields (1.3.57–66); instead his *umbra* will be forced to wander among
those of savages (ll. 61–64). Ovid also introduces other themes not
present in his model. He emphasizes the subject of his own poetic
immortality, announcing that his funeral and tomb are not of crucial
importance ("hoc satis in titulo," l. 77) in comparison with his literary
works, the "maiora...et diuturna magis...monumenta" (ll. 77–78)
which will give him lasting fame, an image which recalls his earlier
reference to the *Metamorphoses* as his "maior imago" at *Tr.* 1.7.11.

The poem therefore stresses Ovid's role and achievements as a poet,
a theme enhanced through its echoes of Tibullus 1.3. Ovid extends this
still further in his own epitaph, which is inspired by Tibullus 1.3.55–
56, but goes far beyond its literary model:

HIC EGO QVI IACEO TENERORVM LVSOR AMORVM
  INGENIO PERII NASO POETA MEO
AT TIBI QVI TRANSIS NE SIT GRAVE QVISQVIS AMASTI
  DICERE NASONIS MOLLITER OSSA CVBENT.   [ll. 73–76]

I who lie here, the poet Ovid, who played with tender
Loves, perished because of my own genius. But let it not
be a hardship for you, the passerby, whoever has been in
love, to say: "May his bones rest in peace!"

We recognize immediately elements common to epitaphs, such as an
address to the traveler and wish for peaceful repose.[11] But Ovid's
inscription also emphasizes his role as elegist: through a deliberate
echo of *Am.* 3.15.1, "quaere novum vatem, tenerorum mater
Amorum," he identifies himself as a "lusor," a sporter or trifler with
elegiac themes, and appeals to all lovers to remember him. At the same
time, he also extends the theme of death-in-exile through a verbal
reminiscence of *Tr.* 2.2, "ingenio perii qui miser ipse meo." Within this
new context Ovid's verb takes on greater force: no longer does "perii"
refer only to the fact of his relegation, as in *Tr.* 2.2. Because Ovid, like
Tibullus, now presents himself as a poet dying away from friends and
loved ones, his death has become both the living death of exile and a
more immediate fate to which he may succumb. Dictating his own
epitaph is therefore doubly appropriate.[12]

   Although the elegy affirms Ovid's poetic immortality (ll. 77–80), its
dominant mood is that of grimness and death. The poet reworks his
Tibullan model to color our initial impressions of his place of exile:
unlike Tibullus's Phaeacia, with its associations of a poetic never-never
land, Tomis is all too real, the place least appropriate for a "tenerorum
lusor amorum." Conditions there are severe, and the poet's health has
suffered. Unlike Tibullus, Ovid cannot hope for a recovery and return.
In this first letter to an individual within the collection, he presents
himself to his wife, and his readers, as a man about to die.

To a Friend: Live for Yourself (Tristia 3.4)

usibus edocto si quicquam credis amico,
   vive tibi et longe nomina magna fuge.
vivi tibi, quantumque potes praelustria vita:
   saevum praelustri fulmen ab arce venit.

If you put any faith in a friend taught by
experience, live for yourself and keep away
from important people. Live for yourself
and, as much as you can, avoid the glitter
of fame. It is from the height of fame that
cruel lightning comes.

Like earlier elegies in *Tr.* 1 on good faith and loyalty, this is a long,
uneven poem. Ovid begins with an Epicurean lecture on moderation,
stating that if he had followed his own advice, he might still be in
Rome (ll. 1–32). He next praises the friend's loyalty (ll. 33–46) before
turning to his own situation (ll. 47–62): at the farthest corner of the
world he vividly recollects the past through a sort of mental vision.
Through the powers of his *oculi mentis* the images of Rome and his
faithful wife remain before him.[13] Finally Ovid addresses his friends
(ll. 63–78): he will not write to them by name because such
recognition will only create difficulties, and perhaps danger, for them.
Yet they should be able to recognize themselves in his verses. Ovid
closes with hopes for their continued loyalty.

The abrupt transition at lines 46–47, where the poet turns from
thanking his friend to describe memories of Rome, has prompted
editors from Heinsius to the present day to begin a new elegy at line
47.[14] Yet most manuscripts show only one poem of seventy-eight lines,
and there are good reasons to treat *Tr.* 3.4 as a single elegy. The
transition is not impossible: Ovid states in line 45 that Scythian Pontus
holds him, then goes on in lines 47–52 to elaborate his situation. Ovid
changes his addressee in mid-poem, writing in lines 1–46 to only one
friend, then collectively to all his friends after line 63, but this sudden
shift does not necessitate division of the poem. Ovid made a similar
change earlier in *Tr.* 1.5, another long poem which began as a letter to
an individual friend, but dropped him for a collective address.

We find another cogent argument for the unity of *Tr.* 3.4 in its
structural plan and development, which are too careful to be
accidental. Ovid begins with a lecture on moderation which consists of
two sixteen-line sections, the lesson illustrated first by Ovid's own
experience and exampla from nature (ll. 1–16), then by mythological
exempla (ll. 17–32); the conventional motif of life's voyage at lines
31–32 echoes that seen earlier in lines 9–16. Ovid next follows with a
central section (fourteen lines) and concludes the poem with two more
sixteen-line sections, a statement that he remembers Rome and those
dear to him (ll. 47–62) and that he will not name his friends (ll. 63–

78). These last two sections of thirty-two lines balance the opening lecture. In the opening lines Ovid cautions his friends about associating with the mighty; at the end he assures all his friends that he will not endanger them by associating their names with himself.

Although Ovid wrote several poems in *Tr.* 1 to unidentified individuals, he gave no explanation why he did not name them openly. This is his first such explanation in the exile poetry. Perhaps his earlier practice had prompted queries from Rome; if so, Ovid provides his explanation in his first epistle within his new collection addressed to an unnamed individual. More important, however, is the question why Ovid declines to name his friends. Within the context of this elegy, his explanation that he does not wish to endanger them directly complements his opening lecture on moderation. But his decision to preserve their anonymity also serves a more important literary purpose. By writing to unnamed individuals Ovid can give full attention to the presentation of his poetic themes. The identity or personality of individual addressees does not color the poems; Ovid has reserved for himself the freedom to treat his subjects, either the journey or Tomis itself, without the complications of particular personalities or friendships. Because they are written to unnamed individuals, elegies to faithful friends or detractors gain a generality of appeal which they would lack if addressed to particular individuals.[15] Ovid's complaints and requests therefore become applicable to all his readers.

To Friends in Rome (Tristia 3.5 and 3.6)

In these companion pieces Ovid defends himself (3.5.51–52, 3.6.25–26) and requests the assistance of his addressee in obtaining a new place of exile (3.5.53–56, 3.6.21–24). Each poem is written to a specific individual: the friend in 3.5 was a recent acquaintance who approached Ovid after his sentence (3.5.1–22); the addressee in 3.6 was the poet's intimate friend before his departure (3.6.1.–16). The first couplet of 3.6 is also modeled on that of 3.5 through the beginning words "foedus amicitiae" (cf. "usus amicitiae," 3.5.1) and repetition of *dissimulare* in the pentameters. The themes of the two poems also complement each other: the first is concerned with good faith and loyalty, the second with reasons for the exile.

To Perilla: On Poetic Fame (Tristia 3.7)

tu quoque, quam studii maneat felicior usus,
  effuge venturos, qua potes, usque rogos.

You too, and may a happier use of your art
await you, escape the coming funeral pyres
in the only way you can.

Ovid's glorification of himself as a creative artist in this elegy was
discussed earlier in Chapter 1, but the poem should be examined
further. Turning from unnamed friends, he now writes to a specific
individual, the poet Perilla, who is perhaps his stepdaughter by his
second wife. What he describes as a letter "subito perarata" (l. 1) is a
carefully developed literary epistle ("sermonis fida ministra," l. 2).[16]
Ovid begins with instructions to his letter (ll. 1–10), which recall those
to his personified book in *Tr.* 1.1: when Perilla asks about him, it
should reply that he lives in exile in a way he does not wish to live
("vivere me dices, sed sic, ut vivere nolim," l. 7). This is an echo of
Tr. 1.1.19 ("vivere me dices, salvum tamen esse negabis" ["you will say
I am alive but deny I'm safe"]). But the contrast between the two lines
is instructive: instead of safety during his heroic journey Ovid now
raises the question of life and death itself.

He next turns to the exact text of his letter (ll. 11–32). His subject is
Perilla's literary endeavors: is she still writing poetry? Ovid served as
her exemplum and was the first to lead her to the Muses. Perilla should
not be discouraged by his own fortune, but should continue writing.
Then he treats the problem of mortality (ll. 33–54). Old age, Ovid
warns, will soon come, but poetic talent and inspiration are immortal.
Even after his death, he will survive and be read. He ends this final
section, like the earlier one, with an injunction: Perilla too must win
her own immortality.

In dealing with the past (ll. 11–20), present (ll. 21–32), and future
(ll. 33–54) of Perilla's life and literary career, Ovid once more assumes
the role of master poet. Having already introduced the theme of death-
in-exile in earlier elegies, he now contrasts human mortality with the
immortality he will gain through his works. Tomis and its hardships do
not figure prominently in the elegy. In contrast to the gloom which
colors most of this collection, Ovid in this literary epistle ends his
series of letters (3.3–3.7) on a proud and confident note.

To an Enemy (*Tristia* 3.11)

As in *Tr.* 1.8, his earlier poem to a faithless friend, Ovid in this poem
does not seem to have a particular individual in mind, but writes to a
lay figure ("quisquis is es," l. 56). We see again conventional topoi

describing cruelty (ll. 7–18–cf. *Tr.* 1.8.37–46) as well as general
complaints about Tomis. Ovid states that he is no longer worthy of
attack, since he is now a dead man ("inanem...umbram," l. 25;
"Manes...meos," l. 32), only the shadow ("simulacra," ll. 30, 31) of
what he once was in Rome (ll. 19–38). His enemy, like Perillus who
designed the bull for Phalaris, will receive the punishment he deserves.
Ovid recounts the legend to illustrate the idea of just retribution (ll.
39–54), then closes with the commonplace warning that Fortune is
changeable (ll. 55–74). Yet there is a significant difference between this
elegy and *Tr.* 1.8. Ovid concentrates here, not on desertion by a friend,
but on the recurring theme of the book, the contrast between his
former life and self in Rome and his present condition.

DESCRIPTIONS OF TOMIS

An Exile's Prayer (*Tristia* 3.8)

cumque locum moresque hominum cultusque sonumque
   cernimus, et qui sim qui fuerimque, subit,
tantus amor necis est, querar ut cum Caesaris ira,
   quod non offensas vindicet ense suas.
at quoniam semel est odio civiliter usus
   mutato levior sit fuga nostra loco.

When I look at this place, the manners of the people, the
way they dress, and their language, and it comes to mind
what I am now and what I was, so great is my desire to
die that I complain that Caesar in his anger did not
punish my wrongs with the sword. But since he once
exercised his hatred for me mildly, I still hope for an
easier exile in a different place.

   With *Tr.* 3.8 we turn from poems written to individuals to more
descriptive elegies. One of the most successful poems in the *Tristia*, it is
divided into two halves: lines 1–22, in which Ovid gives wishes for the
future; and lines 23–42, where he describes his present situation. He
begins with daydreams of an abrupt return from exile: he would like to
mount the chariot of Triptolemus or Medea or take the wings of
Perseus or Daedalus to see again his homeland and household. Yet
Ovid returns to his senses. He can only pray to Augustus, the one
divinity who can bring about his return.[17] Although a recall to Rome is

too much to ask, he hopes that someday, when the emperor has softened his anger ("forsitan hoc olim, cum iam satiaverit iram," l. 19), he may approach him with his request. In the meantime, Ovid asks to go elsewhere. In this way he dismisses fanciful dreams to turn to wishes which may someday be fulfilled. The staccato effect of the individual couplets in lines 11–22 is in direct contrast to the flowing periods of Ovid's imaginative dreams (ll. 1–10).[18]

In the second half Ovid reviews the realities of his exile, treating both the physical conditions (ll. 23–32) and its mental effects (ll. 33–42). The climate, food, and water do not agree with him—complaints seen earlier at *Tr.* 3.3.7–10. He is now sick and cannot sleep at night. He has no appetite, and his color is like that of the autumn leaves. Here Ovid uses a simile directly reminiscent of *Aeneid* 6.309–10, where Virgil compares the souls waiting for passage across the Styx to leaves, to suggest a stage of decay, perhaps even to indicate that he is now in the autumn of his life. He is no healthier in mind than in body, but still hopes for a milder place of exile.

The elegy moves from fanciful visions of return to the reality that recall depends entirely on Augustus. Ovid's description of hardships in Tomis, while general, is the most complete which we have seen thus far in this collection. *Tr.* 3.8 summarizes the mood of this book, the despair and hardships of exile in Tomis and the desire to return.

How Tomis Got Its Name (Tristia 3.9)

Hic quoque sunt igitur Graiae (quis crederet?) urbes
    inter inhumanae nomina barbariae?
huc quoque Mileto missi venere coloni
    inque Getis Graias constituere domos?
sed vetus huic nomen, positaque antiquius urbe,
    constat ab Absyrti caede fuisse loco.

Are there Greek cities then here too (who would
believe it?) among the names of savage barbarism?
Did colonists from Miletus come here too and did
they found Greek cities among the Getae? But this
place has an ancient name, even older than the
founding of the city, clearly derived from the
murder of Absyrtus.

Ovid narrates the legend of Medea and Absyrtus to link his place of exile with inhuman, bloody deeds. He answers his readers' disbelief ("quis crederet," l. 1) by the authority of the myth ("constat," l. 6), demonstrating that Pontus, long associated with colonization by the Greeks, is indeed a world of savage brutality. His juxtaposition of "Getis Graias" (l. 4) is certainly deliberate.[19]

Ovid assumes that his reader is familiar with the legend and concentrates instead on Medea's reaction to her father's pursuit. When her hand is thrown into hurried preparations for flight, she beats her breasts, mindful of the punishment she deserves ("conscia ... meritorum," l. 15), but takes firm steps. When she looks at her brother, she at once realizes that victory is hers ("vicimus," l. 23). She quickly slays him, cuts him up, and scatters the pieces. The actual slaughter is described quickly ("divellit divulsaque," l. 27), with no reactions from Absyrtus who is "ignarus" and "nec quicquam tale timens" (l. 25). Her brother's "pallentesque manus sanguineum caput" (l. 30) remain behind as the grim reminder of the deed, and the elegy closes with emphasis on Aeetes' grief.

Although Ovid presents the main events of the legend, he wishes only to explain the name of Tomis through it, by association with the Greek verb *temno* ("to cut").[20] There is little description of Pontus itself. Although Ovid could easily have commented on Medea's barbarism, comparing it to the barbarism of the place, he is more subtle here: in addition to furnishing an explanation for Tomis's name, he leaves the reader with a feeling of wildness and savagery connected with the origin of the city. From Ovid's first extended treatment of the area in this book, his discussion of its name, we are asked to associate Tomis with cruel, inhuman deeds and death.

Winter and Warfare in Tomis (Tristia 3.10)

sive igitur nimii Boreae vis saeva marinas,
    sive redundatas flumine cogit aquas,
protinus aequato siccis Aquilonibus Histro
    invehitur celeri barbarus hostis equo;
hostis equo pollens longeque volante sagitta
    vicinam late depopulatur humum.

Whether the grim force of the mighty
North Wind freezes the sea's waters or
those of the frozen river, immediately

when the Danube becomes level with the
dry northern blasts, the savage enemy rides
over it on swift horses; an enemy strong in
horses and far-flying arrows devastates the
nearby soil far and wide.

Ovid's first long description of Pontus gives special emphasis to its
harsh winter and the savagery of surrounding tribes. He opens (ll. 1–
12) with a statement of where he is, in "media ... barbaria" (l. 4). The
Danube wards off his savage neighbors during the warmer months, but
in the winter they have easy access to Tomis across the frozen river.

In the next section (ll. 13–50) we see Ovid's famous description of
winter in Tomis: snow which reaches the height of buildings, natives
dressed in skins and trousers, frozen hair and beards as well as frozen
wine, wagons and horses crossing the Danube. Ovid returns to the
problem of credibility raised earlier in *Tr.* 3.9: his readers may not
believe him, but he has no reason to exaggerate. He has actually seen
the sea frozen and walked on it with dry feet: if Leander had lived here,
he would never have perished (ll. 41–42). Like a second allusion to
Acontius appearing later in the poem (ll. 73–74), this elegiac
exemplum touches on a serious theme; in Ovid's land of exile even
legend has lost its meaning.[21] Not all legend, of course, since he used
the Medea myth to demonstrate the savagery of Pontus, but the world
of lovemaking is far removed from Tomis.

In lines 51–66 Ovid turns to the warfare which terrorizes the region.
We meet again the *fera gens* introduced in lines 5–6, tribes which
quickly cross the Danube and devastate the countryside. Some
inhabitants flee, losing all their property, some are led off into
captivity, and others are killed. Even in time of peace, Ovid concludes
(ll. 67–78), men live at Tomis in constant fear and cannot cultivate
their land; the countryside is bare, without leaves or trees. Of all places
in the world, this is the area to which he has been relegated.

Allusions to the Scythian cold are a commonplace of ancient
literature, but Ovid's literary debts in this elegy are more specific: his
account of the Pontic winter is modeled on the famous "Scythian
digression" of the *Georgics* (3.349–83), in which Virgil describes an
extreme winter unsuitable for the keeping of herds. There is no need to
list the many similarities of detail between the two passages.[22] Ovid
follows Virgil's description, but reduces its symbolic role within the
Georgics to a description of external aspects which, following his
custom in the *Metamorphoses* and elsewhere, he emphasizes and

expands. He describes at length unusual phenomena of winter in Tomis, such as icicles in beards, rivers freezing over, and bronze cracking, details to which Virgil only alluded.

Yet Ovid's debts to the *Georgics* are not confined to his description of the winter itself. In his final lines he stresses the plight of the native farmers and describes the countryside as "nudos sine fronde, sine arbore, campos," in a direct reminiscence of *Georgics* 3.352–53, "neque ullae / aut herbae campo apparent aut arbore frondes": Tomis is a land which bears no vines and produces no wine or fruits (ll. 71– 76). Ovid expects his readers to recognize these Virgilian echoes, which show that he must live in a land of extreme cold, quite unlike Italy, the *Saturnia tellus.* He thus gives much greater pathos to his picture of Tomis: exile here is a punishment far too harsh for his offense.

Spring Comes to Tomis (Tristia 3.12)

o quantum et quotiens non est numerare, beatum
    non interdicta cui licet urbe frui!
at mihi sentitur nix verno sole soluta
    quaeque lacu durae non fodiantur aquae.

O how greatly and immeasurably blest is he who
can enjoy Rome, not forbidden to him! But I
experience snow melted by the spring sun and
water that no longer is carved out solid from the
pool.

This variation on a well-known literary model, the return of spring poem, divides itself neatly into halves with a concluding couplet.[23] In lines 1–26 Ovid announces the sudden return of spring ("iam," l. 1) and describes the change of season: the equal days and nights, flowers, birds, and rising grain (ll. 3–12). There are other signs of spring which he cannot see—the vine and tree, which do not grow at Tomis (ll. 13– 16). With the repetition in lines 14 and 16 ("nam procul a Geticis ... abest") Ovid shifts to spring in Rome: there is leisure now in the capital, games, racing, and theatrical performances.

In the second half of the elegy (ll. 27–52) the poet turns to his own situation. He too has small pleasures now that spring has come: the ice and snow are melting, men no longer drive across the Danube, and ships are beginning to come to the city. Ovid will question visitors, and anyone who can bring him news of Rome will be a welcome guest in his home. He then realizes the implication of what he has said: Tomis, not Rome, has become his home (ll. 51–52). He ends with a prayer that Augustus relent and make the region only his "hospitium" (ll. 53–54).

This elegy brings to full development Ovid's contrast between his former life and present circumstances. The fact that he can make a visitor from Rome his "hospes" (l. 50) leads him to an understanding of his situation. The suddenness of his realization ("iamne ... iamque," ll. 51–52) recalls the sudden return of spring in the first line ("frigora iam ..."). With the arrival of warmer weather, Tomis has become less grim and unreal (ll. 27–30); we are no longer in the world of the terrible winter. Yet the small comforts and greater contact with the outside world only reveal to Ovid that Rome is now another world and Tomis his home. The reappearance of spring makes the reality of exile all the more bitter.

LIFE AND DEATH IN EXILE

Better Death than Exile here (Tristia 3.2)

quique, fugax rerum securaque in otia natus,
    mollis et inpatiens ante laboris eram,
ultima nunc patior.

I who avoided the world of affairs and was
born for leisure free from cares, I who was
delicate and unable to bear labor, now am
suffering the most extreme things.

In two short poems placed near the beginning and end of the collection Ovid summarizes the effect of Tomis upon himself: *Tr.* 3.2, which appears immediately after the prologue, is an introduction to more detailed descriptions in subsequent poems, while 3.13 immediately before the epilogue provides a summary of what appeared earlier.

Tr. 3.2 begins with a bitter statement by Ovid: he was fated to live in Scythia, the Muses and Apollo have done nothing to aid a poet in their service, and his personal conduct, far different from that presented by his elegiac Muse, has not benefited him. After his past life, that of an elegist removed from earthly cares, and the dangers of his journey into exile, he is now in Tomis, where conditions and memories of Rome have brought him to complete despair. In the final couplets he laments that he must go on living and asks the gods to hasten his death.

Through its references to the journey and Ovid's argument familiar from *Tr.* 2.353–54 that his personal life is far different from his poetry, this elegy provides a transition from earlier books to the present collection. As in *Tr.* 1, Ovid stresses the traditional role of the poet, removed from the cares and stress of ordinary life (1.1.39–42, 1.11.37–38). But the theme of the journey now figures differently. In his epilogue to *Tr.* 1 Ovid had played on the contrast between his earlier life and the dangers of the stormy sea to excuse any shortcomings within the book (1.11.37–40). That contrast is now abandoned: Ovid's journey has now become a past adventure, a challenge he was able to master (ll. 11–16). With arrival in Tomis, the heroism of the journey is over; the present is much more grim than anything in the past.

As in *Tr.* 3.3, Ovid's death-in-exile theme now also takes on new meaning. The poet no longer asks for divine intervention to save him as at the end of *Tr.* 1.2, but now expresses wishes for death itself as an end to his unhappiness: even death will be better than his present situation. The poem ends with a striking adaptation of a *para-clausithyron* (or elegiac lament before the closed door): Ovid laments that the doors of death ("ianua sepulchri," l. 23; "interitus clausas ... fores," l. 30) are closed to him, that he has knocked so many times in vain.

Through its position within the collection, immediately after the prologue, this elegy, like *Tr.* 1.2, introduces the main theme and dominant mood of its book. Both here are different from those in *Tr.* 1. Now that the journey and its opportunities for adventure are over, the poet must endure the bleakness of an exile far worse than the dangers of the wintry sea. The high spirits of *Tr.* 1 and 2 have been replaced by bitter unhappiness.

A Birthday in Tomis (Tristia 3.13)

non ita sum positus, nec sunt ea tempora nobis,
    adventu possim laetus ut esse tuo.
funeris ara mihi, ferali cincta cupresso,
    convenit et structis flamma parata rogis.

I am not in such a situation, nor are my
circumstances such, that I can be happy at your

arrival. A funeral altar, wreathed with mournful cypress, and fire prepared on an erected pyre
are what is suited for me.

To present the occasion of his first birthday in Tomis, 20 March A.D.
10 (for the date, see *Tr.* 4.10.13–14), Ovid reworks a standard literary
model, a *genethliakon,* or poem written to his birthday god.[24] His tone
is angry as he begins with a direct address to his "natalis" (ll. 1–12): it
should not add to the years of an exile or come so uselessly to Tomis.
It cannot be that Caesar has relegated it as well to Pontus.

In bitter frustration Ovid contrasts the birthday honors customary
in Rome with his present situation (ll. 13–24): the *natalis* cannot
expect a white toga, incense, cakes, and prayers before the altar.
Instead, a funeral is more appropriate. He concludes (ll. 25–28) with
prayers he can properly make on the occasion, that the birthday god
not return to him while he is in Pontus.

At the end of the book, after extended descriptions of Tomis and the
difficulty of life there (3.8,3.9,3.10, 3.12), the poet's death wish
introduced in *Tr.* 3.2 becomes even more compelling. The juxtaposition
of this elegy with *Tr.* 3.12, the return of spring poem, is particularly
effective: with the warmer weather and event of his birthday, Ovid
shows us that life in Tomis must go on, no matter how grim and
unhappy it is. After a total rejection of customary rites, Ovid's only
positive prayer to his *natalis* is to leave Tomis before his next birthday.

EPILOGUE (*Tristia* 3.14)

hoc quoque nescioquid nostris appone libellis
   diverso missum quod tibi ab orbe venit.
quod quicumque leget (si quis leget) aestimet ante,
   compositum quo sit tempore quoque loco.
aequus erit scriptis, quorum cognoverit esse
   exilium tempus barbariamque locum.

Add to my works this something which
comes sent to you from a different world.
When anyone reads it (if anyone will) let him
first keep in mind under what circumstances
and in what place it was composed. He will
be considerate to what I have written when

he knows that its circumstances were exile
and its place a barbaric one.

Ovid first addresses a literary patron (perhaps C. Julius Hyginus,
curator of the Palatine library),[25] asking whether he still keeps his
books: except for the *Ars amatoria*, Ovid's works do not deserve the
exile of their father. The poet also commends to his protection this new
book, an orphan (ll. 1–26).

He next describes the collection itself (ll. 27–52), dropping his
address to the patron for a more general appeal ("quicumque, quis,"
l. 27). Readers must remember the circumstances of its composition:
Ovid's "ingenium" has been weakened by his experience, he has no
books or library, no one to whom he can read his poems, no place of
seclusion for literary activities. He has even begun to forget his Latin,
and there may be barbarisms in his verses.

Much in this epilogue recalls Ovid's prologue: the familiar image of
the book as the poet's offspring and his prayer that it not be exiled like
its father (ll. 11–16—cf. 3.1.73–74), the linking of the collection with
Ovid's earlier works (ll. 25–26—cf. 3.1.65–66), the wish that it enjoy
a favorable reception (ll. 51–52—cf. 3.1.79–82). The relationship
between prologue and epilogue in this collection is therefore much the
same as that in *Tr.* 1: in each epilogue the poet returns to themes of the
first poem. In both collections the prologue is more elaborate and
imaginative, presenting the figure of a personified book; the epilogues
are more simple, direct apologies.

As an epilogue, the elegy is also like that of *Tr.* 1: in both poems
Ovid asks the reader's understanding for shortcomings in his new
verses, pleading the adverse circumstances of their composition. His
choice of the adjective "qualemcumque" (l. 51) to describe the book is
not only an echo of Catullus 1.9 but directly recalls the "carmina ...
qualiacumque" of *Tr.* 1.11.18 and "scripta ... qualiacumque" for which
Ovid apologized in *Tr.* 1.1.46. Yet there are also important differences.
Ovid's apology is much longer than the apologies seen earlier. To
explain the shortcomings of his new book he now cites, not the stormy
seas (*Tr.* 1.11, 1.1.35–40), but his situation: the collection was written
under conditions which he describes as "barbaria" (l. 30—cf.
Tr. 3.10.4, "me sciat in media vivere barbaria"). Ovid no longer
describes his versification as a feat accomplished under hazardous
conditions, with waves splashing the pages (1.11.39–40). This apology
is more direct and serious: hardships at Tomis have made it impossible
for him to write the poetry he would like.

THE BOOK AS A WHOLE

Like its epilogue the collection is also more serious than *Tr.* 1. Ovid no longer plays with the motifs of an heroic journey, but now concentrates on his first year in Pontus, presenting Tomis as a barbarous place which is destroying him physically and mentally. Subordinate themes such as good faith and loyalty and poetic immortality are also present, but Ovid's contrast between Tomis and Rome clearly dominates. He returns constantly to a comparison between the two places, describing his existence in exile in direct contrast to his earlier life. We may note the series of locative pronouns *hic* and *istic* which appear throughout the book:

non domus apta satis, non *hic* cibus utilis aegro. [3.3.9]

There is no home *here*, no food appropriate for
  a sick man.

ergo ego sum dubius vitae, tu forsitan *istic*
  iucundum ... tempus agis? [3.3.25–26]

While I am in doubt for my life, do you
  perhaps lead a happy life *in Rome*?

hic quoque sunt igitur Graiae (quis crederet?) urbes [3.9.1]

Here too then are Greek cities (who would believe
  it?)

siquis adhuc *istic* meminit Nasonis ... [3.10.1]

If anyone *in Rome* still remembers
  Ovid...

non *hic* pampinea dulcis latet uva sub umbra. [3.10.71 – cf. 3.10.74]

The sweet grape does not lie *here* under the
  shade of its cluster.

otia nunc *istic*. [3.12.17]

There's leisure now *in Rome*.

di facit ut Caesar non *hic* penetrale domumque
  ...velit [3.12.53–54)

May the gods bring it about that Caesar not
  wish my home to be *here*....

non hic librorum, per quos inviter alarque
  copia. [3.14.37–38]

There's no supply of books *here*.

Ovid's contrast is also carefully developed through the arrangement of his book. Apart from his prologue and epilogue, which are linked, as in *Tr.* 1, the elegies of this collection are divided into two main groups, the first composed of poetic letters to individuals, family, friends, and a detractor (3.3–3.7, 3.11) and a second of more general poems, laments and descriptions of Tomis. Each of these groups falls generally into separate halves of the book: with the exception of 3.2, the poet's opening lament and death wish, and 3.11, his address to the enemy, the first half of *Tr.* 3 presents letters to individuals, the second more descriptive poems about exile.

This arrangement can be more clearly defined. Like the prologue and epilogue, both *Tr.* 3.2 and 3.13 are linked through parallels of thought and presentation.[26] Both poems are concerned with life and death in exile, both are the shortest elegies in the collection (thirty and twenty-eight lines, respectively), and both are prayers to divinities. *Tr.* 3.2 introduces us to Ovid's state of mind in Tomis and prepares for the elegies which follow; 3.13 summarizes the complaints which have appeared earlier. The elegies occupy positions as the second and the next to the last poems of the book, an arrangement which is no doubt deliberate. In addition, *Tr.* 3.8, which also summarizes Ovid's feelings in Tomis and his desire to leave, shows obvious links with these two elegies. It also appears near the center of the collection, a position which seems deliberately chosen.

The first half of the book begins and ends with two letters to specific individuals, *Tr.* 3.3, Ovid's deathbed letter to his wife, and 3.7, a letter to Perilla; they are the only addressees identified by name. Both poems are also formal letters presenting elements of literary epistles; in each Ovid treats the theme of his poetic immortality. Of the two epistles the deathbed letter appears first, immediately after *Tr.* 3.2, expanding on the general complaints of the preceding poem. In addition, we find three elegies, *Tr.* 3.4, 3.5, and 3.6, addressed to unidentified friends. *Tr.* 3.4 is a long, uneven poem with an abrupt transition near its center, much like *Tr.* 1.5 and 1.9, Ovid's earlier friendship poems. *Tr.* 3.5 and 3.6 are shorter, more direct companion pieces. In these three elegies Ovid treats a variety of themes all familiar from before: gratitude for support, explanations concerning his *error,* and requests for continued assistance.

Ovid's literary epistles in the first half demonstrate his distance both from Rome and loved ones and from his former life, giving much more impact to the descriptive poems which follow. The second half of the collection treats his situation in Tomis, a subject already introduced

(3.2, 3.3.7–14, 3.4.47–52) but now developed more fully.[27] *Tr.* 3.8, Ovid's prayer to leave, returns to themes of the prologue, the contrast between Tomis and Rome and the wish that Caesar relent. *Tr.* 3.8.19 also reintroduces the echo of *Aeneid* 1.203 which appeared at 3.1.75. In *Tr.* 3.9 the poet associates the Pontus region with savagery to color his later descriptions. Next follows *Tr.* 3.10 on winter in Tomis.

Tr. 3.11 is, not primarily descriptive, but an attack on an enemy. As the only poem not chiefly about Tomis in the second half of the book, it provides a change of subject, if not of mood, and reworks a theme previously introduced, the effect of exile upon Ovid himself (3.8.21–40): in Tomis he is no longer what he once was (3.8.38), but only an "umbra inanis" (3.11.25).[28] In his description of spring at Tomis (3.12) Ovid shows what the arrival of warm weather means to him in exile. These five poems of the collection's second half give a carefully developed picture of his year in Pontus. After the cruel winter (3.10) and the coming of spring, the poet realizes that Tomis is his home unless Caesar pardons him (3.12.53–54). After this extended presentation of life in exile, Ovid's bitter birthday poem (3.13) gains greatly in effect.

The book's main subject, to which Ovid returns in elegy after elegy, is his first year in exile: Rome and his former life in the capital, which figure prominently in the prologue and to which he returns in *Tr.* 3.8 and 3.12, become the standard against which the grim conditions of Tomis are measured. In contrast to *Tr.* 1, where we saw a greater variety of poetic themes, that of this collection is generally the same. Ovid therefore organizes his book, not around its themes, as in *Tr.* 1, but through a loose arrangement of its elegies, as shown on page 72. The main sections of the book, letters to individuals, identified and unidentified, and more descriptive poems about exile itself, are framed both by the prologue and epilogue and by 3.2 and 3.13, short elegies in which the poet gives a direct presentation of his state of mind. Ovid first tells his readers that on reaching Tomis he wants only to die (3.2) but after a year there realizes that he must go on living (3.13).[29]

In contrast to that of *Tr.* 1, the tone of this collection is also constant. The playfulness and high spirits seen earlier are gone; gloom and despondency now prevail, and the poet's equation of exile with death takes on a much more sober meaning. As in *Tr.* 1, Ovid reworks literary models, but the effect is to deny their validity in presenting his situation in Tomis. Unlike Tibullus, in *Tr.* 3.3 Ovid cannot portray himself as a dying lover; he is in a sense already dead, and dreams of being reunited with his beloved can no longer be fulfilled. *Tr.* 3.8

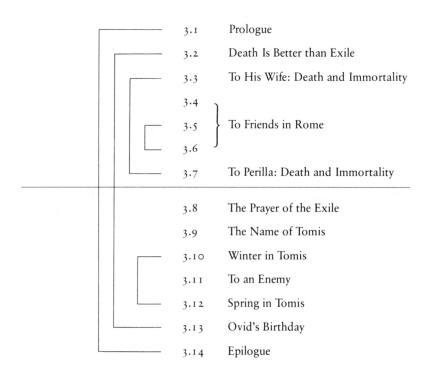

rejects the fantastic means of escape provided by myth to state forcefully that only Augustus can bring the poet back to Rome. *Tr.* 3.10 reworks Virgil's description of Scythia to show that its world of extreme cold and grim existence is actually Ovid's place of exile, one far removed from the fantasy land of romance (3.10.41–42, 73–74). Only the most savage episode of the Medea myth reflects the reality of Pontus which Ovid seeks to portray. *Tr.* 3.10 and 3.12 invert traditional motifs to demonstrate that the return of spring and Ovid's birthday bring him sorrow, not happiness.

Ovid's mood has changed from that of *Tr.* 1 and 2. He no longer attempts to amuse, but seeks to heighten the pathos of his presentation. Indeed, except for the prologue, there is very little humor in this book; we move directly from the amusing picture of the personified book visiting Rome to Ovid's lament in *Tr.* 3.2 that even death would be better than exile in Tomis. The abrupt change in tone is jarring and deliberate. The heroic journey into exile is over, and the Ulysses role prominent in the first collection is discarded. Indeed, it is no longer appropriate. Ovid makes only one reference to Ulysses within the book, at *Tr.* 3.11.61–62, where he compares the wrath of Neptune with that of Jupiter. This couplet does not extend the motif seen earlier, and we should note that the poet also qualifies his comparison ("crede mihi, si sit nobis collatus Ulixes," l. 61). There is nothing heroic or adventurous about Ovid's existence in Tomis as he presents it in *Tr.* 3; his comparison of himself with the dead Hector within the same elegy (ll. 27–28) reflects much more accurately the role he has now assumed.[30]

Ovid's persona has therefore changed from what it was in the first two books. While he again employs literary conventions to express his personal experience and concerns, in this collection he does so with a mood of sustained seriousness unlike anything in his earlier poetry, including the first book of the *Tristia.* Ovid is still aware of his position as a poet and celebrates the power of poetry in *Tr.* 3.3 and 3.7. But now his writing has a more compelling and immediate aim, to present his situation to his Roman readers in an attempt to win support. His personified *libellus,* which acts as his representative in Rome, has a life and a mission of its own (*Tr.* 3.1). The poet restates this theme even more strongly in his epilogue:

est fuga dicta mihi, non est fuga dicta libellis
   qui domini poenam non meruere sui.   [3.14.9–10]

Exile has been imposed on me, but not on
my books, which have not deserved the
punishment of their master.

Ovid presents himself as dead in exile, but the poetic book he has created still has life in the capital; it is therefore through his book, and the extended picture of Tomis which it develops, that he seeks an improvement of his status. The message is clear: exile in Tomis is far too harsh. Ovid deserves a recall to the capital or at least a better place of relegation. By presenting Tomis and its conditions in stark contrast with memories of his former life in Rome, he seeks to make his case much more forceful. We are left with the feeling that after his playful treatment of his journey one year earlier, Ovid hoped to surprise or even to shock his Roman audience with this book. Only through such a grim presentation did he think he could win sympathy for his situation.

iam subeunt anni fragiles et inertior aetas,
  iamque parum firmo me mihi ferre grave est.

Now frail years and an inactive life are creeping
up on me, and in my present weakness it is hard
for me to bear up.

IV TRISTIA 4 Old Age in Exile

OVID'S NEXT COLLECTION, written during his second year at Tomis, A.D. 10–11, invites comparison with *Tr.* 3.[1] The two books have similar structural plans. Like the earlier collection, *Tr.* 4 is divided into two halves, the first devoted mainly to individual letters (4.3–4.5), the second presenting more descriptive elegies (4.6, 4.8). As in *Tr.* 3, an address to an enemy also appears near the end of the book (4.9). These parallels in structural arrangement suggest that Ovid organized this book like *Tr.* 3 and that his intentions were the same in publishing the two collections.

Indeed, both books aim at persuasion. In *Tr.* 3 Ovid contrasted his situation in Tomis with his former life in the capital in an attempt to win support. In this collection, which presents his second year at Tomis, his aims are still the same: to obtain a better and more comfortable place of relegation, if not a complete pardon. Yet the theme of this new book is different. Ovid's principal subject, on which he bases this second appeal, is now his old age in exile. As readers we are asked to see him as a poet near death; the grimness and hardships of exile are presented through the framework of his old age. Ovid's plight in Tomis therefore gains in pathos.

Ovid may well have intended *Tr.* 4 to be a final book, a last address to his readers in Rome; scholars have recognized a tone of finality within the collection, especially in the poet's autobiography, which closes the book.[2] The size of the collection is also smaller than the size of the two books which Ovid had sent to Rome in earlier years: *Tr.* 4 contains only ten elegies (678 lines), in contrast to the eleven and fourteen elegies of *Tr.* 1 and 3 (738 and 788 lines, respectively). Perhaps the poet wished to suggest to readers that his energy and creative powers were flagging. Or he himself may have been less enthusiastic about writing this second book from Tomis. *Tr.* 3, in which he dramatically presented the hardships of exile in contrast to his former life in Rome, had failed to win him a change in exile, much less a pardon.

Despite its shorter length, the book is no less ambitious than *Tr.* 3. In his collection of a year earlier, Ovid gave prominence to his first year in Tomis to seek a pardon or a new place of exile; although he celebrated his position as writer in several elegies, this theme was secondary to his main subject, the contrast between Tomis and Rome. In *Tr.* 4 the theme of Ovid's poetry takes on new significance: he presents his old age in exile not only to win support but also to justify his entire life and literary career. The self-glorification seen earlier in *Tr.* 1.6 and 3.7 now becomes more extensive, especially in the final elegies of the book.

Although Karl Herrmann and R. J. Dickinson have discussed the collection as a whole and Georg Luck and T. J. De Jonge have provided detailed commentaries on the book, most study of *Tr.* 4 has centered on its epilogue, Ovid's famous autobiography.[3] In Chapter 1 we treated three elegies within the book: 4.2, Ovid's account of Tiberius's triumph in Rome; 4.4, his address to an unnamed friend; and 4.8, his description of old age in exile. Our discussion, like that of earlier books, will be organized around the main groups of poems in the collection, with separate examination of the prologue and epilogue.

PROLOGUE (*Tristia* 4.1)

iure deas igitur veneror mala nostra levantes,
  sollicitae comites ex Helicone fugae,
et partim pelago partim vestigia terra
  vel rate dignatas vel pede nostra sequi.
sint, precor, haec saltem faciles mihi! namque deorum
  cetera cum magno Caesare turba facit.

I am right then to worship the goddesses who relieve
my misfortunes, comrades from Helicon of my
troubled exile, who deigned to follow my steps partly
by sea, partly on land, now by ship, now by foot.
May they at least, I ask, be propitious to me, for the
rest of the gods are on great Caesar's side.

This prologue plays on paradoxes and contrasts: writing, the activity
which sent Ovid to exile, is also the only resource available to him to
relieve his misery. Yet his hardships are so great that he cannot write as
he would wish.[4] Opening and closing with a direct address to the
reader ("lector," l. 2; "quisquis es … legas," l. 104), the poem is divided
into two main sections. In the first half (ll. 1–52) Ovid illustrates a
familiar theme, the consolation of song, through exemplum after
exemplum, some of them borrowed from Tibullus and Propertius:[5] he
too writes, not for glory, but to forget his troubles. Versification in
exile, which some may think is madness, is therefore a useful activity.

This optimism ends in mid-poem as Ovid turns to an extended
account of his misfortunes (ll. 53–106). He expands on one aspect of
his situation, the insecurity of Tomis, asking his readers to imagine him
dependent on only walls and gates for his safety. Next follows an
apology for his verses: in his frustration Ovid often throws the poems
he has written into the fire. He asks that Rome think well of the few
which survive.

This prologue is markedly different from the prologues of the two
earlier books. Ovid apologizes for his book directly and does not
introduce the figure of a personified *libellus*. He therefore avoids the
playfulness seen previously: there is no physical description of the
book, no linking of it with its *fratres*, and no scene of a reception in
Rome. Although "tear-stained pages" appear again (4.1.95–96),
Ovid's use of them is now more serious: they do not describe his
physical book, but directly reveal his state of mind in exile.

Ovid's defense of his work is based on arguments seen earlier in the
epilogue to *Tr.* 3: poetry as consolation, the difficulties of composition,
and the lack of an audience. There are indeed striking parallels between
the two poems.[6] But such an apology now appears in the prologue,
creating a distinctive tone for Ovid's new book. His opening thoughts
on the consolation of poetry are deliberately answered by an extended
description of his hardships. The second half of the prologue
contradicts its initial optimism: for Ovid in Tomis, poetry is no longer

a means to forget his troubles (ll. 35–40), but only reminds him of the past (ll. 97–100).

Yet Ovid establishes his role as that of a poet, even in exile, a theme not fully developed in earlier prologues. Closely linked to this picture of a poet among barbarians is that of Ovid, an old man in the midst of continual warfare. Hostilities in Tomis had figured prominently in *Tr.* 3.10, but in that poem Ovid, although endangered, did not appear to be directly involved with them. Now he takes on the role of full participant as he gives a picture of himself forced to bear arms at an advanced age:

> aspera militiae iuvenis certamina fugi,
>   nec nisi lusura movimus arma manu;
> nunc senior gladioque latus scutoque sinistram,
>   canitiem galeae subicioque meam.   [ll. 71–74]

As a young man I avoided the rough struggles
of warfare and took to arms only to play. Now
in my old age I gird my side with a sword, my
left hand with a shield, and put a helmet on my
gray head.

This portrait of Ovid complete with shield and sword has given rise to speculation concerning his service in Tomis's "Home Guard." Rather than accept it as autobiographical detail, we must recognize his play on the anti-military conventions of Roman elegy, the contrast between the young poet who shirked duty and the old man now pressed into service. Ovid may also invite comparison of himself to the aged Priam donning arms at *Aeneid* 2.509–11.[7] We see in this prologue an Ovid different from the protagonist of *Tr.* 1 and 3 represented in the capital by his personified *libellus*. He is still very much concerned with his poetic calling, even in a situation hardly favorable to it, but now an old man.

TO HIS WIFE (*Tristia* 4.3)

> nec tibi, quod saevis ego sum Iovis ignibus ictus
>   purpureus molli fiat in ore pudor.
> sed magis in curam nostri consurge tuendi,
>   exemplumque mihi coniugis esto bonae,
> materiamque tuis tristem virtutibus inple.

Do not let a crimson blush appear on your fair
face because I have been struck by Jupiter's
cruel thunderbolts, but rather arouse yourself to
the task of defending me and be for me the
model of a good wife. Fill with your virtues the
sad role given to you.

Ovid's third letter to his wife in the books from exile plays on
themes introduced in previous epistles. Elegiac topoi seen earlier are
now even more fully developed. In an opening address to the stars
questioning whether his wife is faithful to him during his absence
(ll. 1-20), Ovid describes her as his "domina" (l. 9) and presents
himself, like most anxious lovers, as overly fearful ("spes ... mixta
metu," l. 12; "desine tuta vereri," l. 13). When he addresses her directly,
he first questions her state of mind without him (ll. 21–30), with
references to her empty bed ("lectus locusque," l. 23), lonely nights,
and symptoms of elegiac lovesickness.[8]
    Ovid then instructs her how to behave in his absence (ll. 31–84).
His lecture is an expansion of themes seen earlier in *Tr.* 3.3: he is sure
that his wife is appropriately sorrowful (ll. 31–38—cf. 3.3.25–28). He
also treats the notion of his death away from her: he would have
preferred to die in her arms, comforted by her tears and the customary
funeral rites (ll. 39–48—cf. 3.3.29–46). Finally Ovid discusses his
relegation as her opportunity for glory (ll. 49–84). His wife should be
grieved by his absence, but must not be ashamed of him now; by
enduring a difficult situation she will win lasting fame. Indeed, because
of the recognition she will receive she has no other choice than to
remain faithful.
    Although its themes are familiar, the poem is significantly different
from *Tr.* 1.6 and 3.3. In his first address to his wife, Ovid commended
her loyalty and in return promised her poetic immortality, linking, like
other elegists, praise of his beloved to his own self-glorification. Ovid's
deathbed letter was directly inspired by a well known elegiac model.
Its readers were invited to think of Tibullus on Phaeacia; indeed,
literary echoes gave the elegy much of its force. This poem marks a
departure from earlier use of more traditional motifs. Ovid begins as a
conventional lover questioning the stars about his beloved but drops
the pose midway through the poem to deliver a lecture on her
responsibilities to him.
    His tone of superiority is not new. In *Tr.* 1.6 Ovid declared his power
to confer poetic immortality, and in 3.3 he dictated detailed instruc-

tions about his funeral at the same time as he declared his fame would survive. But his concerns in this elegy are much more insistent, focused, not on romantic faithfulness, but on his wife's larger responsibilities to him in exile. His lecture on responsibilities is, not praise for past actions, but an exhortation for the future: his wife must not desert him now.

Ovid's tone may surprise modern readers. He addresses his wife, as his Roman readers would expect, in the spirit and with the authority of a paterfamilias. But his lecture also points to a greater distance between himself and his addressee, an increased insecurity or doubt about her state of mind. In contrast to the "dolor" which he expects his wife to suffer because of their separation, Ovid hopes that "pudor" will not cause her to abandon him (ll. 61–62). Unlike earlier collections, it is now Ovid's wife, not a loyal friend (*Tr.* 1.5), to whom he directs a good faith and loyalty lecture reinforced by ethical stereotypes and exempla (ll. 63–68, 73–80). Ovid presents himself as much more than merely a lover in verse, celebrating his beloved or lamenting his separation from her. In this elegy he takes on the role of a husband beset by worries that he has been forgotten, appealing to the obligations and demands of marriage.

GOOD FAITH AND LOYALTY (*Tristia* 4.4, 4.5, 4.7)

mitius exilium pauloque propinquius opto,
    quique sit a saevo longius hoste locus;
quantaque in Augusto clementia, si quis ab illo
    hoc peteret pro me, forsitan ille daret.

I want a place of exile that is milder and a bit
closer, a spot which is farther away from the
savage enemy. And so great is Augustus's
clemency that if someone were to ask this of
him for me, perhaps he would grant it.

Ovid's lecture to his wife introduces three more elegies on the good faith theme. The first, *Tr.* 4.4, to an unnamed friend, merits detailed examination. As *Tr.* 4.3, as an address to Ovid's wife, showed similarities to 3.3, *Tr.* 4.4, written to an unnamed friend, also resembles 3.4. Ovid again concerns himself with the problem of not naming

friends in his verses (ll. 7–26–cf. 3.4.63–72). Yet this poem too is
different; while not naming his friend directly, Ovid departs from his
earlier practice and deliberately supplies so many details about his
family and background that he can be identified almost certainly as
M. Valerius Corvinus Messallinus, the son of Ovid's literary patron
Messalla Corvinus.[9] In fact he shows no hesitation in doing so, stating
that Messallinus's known qualities betray him.

The theme of this elegy is also new. Although Ovid discusses the
dangers of association with himself, his main subject is now a specific
request: he wants Messallinus to intercede with Augustus in his behalf.
Ovid had expressed hopes for a new place of relegation at *Tr.* 2.185–
86 and 577–78 (directly echoed in this elegy at l. 51). But now his
request is stronger and more forceful. He even distinguishes between
what are long-range goals, a pardon and return to Rome, introduced,
as in *Tr.* 3, by an echo of *Aeneid* 1.203 ("forsitan hanc ipsam, vivam
modo, finiet olim," l. 47), and his immediate desire, another place of
relegation. Ovid hopes that Messallinus will champion his cause.

The elegy follows a structural plan similar to that of *Tr.* 3.4, with a
central section framed by two sections of equal length. Ovid first
praises Messallinus's character and rhetorical ability. Through panegyric of Augustus discussed earlier in Chapter 1 he explains that his
act of *officium* will not be harmful and appeals to the memory of
Messallinus's father, who encouraged him in his earlier career (ll.
1–34). He next defends his life and requests Messallinus's assistance
(ll. 35–54), then turns to a description of Tomis (ll. 55–84). To
illustrate its savagery Ovid recounts the Iphigenia legend: Pontus is
close to the spot where Iphigenia made human sacrifice.

Tr. 4.4 presents an abrupt change in tone from the elegy which
precedes it. After the superiority of his lecture to his wife, the poet is
flattering and obsequious to the son of his former patron. In contrast
to elegies in earlier books addressed to unidentified friends, this is also
a highly personal poem. Ovid thanks Messallinus for past favors and
praises his family but also requests assistance: he should approach
Augustus in Ovid's behalf. Although his addressee is not named, Ovid
makes his appeal publicly. The poem is, in effect, an open letter to
Messallinus to help him. Ovid writes to a prominent member of one of
the most important families in Rome, exploiting a personal relationship to achieve an immediate goal. In this way *Tr.* 4.4 looks ahead to
requests in later books from exile, particularly the *Epistulae ex Ponto.*

Tr. 4.5 to a loyal friend is much more perfunctory. Ovid appears to
have a particular individual in mind, but gives no clues concerning his

identity.[10] In contrast to the specific request made to Messallinus, we are given only a second explanation why the poet does not name his friends openly (ll. 1–16), platitudes about loyalty, and a request for continued support (ll. 17–34).

In *Tr.* 4.7, a good-natured reproach to an old friend from whom he has received no letters, Ovid declares that he will believe all the wonders of mythology before he believes that his friend has forgotten him (ll. 1–18). Since he is distant, there are many reasons why the letters have not arrived, and the friend should write more frequently: Ovid will then not be forced to make excuses for him (ll. 19–26). The center of the poem is devoted to a catalog of mythological figures, with two pentameters, "tergeminumque virum tergeminumque canem" (l. 16) and "centimanumque Gyan semibovemque virum" (l. 18), which recall the famous anecdote of the elder Seneca about the three lines which Ovid's friends wished to remove from his corpus (*Controversiae* 2.2.12). The poet may have been thinking of this episode; "semibovem-que virum" is half the line of *Ars* 2.24 quoted by Seneca. Ovid's addressee appears to be a poet from whom he expects verses ("tempore tam longo cur non tua dextera versus / ... officiosa fuit," ll. 3–4). He may be writing to Albinovanus Pedo, whom he addresses in *P.* 4.10 and whom Seneca mentions as the source of his anecdote and one of the judges who chose the three lines. In contrast to the other elegies in the collection, Ovid here gives lighthearted treatment to a principal theme, the passage of time and separation from friends.

DESCRIPTIONS OF EXILE

The Passage of Time in Tomis (Tristia 4.6)

nos quoque quae ferimus, tulimus patientius ante:
    vae, mala sunt longa multiplicata die.
credite, deficio, nostroque a corpore quantum
    auguror, accedunt tempora parva malis.
nam neque sunt vires.

I too long ago bore with greater endurance what I
am bearing now. Alas, my misfortunes have been
multiplied by the passage of time. Believe me, I
am failing, and to the extent that I can judge from

my physical state, there is little time to be added
to my sorrow. For I have no strength.

Ovid opens with a literary commonplace, the changes brought about
by time.[11] Time can cure everything but his own troubles; although two
autumns have come since he left Rome, his grief is still fresh (ll. 1–22).
He then elaborates his condition (ll. 23–50): with time some things
actually grow worse, and his own troubles are increasing. He has
neither the strength nor health which he had before and is even sicker
in mind than in body. There is only one hope for him, he concludes—
that death come to end his misfortunes.

Ovid adapts a topical theme to demonstrate that it does not apply to
his own situation. With the passage of two years in exile (ll. 19–20),
he is much worse than before. His deterioration in Tomis, a subject
treated in his earlier book (3.3.7–8, 3.8.27–34, 3.11.25–26) and in
the prologue to this collection (4.1.71–74, 99–100) therefore becomes
much more pathetic.

Old Age in Exile (Tristia 4.8)

tempus erat nec me peregrinum ducere caelum,
   nec siccam Getico fonte levare sitim,
sed modo, quos habui, vacuos secedere in hortos,
   nunc hominum visu rursus et urbe frui.

Now it would be time not to breathe foreign air
or relieve my parched thirst with Getic water, but
to withdraw to the secluded gardens which I
had, to enjoy again the sight of men and the city.

This elegy, already treated in Chapter 1, must be discussed in detail.
One of the most thoughtful and subtle in the exile poetry, it brings to
full development the theme of old age seen in the prologue and Tr. 4.6.
Ovid contrasts his former hopes for retirement with the actual turn of
events: his relegation has destroyed what should naturally have been
happy last years.

He begins (ll. 1–16) by describing old age coming upon him in terms
strongly reminiscent of love elegy: his hair is turning white ("mea
cycneas imitantur tempora plumas / inficit … nigras alba senecta
comas," ll. 1–2), and he has reached the age of idleness ("inertior
aetas," l. 3). We may compare Propertius 3.5.24 ("sparserit et nigras

alba senecta comas") and Tibullus 1.1.71 ("iam subrepet iners aetas").
Ovid's swanfeather hair is also a deliberate echo of Horace's white
plumage in *Carmina* 2.20.9–12, an image particularly appropriate for
an aging poet close to death and his last songs.[12] He then contrasts
what he had expected for his last years, an idyllic picture of retirement
("parvam ... domum veteresque Penates / ... rura paterna," ll. 9-10)
with his wife and comrades ("in sinu dominae carisque sodalibus
inque," ll. 11) with present reality: instead of peaceful detachment in
the company of loved ones, the gods exposed him to the hardships of
Pontus.

Ovid reworks the same idea in the next section (ll. 17–32), his
georgic scene now replaced by exempla echoing those of *Tr.* 4.6. As
weather-beaten ships are placed in dry dock (cf. 4.6.35–36),[13] an aging
horse is sent to pasture (cf. 4.6.24), and an old soldier takes off his
armor (a variation of 4.6.31–34), the poet expected an honorable and
easy retirement. Instead his fates gave him a comfortable youth and
grim old age ("tempora prima / mollia praebuerint, posteriora grav-
ant," ll. 31–32). Ovid again plays on a standard motif of love elegy,
recalling his presentation of himself in the prologue as a young man
who avoided hardships ("aspera ... certamina fugi") but must be a
soldier in his last years (4.1.71–74). This second section ends like the
first, contrasting expectations with reality. The "fata" of its last couplet
(l. 31) correspond to "dis" in the final couplet of the opening section
(ll. 15–16); "quondam" in the next to the last couplet (l. 29) recalls
"quondam" in a corresponding position above (l. 13).

Ovid now reflects upon his situation, overwhelmed after fifty years
of an upright life (ll. 33–44). He again comments on the unnaturalness
of his relegation: if Delphi or Dodona had predicted this old age (cf.
"animo ... non divinante futura," l. 29), he would never have believed
them. The final lines (ll. 45–52) give conclusions which have arisen
from his reflections: nothing is so strong that it can withstand divine
control. Ovid applies these generalizations to his own case: although
he drew his misfortune upon himself through his own fault, Augustus's
anger has given him greater ruin.

The elegy's conclusion was discussed earlier in Chapter 1. An
elaborate exercise in imperial flattery, it presents a carefully developed
challenge to the emperor: if Augustus is to be celebrated for his
clementia, he should demonstrate it now. Yet the poem is not directed
to the emperor, but is rather a general appeal for the reader's sympathy.
Ovid presents himself as an unhappy and broken old man, enduring an

old age both unnatural and unexpected, the antithesis of elegiac retirement.

TO AN ENEMY (*Tristia* 4.9)

trans ego tellurem, trans altas audiar undas,
    et gemitus vox est magna futura mei.
nec tua te sontem tantummodo saecula norint:
    perpetuae crimen posteritatis eris.

Across the land, across the deep waves will I
be heard, and great will be the voice of my
lament. Nor will your generation alone know
that you are guilty; you will be an object of
disgrace for posterity forever.

This poem is best discussed separately, in its position near the end of the collection. The enemy himself, like the enemies of earlier books, is not identified, and Ovid gives no indication that he has a particular person or offense in mind ("nomen facinusque tacebo," l. 1). Instead the poem inverts the poetic immortality theme seen earlier in *Tr.* 1.6 and 3.7: as Ovid can make friends and supporters immortal through praise in his verses, he can also give his enemies lasting infamy.[14]

The elegy is divided into two halves, each containing sections of six and ten lines. Ovid first promises to conceal the enemy's name if he will repent of his hostility (ll. 1–6); if he continues, the poet announces that he will take up the arms of the Muses (ll. 7–16). The second half gives us Ovid's counterattack: he could disgrace the enemy (ll. 17–26) but will recall his forces and give his detractor a chance to come to terms (ll. 27–32).

Ovid's self-confidence is in direct contrast to the gloom prominent in other elegies of the book, particularly in its second half. His assertion that an oak blasted by Jupiter's thunderbolt often becomes green again ("saepe Iovis telo quercus adusta viret," l. 14) directly contradicts his earlier statement in 4.8.45–46, "nil adeo validum est ... / ut maneat rapido firmius igne Iovis." Although unsuited for the rigors of warfare in Tomis (4.8.21–24—cf. 4.1.71–74), Ovid is prepared to take up the weapons of poetry (ll. 15–16). The two elegies present a striking change of mood: while 4.8 deals with the helplessness and frustration of Ovid's old age, 4.9 gives a proud declaration of his creative power.

As a poet Ovid is in full control of his situation. He can immortalize or defame the subjects of his verses and even refers to his own "clementia"(l. 3) and "ira" (l. 10): his position as poet gives him powers comparable to those of temporal authority.[15] Ovid stresses his self-confidence and power as a poet, in marked contrast to the gloom in *Tr.* 4.6 and 4.8, to prepare for the proud poetic autobiography which follows.

EPILOGUE: OVID'S AUTOBIOGRAPHY (*Tristia* 4.10)

saepe pater dixit "studium quid inutile temptas?
　　Maeonides nullas ipse reliquit opes."
motus eram dictis, totoque Helicone relicto
　　scribere temptabam verba soluta modis.
sponte sua carmen numeros veniebat ad aptos,
　　et quod temptabam scribere versus erat.

Often my father said, "Why put your effort in a
worthless pursuit? Homer himself left no great
legacy." Influenced by his words I abandoned
all of Helicon and then tried to write words free
from poetic measures. Of its own accord,
poetry kept coming in the right rhythms, and
whatever I tried to write was verse.

Ovid makes frequent references to his earlier life in the books from exile, usually to argue that it was untouched by scandal and quite unlike his poetry; we may cite *Tr.* 4.4.35–36 within this book as an example. This collection also presents other references to his earlier poetic career. Ovid treated his activity in Messalla's circle in 4.4.27–32 and twice mentioned an earlier life of elegiac detachment, in contrast to the rigors of exile, in 4.1.71–74 and 4.8.31–32; such "otia ... in studiis" were also among his desires for a happy old age (4.8.7–8). These themes now reappear in his epilogue.

Because *Tr.* 4.10 has received considerable study in recent years, our discussion will center on its function within the book.[16] As epilogue to the collection it picks up themes introduced in the prologue: a tribute to Ovid's Muse as his companion in exile (4.10.115–22—cf. 4.1.19–28, 49–52); the popularity of his earlier writings (4.10.55–60—cf. 4.1.68); his present old age (4.10.93–94—cf. 4.1.73); an explanation why he continues to write (4.10.111–14—cf. 4.1.37–48); and the pose of burning less successful poems (4.10.61–64—cf. 4.1.101–4). But *Tr.* 4.10 is much more than simply an epilogue to the book. It also carries forward the theme of creative immortality seen in the preceding elegy, as Ovid adopts motifs of a conventional *sphragis,* or poetic autobiography, to present an account of his life and justification of his literary career.

Two couplets addressed to the reader frame the major sections of the elegy: "candide lector" at the end (l. 132) directly recalls "quem legis" (l. 2) in the beginning couplet. In the first half of the poem (ll. 3–64) Ovid discusses his background and career up to the time of his relegation: his birthplace and family (ll. 3–14), early education (ll. 15– 26), short-lived legal career and the death of his brother (ll. 27–40), and his early literary endeavors (ll. 41–64). Ovid's brother, born on the same day but a year earlier, who chose a public life, appears to symbolize a conflict of interests within Ovid himself, the pursuit of a political career in contrast to his much stronger love of poetry. After his brother died at the age of twenty, Ovid's public life died as well. He discusses the poetic circle to which he belonged, lists poets whom he knew, and describes his first love elegies.

Ovid next treats his personal life (ll. 65–130). He defends his morals (ll. 65–68), reviews his three marriages (ll. 69–70), and tells of the death of his parents (ll. 77–80) whom he addresses directly (ll. 81– 92): they must know that *error,* not "scelus," was the cause of his exile. In his old age ("canities ... / ...antiquas miscuerat comas," ll. 93–94) Ovid was ordered to Tomis (ll. 93–130). He treats at length the literary pursuits which relieve his cares and thanks his Muse for granting him glory. If prophecies are true, he will enjoy immortal fame.

In this autobiography Ovid is allusive in his account of his early life and selective in his details. He makes only passing reference to his greatest work, the *Metamorphoses* (ll. 63–64—cf. *Tr.* 1.7), not because it was unfinished,[17] but to heighten an intentional contrast in the poem between the *Amores,* his earliest elegiac works, and his present elegies from exile. There are other contrasts as well. Ovid invites us to compare the death of his brother and the deaths of his parents, events which preceded major phases of his poetic career, his decision to abandon politics, and his relegation to Tomis. He also contrasts his earlier company in a circle of poets with his present isolation, and, as in previous epilogues, the poetry of earlier days with that of exile (cf. *Tr.* 1.11.37–38, 3.14.13–26).

Yet the scope of this epilogue is much broader. As in his poetic epitaph (*Tr.* 3.3.73), Ovid again introduces himself as a "tenerorum lusor amorum," calling attention to his elegiac achievements. He not only apologizes for this poetic book but ends his collection with the most extensive piece of self-glorification in all of his writings, a complete justification of his career. As an account of a life and accomplishments, very much in the spirit of ancient biography, it affirms that Ovid's calling, although regarded by some as a "studium inutile" (l. 21) has given him a purposeful life, both before and during his exile.[18] Ovid's creativity has enabled him to resist the hardships of Tomis; the secure detachment ("tuta ... otia") to which the Muses had persuaded him early in his career (ll. 39–40) has now been forgotten (105–6—cf. *Tr.* 3.2.9, "fugax rerum securaque in otia natus"). Poetry has allowed Ovid to surmount present difficulties (ll. 111–20) but, even more important, promises him immortal fame after death (ll. 121–30). Thus his life as a poet has been far from "inutile," and he ends this book with this proud declaration.

THE BOOK AS A WHOLE

Did Ovid intend this book to be the last published from Tomis? His autobiography gives the collection a distinct tone of finality, and *Tr.* 4.6 and 4.8 present a picture of the poet near the end of his life. The prologue, which introduces this theme, is more serious than earlier ones, without the playfulness of *Tr.* 1.1 and 3.1. The epilogue can also be read as a poetic testament, Ovid's review of his literary career from his first elegiac poetry to his last. It might even be suggested that Ovid planned his collections from exile as a four-book block of poetry, analogous to the four books of Cornelius Gallus and Propertius.[19] The poet indeed refers to *Tr.* 1–4 as a separate corpus in the first couplet of his next collection from Tomis (*Tr.* 5.1.1–2). Yet, as we have seen, each of the individual collections is different, and examination of *Tr.* 4, in comparison with earlier books, indicates that whatever Ovid's intentions, it was planned and published like others as a single book reflecting one year of his relegation.

Ovid's summary of his career and presentation of old age in exile by no means indicate that he is now resigned to his situation. As in earlier collections, we see continued emphasis on his separation from his family, friends, and life in the capital. In his triumph poem Ovid directly contrasts his isolation with the happiness of those who can participate in the public life of Rome (4.2.65–70). *Tr.* 4.3 treats his separation from his wife with hopes that she not desert him, and 4.4 is a direct request to Messallinus to work for a recall. In keeping with the theme of his old age Ovid now qualifies the Virgilian echo seen earlier in *Tr.* 3 to describe hopes for a pardon:

forsitan hanc ipsam, vivam modo, finiet olim
    tempore cum fuerit lenior ira, fugam.   [4.4.47–48]

Perhaps someday, if only I am alive, he will
end my exile itself, when his anger softens
with time.

Yet he still wants Messallinus to approach the emperor in his behalf. In its carefully developed picture of Ovid's declining years, *Tr.* 4.8 is a challenge to Augustus to demonstrate his *clementia.* The enemy poem also presents hopes, again qualified, for a return to Italy ("et patriam, modo sit sospes, speramus ab illo," 4.9.13).

The collection is shorter and more loosely organized than earlier books. As in *Tr.* 3, we have an even number of elegies within the collection, divided into two halves, with a linked prologue and epilogue but no center poem. Within the first half, *Tr.* 4.2, the triumph poem, follows a pattern already seen in *Tr.* 1 and 3, providing a change of mood from that of the prologue. Here the transition, from Tomis back to Rome, is reversed from that of earlier books, in which Ovid moved from Rome to exile itself. The two elegies which follow are both written to particular individuals: as in *Tr.* 3, Ovid's first letter is to his wife, whom he lectures on her responsibilities to him. In *Tr.* 4.4 we see a change of tone as Ovid assumes the role of a respectful client in addressing Messallinus. The first half is completed by *Tr.* 4.5, a short request to an unidentified loyal friend, which adds little to the book and is perhaps a filler poem, composed earlier and then included to round out the collection.

In the second half Ovid turns to more descriptive poems. *Tr.* 4.6 treats the passage of time, a theme developed further in 4.8. In contrast, *Tr.* 4.7 and 4.9 provide a change of mood. *Tr.* 4.7, to a friend who has not written, also gives additional emphasis to the passage of time, Ovid's absence of two years (4.7.1–2), and 4.9, which demonstrates the power of poetry, prepares the reader for Ovid's autobiography and epilogue.

The arrangement of the collection can be represented as shown. As in *Tr.* 3, the enemy poem appears near the end of the collection; yet

	Prologue: Poetry in Exile	4.1
Two Years in Exile	4.6
To a Friend: No Letters	4.7
Old Age in Exile	4.8
To an Enemy	4.9
Epilogue: Autobiography	4.10

The Triumph — 4.2
To His Wife: Responsibilities — 4.3
To Messallinus: Request — 4.4
To a Loyal Friend — 4.5

through its emphasis on the power of poetry it plays a much more important role in the thematic development of its book. The structural arrangement itself is much less complex than that of *Tr.* 3: there are no formal epistles framing other letters such as 3.3 and 3.7, but more simple juxtaposition of poems presenting changes of mood.[20]

Because *Tr.* 4 is shorter and simpler in its organization than the two earlier collections, it might appear less ambitious. Yet the book must be assessed, not from its size or arrangement, but from its contents. Ovid's emphasis on his old age throughout it and his closing autobiography lend an unmistakable tone of finality. We may be led to conclude that the poet indeed thought he was near the end of his life and decided to compose a farewell to his Roman audience. The tone of finality may also reflect an increasing awareness of his break with Rome and the impossibility of returning to his former life, which may well have prompted him to move beyond the immediate context of his poetic book to give an autobiographical summary of his life and career at its end. We might even interpret this farewell tone as an announcement by Ovid that his literary career, responsible in part for his relegation, is now ended and that he does not intend to publish additional works. If so, he implies that his literary activities will no longer offend anyone, that Augustus should now allow him to return. In this way his presentation of himself as an old man strengthens his pleas.

But we must also view the autobiography as part of its poetic book. Ovid's earlier plea for a recall in *Tr.* 3, based on an extended contrast between the capital and his place of exile, had not been successful. Now he tries one more time, concentrating, not on a contrast of external environments, Tomis and Rome, but on himself, stressing the length of his absence and the steady decline of his health and spirit. Because Ovid was already in his second year of residence at Tomis, elegiac themes such as the passage of time and advancing age easily lent themselves for reworking. We find in the book little extended description of Pontus itself or conditions there. Tomis is now not so much an unreal, cruel world where existence is a living death, as it was in *Tr.* 3, as the scene of Ovid's own deterioration.

Ovid's subject also gave him an opportunity to treat at greater length his position as poet, both at the beginning of his career and at the present time, in exile. Conditions in Tomis allowed him to play on the traditional role of the love elegist, removed from dangers and worldly concerns, demonstrating that for him such a life is no longer valid. To reinforce this contrast between his previous life and present situation, Ovid makes many references within the book to his earlier poetic career. He celebrates Tiberius's Pannonian triumph in a poem reminiscent of earlier treatments of this theme in the *Amores* and *Ars amatoria* only to demonstrate his separation from his former world (*Tr.* 4.2.67–70). In his request to Messallinus he appeals to the patronage of Messalla Corvinus which he enjoyed as a youthful poet. *Tr.* 4.7 to a poet friend presents deliberate play on some of Ovid's most notorious elegiac lines. Then the final elegies bring to full development the contrast between Ovid's beginning career and his last years. While echoes of Propertius and Tibullus demonstrate that old age in Tomis is far different from idyllic retirement, Ovid's reminiscence of Horace, *Carmina* 2.20 introduces another, quite positive theme, the poetic self-glorification of the last two poems. In his autobiography Ovid again proclaims himself a "tenerorum lusor amorum": he answers the pessimism of the prologue through a proud review of his career and an affirmation of the power of poetry.

But along with its self-glorification, this collection appeals for sympathy and support. Although Ovid takes pride in his poetic achievements, his plight in exile is still compelling. His presentation of himself has now also become more self-reflective: as poet he emphasizes not so much external conditions as the effect they have on him as a writer. The purpose of his versification is no longer to achieve immortality, something which earlier works have brought him

(4.10.121–30), but to forget his troubles (4.1.3–4, 35–48; 4.10.111–20). Ovid is still aware of his position as poet; indeed, the contrast between the temporal authority of the emperor and his own creative power becomes in *Tr.* 4.9 and 4.10 even more striking than it was in *Tr.* 3.7. Yet Ovid as a writer must endure an old age and punishment far too harsh for his offense. His immediate unhappiness cannot be offset by the promise of immortality to come. All of this strongly reinforces his requests to his wife and friends for support and his open invitation to Augustus to pardon him.

Hunc quoque de Getico, nostri studiose, libellum
  litore praemissis quattuor adde meis.
hic quoque talis erit, qualis fortuna poetae:
  invenies toto carmine dulce nihil.

Add this book too, devoted reader, to the four already
sent from the Getic shore. This one too will be like its
poet's fortune. In all of its poetry you'll find nothing
sweet.

V TRISTIA 5 Another Book from Exile

THE FIRST COUPLETS (Tr. 5.1.1–4) of Ovid's next collection
immediately raise questions about its relationship to the first four
books. Ovid introduces his new book as an addition to those already
published, treating Tr. 1–4 as a corpus already completed and separate
from his present undertaking. We could even read the first line as
evidence that Ovid did not intend to publish another poetic book when
he finished Tr. 4. The finality of tone noted in the earlier collection
would support this view.

If this were Ovid's original intention, he definitely changed his mind,
for in the third year of his relegation, A.D. 11–12 (Tr. 5.10.1–2), we
find another collection quite different from earlier books. The poet
himself now also seems to have undergone significant changes in his
attitude toward exile, his poetry, and his hopes for a return. We are no
longer given, as in Tr. 4, a picture of a wretched exile near the end of
his life. Ovid declares early in the book that he is still alive and even
healthy (Tr. 5.2.3–6). At the same time, however, he returns in poem
after poem to a familiar theme: he urgently desires to leave Tomis.

With fourteen elegies of 750 lines, Tr. 5 is somewhat longer than the
collection which precedes it (ten poems of 638 lines). Also noteworthy

is the much larger number of poems within the book addressed to specific individuals, either friends in Rome or Ovid's wife. Unlike earlier collections, the book contains few elegies which are primarily descriptive. All but the prologue and *Tr.* 5.10 are written to specific individuals, and in *Tr.* 5.10 Ovid also directly addresses friends ("amici," 5.10.47). In addition, the theme of poetic apologia is given greater prominence. Ovid not only uses the prologue to defend his exile poetry but returns to this subject in *Tr.* 5.7 and 5.12.

Previous study of *Tr.* 5 has been even more limited than that of earlier books. Although there are commentaries by Georg Luck and J. T. Bakker,[1] only Karl Herrmann and R. J. Dickinson have discussed the collection itself at any length, and none of its individual elegies has received the attention given poems in other books. Our analysis of the book will begin with its prologue and will then be organized according to the addresses of individual elegies: Ovid's poems to unidentified friends, which vary in length, importance, and subject matter, his single address to an enemy, and the four poems to his wife, the last of which also functions as the epilogue.

PROLOGUE: POETIC APOLOGIA (*Tristia* 5.1)

delicias siquis lascivaque carmina quaerit,
  praemoneo, non est scripta quod ista legat.
aptior huic Gallus blandique Propertius oris,
  aptior, ingenium come, Tibullus erit.
atque utinam numero non nos essemus in isto!
  ei mihi, cur umquam Musa iocata mea est?
sed dedimus poenas, Scythicique in finibus Histri
  ille pharetrati lusor Amoris abest.
quod superest, animos ad publica carmina flexi
  et memores iussi nominis esse mei.

If someone is looking for lovemaking or playful poems, I warn him ahead of time, it is better that he not read these. Gallus will be better for him, and Propertius with his seductive voice, better too Tibullus, that agreeable wit. And would that I were not in their number! Alas, why did my Muse ever play? But we have paid the penalty, and in the territory of Scythian Danube the poet who played with quivered

Amor is absent. For the future, I have turned my
mind and those of my readers to poems intended
for everyone, which everyone may read, and I
have asked them to remember me.

The theme of poetic apologia, which figured earlier in the epilogue
to *Tr.* 3 and Prologue to *Tr.* 4, now reappears in Ovid's most extensive
apology for the exile poetry seen so far. Like *Tr.* 4.1, this prologue is an
introduction to and defense of its book, based on arguments already
familiar, the direct relationship between Ovid's poetry and his
condition in exile. But Ovid now goes much farther than before,
describing in strikingly blunt terms the shortcomings of his verses. *Tr.*
5.1 is therefore much more than an introduction to its collection. It
becomes a poetic self-assessment, Ovid's analysis of the elegies from
Tomis, their inspiration, purpose, and weaknesses.

Because of its apologetic theme, *Tr.* 5.1 has been compared to three
program poems in Ovid's *Amores.*[2] *Am.* 1.1 presents one point of
comparison, that of poetic *materia,* or subject matter: when Amor
stole a foot from the second line of Ovid's imaginary epic, he decided
to write elegy although he lacked the *materia* for its composition (*Am.*
1.1.19–20). Here Ovid stresses, not the contrast, but the correspondence between his *materia* and poetry. Since it is directly related to
its subject, his unhappy situation, its mournful tone is appropriate
(5.1.5–6, 27–28). The prologue also recalls *Am.* 2.1, which contrasted
elegy with epic: in both poems Ovid states that his new book is similar
to early poetry (cf. *Am.* 2.1.1–4 and *Tr.* 5.1.1–4), informs readers that
its contents are autobiographical (*Am.* 2.1.2, *Tr.* 5.1.10), and warns
them about the collection (*Am.* 2.1.3–4, *Tr.* 5.1.15–18).

The third program poem of the *Amores* presents a debate between
Elegy and Tragedy, each making claims on Ovid. Tragedy rebukes the
poet for continuing to write elegy and criticizes his Muse as childish
(*Am.* 3.1.27–28). In this prologue we find these themes reworked: an
interlocutor makes similar objections to Ovid's continuing to write the
same kind of poetry from Tomis (5.1.35), and the poet himself
describes his earlier writings as juvenile and frivolous (5.1.7–8, 19–
20), in contrast to his present works.

Yet the differences between this program poem and those poems of
the *Amores* far outweigh the parallels. As in his poetic autobiography,
Ovid does not compare elegy with other verse forms, but compares
two types of elegy itself, his youthful productions and his present
verses. He begins the prologue with the announcement that he has

abandoned love elegy and turned to something new, "publica carmina," or "public poems." His phrase is significant. Within his immediate context Ovid presents *publica carmina* as quite different from the love elegies ("delicias ... lascivaque carmina," l. 15) he composed in his earlier career. But his adjective *publica* suggests more than one meaning.

Ovid's term "public" certainly has overtones of "ordinary," "commonplace" or "not refined." We may compare a later characterization of his poetry at *P.* 4.13.3–6:

unde saluteris, color hic tibi protinus index
    et structura mei carminis esse potest.
non quia mirifica est, sed quod non publica certe est:
    qualis enim cumque est, non latet esse meam.

The source of your greetings the tone and structure
of my verse can immediately tell you, not because it
is marvelous but because it is at least not ordinary.
Indeed whatever sort it is, it's no secret it's mine.

Publica carmina would therefore be ordinary poems, the sort anyone can write. But there is more to Ovid's meaning. His addresses to his wife and friends are "public" in that they are, not private letters, but poems sent to Rome for publication, poetry intended for everyone, which everyone may read.[3]

Ovid also states why he writes these *publica carmina.* Comparing himself to a dying swan, he announces that his purpose is to broadcast his death in exile (ll. 13–14). But he goes still farther in this declaration of poetic intentions, separating himself from the tradition of amatory elegy and from Gallus, Propertius, and Tibullus, the same elegists with whom he had proudly associated himself in *Tr.* 4.10.51–54: he is no longer a *lusor Amoris.* Indeed, he expresses regrets for ever having been part of that tradition.

The rest of the prologue presents a dialogue between Ovid and an interlocutor ("ex vobis aliquis," l. 25), who raises specific objections to the exile poetry (ll. 25–80). First, why does he continue to write? Ovid returns to the theme of the opening lines: his books illustrate the direct relationship between his situation and his poetry. If Caesar relents, so will Ovid's mood, but he will not be playful as before. Now he will write what the emperor himself will approve (ll. 25–48).

Next, can't he endure his troubles better by keeping silent? Ovid replies that "dolor" unlamented becomes more painful to bear, introducing exempla to show that his exile poetry is merely a means of expressing grief (ll. 49–68). The next objection is simple and direct: the poems are bad (ll. 69–78). Ovid admits this ("fateor," l. 69), but replies that no one is forced to read them. Moreover, he explains, he will not revise them, but wants them read as they were written: they are no more barbarous than Tomis itself. As a poet he is no longer to be judged by Roman standards. A final question remains: why then does he send the poems to Rome? Ovid wants to be with his readers in whatever way he can (ll. 79–80).

The contrasts with earlier prologues are striking. Ovid's apologia is his principal and only theme. There is no attempt to amuse, as in *Tr.* 1.1 and 3.1, and no description of Tomis and old age as in *Tr.* 4.1. Although Ovid returns to a theme seen earlier, poetry as consolation, he no longer considers his verses art, but merely an expression of grief (ll. 27–28). Ovid mentions the "Pieridum mora" as a means of consolation (l. 34), but we see no tribute to the Muses (cf. 4.1.19–28, 49–52, 87–88, and 4.10.117–22) or concern for artistic standards implicit in the pose of burning the worst poems (4.1.99–104). Instead Ovid presents himself totally indifferent to the reception his book will have: readers can disregard it if they wish (ll. 69–70), since he no longer seeks the "fama" which encourages poetic talent (ll. 75–76—cf. *Tr.* 4.10.125–26). Following immediately after Ovid's autobiography, this prologue seems a deliberate renunciation or denial of his poetic calling and the self-glorification seen in that poem. As he rejects the "laeta et iuvenalia" of his earlier career (ll. 7–8), which he celebrated at length in *Tr.* 4.10, Ovid states bitterly that his present literary efforts are no more uncouth than his situation. Readers are therefore alerted that this new book will be quite different from the others.

LETTERS TO FRIENDS

To Fellow Poets: Bacchus's Festival (Tristia 5.3)

huc ades et casus releves, pulcherrime, nostros,
  unum de numero me memor esse tuo.
sunt dis inter se commercia. flectere tempta
  Caesareum numen numine, Bacche, tuo.
vos quoque, consortes studii, pia turba, poetae
  haec eadem sumpto quisque rogate mero.

Attend and relieve my misfortunes, most
beautiful one, remembering that I am one of
your number. There are dealings among the
gods. Do try, Bacchus, to influence Caesar's
divine power through your own. You too,
devoted band of poets who share in my
pursuit, make the same prayer, each one of
you, with unmixed wine in hand.

After renouncing his earlier verses and the elegiac tradition in his
prologue, Ovid here treats his poetic role much more positively by
reworking a well-known literary model, a hymn to Bacchus (cf. Horace
Carmina 2.19, Propertius 3.17). But unlike earlier Augustan poets,
Ovid turns to the god not as a present source of inspiration, but a
means to recall past associations. He uses the occasion of the Liberalia
to introduce two appeals, one to Bacchus, the second to former
colleagues in Rome.

Ovid opens with a description of festival rites in which he used to
participate (ll. 1–12) as a poet favored by the god ("non invisa tibi pars
ego saepe fui," l. 6), then turns to Bacchus with a prayer for help (ll. 13–
46). He bases his appeal, introduced through an aretalogy, or catalog
of virtues, of the god (ll. 19–26), on the obligations Bacchus must feel
toward a priest ("vatem," l. 31) and worshipper ("e sacris hederae
cultoribus unum," l. 15; "cultor," l. 34). Finally he addresses his fellow
poets: may they feel his absence from their company
(ll. 47–58).

Ovid's description of his friends as a "pia turba" (l. 47) links the
main sections of the poem. Like Ovid himself, they are loyal to their
patron deity, but they should also remember their former colleague.
Ovid's hope that someone will notice his absence (ll. 51–52) also
recalls his prayer to Bacchus that the god himself not forget him
(ll. 33–34).[4] His friends too must remember that he was once a valued
member of their company ("si vestrum merui candore favorem," l. 53).
The closing request ("quod licet, inter vos nomen habete meum," l. 58)
returns to a theme introduced in the prologue, Ovid's desire to keep his
name alive in Roman literary circles (5.1.24, 79–80).

To Friends: Life in Tomis (Tristia 5.7 and 5.10)

ille ego Romanus vates (ignoscite, Musae)
  Sarmatico cogor plurima more loqui.

en pudet et fateor, iam desuetudine longa
  vix subeunt ipsi verba Latina mihi,
nec dubito quin sint et in hoc non pauca libello
  barbara: non hominis culpa, sed ista loci.

I, a Roman poet (forgive me, Muses!), am
forced to say most things in Sarmatian language. I am really ashamed, I confess it; from
long lack of practice scarcely do Latin phrases
come to me, and I have no doubt this book
contains not a few barbarisms. This is the fault
of the place, not of me.

The first of these two elegies, a literary epistle to a friend in Rome
(ll. 1–4), expands on the theme of the prologue, treating the problem
of writing in exile through an extended description of Tomis. The
friend has asked about Ovid's health (ll. 5–6) and the area of Pontus
(ll. 9–10), and this poem is his reply.

Ovid's description has two main parts, each dealing with Tomis and
its relationship with his poetry.[5] He begins with an expansion of his
account of warfare in *Tr.* 3.10 and 4.1 (ll. 11–40), describing the
inhabitants, some Greeks, but mostly Getae, who ride freely through
the streets with quivers of poisoned arrows, have uncut hair and
beards, and carry knives: these are the people among whom he must
live as a "vates" (l. 22). Ovid's choice of this term, "poet-prophet,"
more solemn than the usual *poeta*, underscores the incongruity of his
situation. He next returns to his literary activity: although he is happy
to hear that his poems are being pantomimed in Rome, he reminds his
friend that he does not seek applause. He is grateful that such
performances are keeping his name alive ("profugi nomen in ora refert,"
l. 30), a theme introduced in the prologue (5.1.24–cf. 5.3.58), but
now he writes only to forget his troubles.

The second half of the elegy (ll. 41–68) begins like the first, with
questions: what else can Ovid do except write poetry? He rejects two
other possible diversions, Tomis itself (ll. 43–44) and its inhabitants
(ll. 45–46), expanding on the latter. Ovid discusses at length the most
telling characteristic of their barbarity, their language. Few speak
Greek, and those who do speak it badly (cf. ll. 11–12, where Ovid
stressed the predominance of the Getic population). No one can speak
any Latin at all, and Ovid himself, a Roman poet ("vates," l. 55–cf

l. 22), must use Sarmatian to communicate. To avoid forgetting Latin completely, he talks to himself and has returned to writing verse. In this way he keeps himself from thinking about his troubles; this is sufficient reward.

Scholars have interpreted Ovid's announcement that he is learning Getic as evidence that he adjusted to Tomis or, at least in part, became reconciled to his situation.[6] His statement that he is learning the local language, even though he considers it disgraceful ("en pudet," l. 57), may be autobiographical fact; yet we must also recognize it as a poetic element introduced to excuse the shortcomings of his verse. Ovid's statement may reflect a change in attitude: by announcing that he is learning Getic, he may wish to demonstrate that he does not expect to leave Tomis in the near future, that he must attempt to make the best of things.

Yet such admissions are far from evidence of an adjustment, but are rather to be read in the spirit of the prologue, revealing a bitter and ironic self-awareness. Ovid now seems to understand his situation, one much bleaker than that presented in earlier books. His break from his earlier life seems more complete. He has forgotten his earlier love poetry ("lusorum oblitus amorum," l. 21) and fears that Rome has forgotten him in turn ("oblivia nostri," l. 29). Versification has become for him merely a means of forgetting his troubles ("miserarum oblivia rerum," l. 67). In light of the distance he has fallen from his own former self-esteem and his standing in the capital, Ovid's characterization of himself as "ille ego Romanus vates" (l. 55) becomes bitterly sarcastic.

In *Tr.* 5.10, a second description of Tomis, Ovid presents constant warfare and Getic barbarity, not to excuse his poems, but to portray Pontus as an unreal and unnatural world. The poem, unlike the others in this collection, is primarily descriptive and not a literary epistle. Although Ovid addresses friends near the end ("amici," l. 47), he concentrates on a picture of exile as a paradoxical and impossible world.[7]

Ovid first expands a simple chronological statement: he has been here three years, but they seem like ten. Time seems to stand still, indeed, the "rerum natura" (l. 9) appears to have changed (ll. 1–14). He next treats the themes of warfare (ll. 15–26) and barbarism (ll. 27–44), again stressing their unnatural aspects ("cum minime credas," l. 19). Nothing outside the walls is safe, the enemy fly as thick as birds, people pick up poisoned arrows in the streets. Ovid expands his picture though a comic inversion of georgic and pastoral motifs:

shepherds wear helmets; men carry weapons in one hand while they plow with the other (ll. 23–26).

As in his first account, Ovid describes the long hair and trousers of the Getae (ll. 31–32—cf. 5.7.49–50) as well as their violence (ll. 43–44—cf. 5.7.47–48), but gives greatest emphasis to their language (ll. 35–42). But in contrast to *Tr.* 5.7.55–56, where he was forced to speak Sarmatian, his situation has become even more grotesque. Ovid has no "commercia linguae" with the natives (l. 35—cf. *Tr.* 3.11.9, 5.7.61) and must use gestures to communicate. They regard *him* as the barbarian and laugh at the sound of Latin. They even talk openly about him in their language, perhaps in mockery, but Ovid cannot reply. They think him insane if he nods yes or no to something they say. This ultimate indignity, a complete reversal of roles between Roman and barbarian, introduces a closing lament (ll. 45–52).

On Writing in Tomis (Tristia 5.12)

nec tamen, ut verum fatear tibi, nostra teneri
    a conpondendo carmine Musa potest.
scribimus et scriptos absumimus igne libellos:
    exitus est studii parva favilla mei.

But, to confess the truth to you, my Muse
cannot be restrained from writing poetry. I
write and burn the books I have written. A
bit of ash is the outcome of my poetic
activity.

This literary epistle answers a friend's suggestion that Ovid turn to "solacium in litteris" and write poetry as a means of spiritual consolation. He repeats arguments seen in the prologue and *Tr.* 5.7 emphasizing the distinction between his present poems and ordinary "carmina," a "laetum ... opus" which requires "pax mentis" (ll. 3–4). His books from exile are not the product of normal poetic activity ("studio," l. 9—cf. "studio," l. 1) but an expression of personal grief (ll. 1–10). Ovid further declares that for him consolation is not possible in philosophical or spiritual terms: even Socrates would have been overcome by conditions in Tomis (ll. 11–16). The poet may be able to forget what he has lost ("oblivia," l. 17—cf. 5.7.67), but his mind is never at ease (ll. 17–20).[8]

He next expands arguments seen earlier in *Tr.* 3.14.33–36: his talent has been dulled by his misfortune and inactivity; whatever poetry he produces is that worthy of his situation (ll. 21–36). More suggestions for continuing to write are rejected in turn. Ovid is no longer interested in glory (ll. 37–50—cf. *Tr.* 5.1.75–76, 5.7.37–38), and he has no audience in Tomis (ll. 51–58—cf. *Tr.* 3.14.39–40, 4.1.89–94).

Finally Ovid declares that he is still writing, but burning what he writes: only that which escapes the flames reaches his Roman audience, and would that he had burned the *Ars* (ll. 59–68)! We are reminded of similar admissions of burning the worst poems in Tomis (*Tr.* 4.1.99–102) or the "unfinished" *Metamorphoses* (*Tr.* 1.7.15–26). But here Ovid's tone is different. He no longer seems concerned with poetic standards and presents no apology for the verses which survive. Instead, he announces bluntly that out of compulsion he is writing bad poetry, then burning it. His verses, bad as they are, merely reflect his situation.

Other Letters to Friends (*Tristia* 5.4, 5.6, 5.9, 5.13) and an Enemy (*Tristia* 5.8)

The remaining epistles to friends are shorter and less important. *Tr.* 5.4, an address to a loyal friend by a personified letter, describes Ovid's misfortunes and defends him (ll. 1–22), then praises the friend's loyalty and asks that it continue (ll. 23–50). Both themes and the exempla illustrating the friend's devotion (ll. 25–26) are familiar. The addressee may well be the intended recipient of *Tr.* 3.5; both elegies express similar sentiments about a friend who remained loyal after Ovid's relegation. In both the friend is described as "carus" (3.5.17–18, 5.4.23), and *Tr.* 5.4.34, "nec vellent ictae limen adire domus," directly recalls 3.5.8, "et deploratae limen adire domus." Ovid's personification of his epistle, reminiscent of *Tr.* 1.1 and 3.1, also gives greater objectivity to his account of his troubles: his letter becomes both his witness and spokesman.[9]

Tr. 5.6, to a faithless friend, reworks the good faith and loyalty theme already seen in *Tr.* 5.3 and 5.4 reproaching abandonment after a long friendship. In *Tr.* 5.9 Ovid returns to the theme of not naming his friends, seen earlier in *Tr.* 1.5, 3.4, 4.4, and 4.5. His statement that his addressee stood by him to keep him alive after his relegation (ll. 13–20) recalls similar thoughts in *Tr.* 1.5.3–6; both poems may be addressed to the same individual.

Tr. 5.13, a mild reproach to a friend for not writing, recalls a similar complaint in *Tr.* 4.7. Ovid begins (ll. 1–18) with an explanation that he is sick in body and hopes the friend is well ("si tamen ipse vales, aliqua nos parte valemus," l. 7) reworking the epistolary formula, *si vales, valeo,* and concludes (ll. 19–34) with praise of the friend's loyalty, introducing an idea seen earlier at *Tr.* 3.7.2, that the exchange of letters must take the place of earlier conversation.[10]

The last poem in this group, *Tr.* 5.8, is Ovid's only address to an enemy in the collection. Ovid lectures his detractor on the mutability of Fortune (ll. 1–20) and treats his own situation (ll. 21–38): the enemy may live to see the poet pardoned and back in Rome.

LETTERS TO HIS WIFE

A Request for Support (Tristia 5.2)

quid dubitas et tuta times? accede rogaque:
    Caesare nil ingens mitius orbis habet.
me miserum! quid agam, si proxima quaeque relinquunt?
    subtrahis effracto tu quoque colla iugo?

Why do you hesitate? Why be afraid when there is no
danger? Go and ask. The great earth contains nothing
more gentle than Caesar. Poor me! What shall I do if
those nearest to me forsake me? Do you too withdraw
your neck from our broken marriage yoke?

This letter, which appears immediately after the prologue, is a direct appeal for aid. Ovid introduces the poem as an "epistula" (l. 1), a term which recalls *Tr.* 3.3. Yet the letter shows few of the elegiac motifs seen earlier. Instead of presenting himself as a dying lover, Ovid announces that he is no longer in danger (ll. 3–6); moreover, in contrast to a poetic role assumed earlier, that of an elegist removed from worldly concerns (*Tr.* 4.1.71–72), he declares that hardships have toughened him. There is little expression of affection or feeling for his wife: from the first line, "ecquid ubi a Ponto nova venit epistula, palles," we find a tone even more persistent than that in previous letters to her. Indeed, Ovid says so little about his marriage that Ronald Syme has suggested that the letter is not addressed to his wife at all. [11]

The elegy, like others seen earlier, has a sudden shift near its center. Ovid first laments his situation: while his body can withstand hardships, his mind is still afflicted, and the passage of time has not healed his wounds (ll. 1–12). But he has hopes that Augustus will relent. If his wife were concerned for him, he would win a transfer (ll. 13–36).

This indirect appeal next leads to a more insistent tone marked by imperatives and rhetorical questions (ll. 37–46): why does she hesitate? Where can Ovid turn if his wife deserts his cause? In frustration the poet finds an outlet in his own direct prayer to the emperor (ll. 47–78) discussed at length in Chapter 1.[12]

This elegy is not unlike *Tr.* 4.2, the first poem after the prologue in the preceding collection. Both poems present flattery of Augustus, 4.2 through its description of the triumph and 5.2 through a direct appeal to the emperor. But here Ovid's panegyric appears within the framework of a letter to his wife asking her to take some action in his behalf. When he is frustrated by her apparent reluctance or refusal, he himself turns to the *princeps,* restating arguments already seen in his address to his wife: because warfare and the constant fear of death make Tomis intolerable (ll. 63–72—cf. ll. 29–32), he seeks another place of exile (ll. 73–78—cf. 33–34). Thus the opening section (ll. 1–36) and Ovid's appeal (ll. 47–78) are balanced within the poem, linked by the central passage of frustrations (ll. 37–46).

Ovid's treatment of his wife is surprisingly harsh. The elegiac conventions seen in earlier letters are all but discarded: we are given the impression that she has no concern for her husband (ll. 33–34), is unable or unwilling to help him (l. 37), and has even abandoned him (ll. 39–40). We have noted in earlier books that the elegy immediately after the prologue set a tone or mood for its collection. Here Ovid's request for aid shows him impatient and exasperated at his wife's failure to support him. Since he expects and deserves better from her, the urgency of this epistle underscores his own direct appeal to Augustus and adds force to other letters to friends which follow.

His Wife's Birthday (*Tristia* 5.5) and Ovid's Status (*Tristia* 5.11)

nata pudicitia est, virtus probitasque fidesque,
  at non sunt ista gaudia nata die,
sed labor et curae fortunaque moribus inpar,
  iustaque de viduo paene querela toro.
scilicet adversis probitas exercita rebus
  tristi materiam tempore laudis habet.

On this day of your birth was born chastity,
virtue, uprightness, loyalty. But joyfulness was
not born then—rather hardship, cares, fortune unsuited to your character, and just
laments for a marriage bed almost widowed.
But I tell you, uprightness schooled by misfortunes furnishes in times of sorrow a subject
for praise.

Ovid's celebration of his wife's *natalis* invites comparison with *Tr.*
3.13, his earlier birthday poem. Here we see, not an inversion of a
genethliakon, or birthday poem, but reworking of its conventions to
stress the theme of exhortation seen earlier in *Tr.* 5.2 and 4.3.71–84:
his wife should gain fame through her loyalty. Ovid first assumes the
poetic role of priest, describing preparations for the birthday sacrifice
(ll. 1–12). He identifies himself with Ulysses, but in contrast to *Tr.* 1,
his comparison here is selective: Ovid presents himself simply as the
husband of a loyal wife whose birthday the hero celebrated away from
home (ll. 3–4). He then prays to the *natalis* that it come favorably,
that his wife be happy in everything except the loss of her husband
(ll. 13–40). Ovid continues with reflections about her, a woman of
character similar to that of legendary heroines. Like Penelope, Evadne,
Alcestis, and Laudamia, she too would be unknown if Ovid had
remained in good fortune (ll. 41–60).

The poem concludes with a prayer to Augustus to end his wife's
unhappiness (ll. 61–64). After several allusions to his own situation,
Ovid's closing plea is nothing more than an indirect appeal for himself:
his return would be his wife's best birthday gift.[13] His observations
about the sacrificial smoke (ll. 29–40) also support his request: like
the winds in *Tr.* 1.2.91–92 and 1.4.17–22 which threatened to blow
his ship back to Italy, those carrying the incense in that direction reflect
divine approval of his appeals. Nature herself appears to oppose his
exile in Tomis.

In *Tr.* 5.11, a third, much shorter letter to his wife, Ovid discusses his
status in Tomis. She has complained in a letter ("littera questa tua est,"
l. 2) that someone called her the wife of an exile. Ovid explains the
technicalities of his sentence, praises Augustus, and warns the detractor
not to describe him by a false name. The epistle therefore reinforces the
theme of *Tr.* 5.2.

POETIC GLORY (*Tristia* 5.14)

quod numquam vox est de te mea muta tuique
   indiciis debes esse superba viri.
quae ne quis possit temeraria dicere, persta,
   et pariter serva meque piamque fidem.

[Consider too] the fact that my voice has never
been silent about you and that you ought to be
proud by reason of your husband's testimony.
Continue to take care so that no one can say
my words are rash. Preserve both me and your
devoted loyalty.

In the final poem of the collection Ovid focuses on the immortality which he has given to his wife in his verses. *Tr.* 5.14 is therefore an expression of literary self-glorification not unsuitable to end the book in place of a more formal epilogue. Through its stress on poetic immortality the elegy reminds us of *Tr.* 1.6, Ovid's first poem to his wife, where he promised her fame in return for past loyalty. Both elegies link her virtues to immortality in his verse, but here the earlier situation is reversed: Ovid now treats his celebration of his wife as past action and urges her to continued loyalty in the future. His poem is, not praise, but exhortation.

Ovid first describes the "monumenta" which he has already given his wife in his verses (ll. 1–18), then turns from the past to the future, urging her to continue in her faithfulness (il. 19–46). Stock exempla support the appeal, climaxing in that of Laudamia who appeared earlier at *Tr.* 5.5.57–58. Ovid quickly adds that he does not ask his wife to sacrifice her life for him. He does not lecture her, because she is not acting; his admonition is to be considered acknowledgment of her deeds. Yet this final praise does not invalidate earlier exhortations. By calling his wife's attention, and that of his readers, to the fame which his works have already given her, he stresses the repayment he expects. The book therefore ends, not on a note of apology for itself, but with a request for aid, in significant contrast to earlier collections.

THE BOOK AS A WHOLE

Ovid's epilogue is an appropriate starting point for discussion of the book. The poet replaces his usual apology for his collection with a request to his wife for continued support. Her importance in the final poem also reflects the greater role which she plays in the book itself. In contrast to earlier books, where she appeared only once in each collection, four elegies here are addressed to her: *Tr.* 5.2, Ovid's exhortation to plead his case before Augustus; 5.5, addressed to her *natalis* but urging her to win fame through loyalty; 5.11, Ovid's declaration that she is not an exile's wife; and 5.14, the final poem.

This collection is also different from earlier books because of the many poems within it addressed to friends in Rome: *Tr.* 5.3, the poem on Bacchus's festival; 5.4, the personified letter to a faithful friend; 5.6, an exhortation to remain loyal; 5.7, a description of Tomis in answer to a friend's letter; 5.9, an expression of gratitude to an unnamed friend; 5.12, an explanation to a friend about writing in Tomis; and 5.13, a reproach to a friend for not writing. Seven elegies in all are addressed to individuals or specific groups of friends, in contrast to the much smaller number of individual addresses in earlier books: three each in *Tr.* 1, 3, and 4.[14]

Like earlier books, *Tr.* 5 contains one poem to an enemy in Rome (5.8); it occupies a position at the center of the collection, not near its end, as in *Tr.* 1, 3 and 4. Only one elegy in the entire book cannot be considered a letter to a specific individual or group, 5.10, in which Ovid treats life in Tomis. We may compare the much larger number of nonepistolary, more descriptive poems in earlier books: five in *Tr.* 1, four in *Tr.* 3, three in *Tr.* 4.[15]

Ovid's arrangement of his book appears to have been directly influenced by his poetic format: he presents a book of elegiac letters addressed primarily to individuals in Rome, both his wife and friends. Within it he does not introduce new descriptions of exile, but focuses instead on only two aspects of Tomis already treated earlier, its hostile conditions and the barbarity of the inhabitants. These are the subjects to which he returns in poem after poem.

In contrast to previous collections, we see in *Tr.* 5 a uniformity of theme treated in different letters to specific individuals. Because Ovid does not concern himself with a variety of subjects, his arrangement of elegies is based, not on theme, but on his individual addressees. The elegies which follow the prologue, *Tr.* 5.2 through 5.14, are arranged so that two poems addressed to friends are offset by single elegies addressed to Ovid's wife and a central poem addressed to the enemy.[16] Thus we have the representation of Ovid's plan as shown.

Although he organizes his collection by addressee, not subject matter, Ovid still makes some attempt at *variatio* of theme. *Tr.* 5.3 and 5.5 can be described as occasional poems, one on Bacchus's festival,

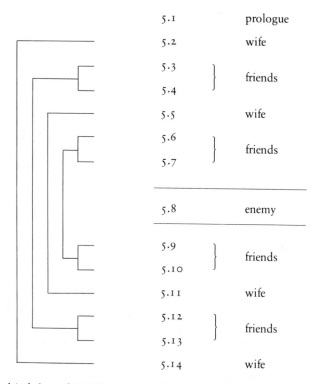

5.1		prologue
5.2		wife
5.3	⎫	
5.4	⎬	friends
5.5		wife
5.6	⎫	
5.7	⎬	friends
5.8		enemy
5.9	⎫	
5.10	⎬	friends
5.11		wife
5.12	⎫	
5.13	⎬	friends
5.14		wife

the other on the birthday of Ovid's wife; both are offset by 5.4, the personified letter to a loyal friend. *Tr.* 5.6, Ovid's reproach to the faithless friend, and 5.8, the enemy poem, frame 5.7, on life and writing in Tomis. *Tr.* 5.9, 5.11, and 5.13, three shorter elegies treating themes seen in earlier books (naming friends openly in the poems, Ovid's status as a *relegatus,* and no letters), offset two longer and more important poems, 5.10 on Tomis and 5.12 on why Ovid continues to write. We may compare Ovid's earlier arrangement of individual elegies in *Tr.* 3, where his poems on winter and spring at Tomis (*Tr.* 3.10 and 3.12) were offset by his address to the enemy, and in *Tr.* 4, where 4.7, a good-natured reproach for not writing, appeared between two longer, more descriptive elegies on the passage of time and old age.

We cannot deny that in this collection, as in earlier ones, Ovid arranges elegies to avoid monotony. But such an arrangement does not reflect a general plan for the entire book; Ovid replaces *variatio* of theme with a symmetrical arrangement of elegies by addressee. *Tr.* 5 is also different in other ways from earlier collections. There is no central theme dominating the entire book such as the journey into exile in *Tr.* 1, Ovid's comparison of Tomis and Rome in *Tr.* 3, or his old age in *Tr.* 4. The poet's concern is now not so much that of developing a picture of himself or his situation in exile as presentation of "publica carmina" (5.1.23). He gives much greater emphasis to poetic epistles, stating that letters in verse must take the place of earlier conversations and direct contact (5.13.27–30). He now seems to be aware that he may not be able to return to Rome (5.1.45–46, 5.2.77–78, 5.10.49–50), that poetic books such as this are the only way to keep in touch (5.1.79–80, 5.3.47–52).

Ovid presents himself in this collection a correspondent in verse rather than a poet as in *Tr.* 1, 3, or 4. He separates this book from both his earlier amatory elegy (5.1.17–22) and from other books of the *Tristia* sent to Rome in earlier years (5.1.1–4) and declares that for him versification has become simply an expression of personal grief, distinct from real poetry, which demands mental and spiritual tranquillity (5.12.3–4). Because he writes through some compulsion (5.12.59–60), to get his mind off his troubles (5.1.77–78, 5.7.37–40, 65–68; 5.12.17–18), he can no longer produce anything but bad poems. In contrast to earlier books where Ovid presented his place of relegation, or old age, in literary terms to his Roman audience, he has now assumed the role of poetic letter writer, expressing his unhappiness in separate epistles to his wife and friends. He returns to literary self-glorification in the final poem, but with a purpose different from that in earlier books: now he links his wife with the fame he has given her as an incentive to act.

Ovid's reassessment of his position as poet may indicate a diminished faith in his own talent or in his literary audience at large: he writes public poems to his wife and friends because he can no longer address a larger, more general readership. But along with his bitter condemnation of his present writing which appears throughout the book, Ovid is still aware of his position as poet. *Tr.* 5.3 on the Liberalia recalls his former standing among literary colleagues in Rome. His characterization of himself as a Roman "vates" among barbarians (5.7.55) plays on the solemnity Augustan poets attached to their calling. His final address to his wife cites the "monumenta" she has already received in his works (5.14.1). Because Ovid still considers himself a major poet, his decision to present a book of poetic epistles rather than a book about exile itself must be viewed as a change in literary strategy.

One theme figures prominently in these separate communications, Ovid's desire to leave Tomis for another place of relegation. He introduces this wish in the prologue (5.1.45–46), then devotes the next elegy, the longest in the book, to a full presentation of it, prodding his wife to speak in his behalf and sending his own direct appeal to Augustus. He returns to the same subject in subsequent letters to both his wife and friends, reinforcing the insistence of his appeal in 5.2: they should work to obtain at least a partial remission of his sentence. Apologies for the exile poetry, both in the prologue and in *Tr.* 5.7 and 5.12, are longer and more elaborate than before. All, however, are variations on the same theme, that Ovid's situation produces bad poetry. His troubles are such that he cannot master them philosophically (5.12.11–16). Readers cannot expect better from any poet, even a master poet, in Tomis.

To reinforce the urgency of his plight Ovid presents a bitter awareness that his break with Rome is becoming more and more complete, that chances for a full pardon and return are less and less, that he must try to gain what he can. The spirit of artistic independence noted in earlier books has now disappeared (5.1.45–46), and imperial flattery has become more blatant and expansive (5.2). Ovid now describes his place of exile mainly to excuse the poor quality of his verses. He is no longer writing real poetry, something impossible in Tomis, but presents himself demoralized and reduced to a lesser artistic role, that of a poetic correspondent, a writer of appeals in verse attempting to gain assistance in the one way he can. In this way *Tr.* 5 is different from what we saw before, a bridge between earlier books of the *Tristia* and the *Epistulae ex Ponto,* where Ovid's requests become even more open and compelling.

invenies, quamvis non est miserabilis index,
    non minus hoc illo triste, quod ante dedi.
rebus idem, titulo differt; et epistula cui sit
    non occultato nomine missa docet.
nec vos hoc vultis, sed nec prohibere potestis
    Musaque ad invitos officiosa venit.

Although its title is not in itself sorrowful,
you'll find that this work is no less sad than
my previous one. It is the same in theme,
different in title; and each letter tells to
whom it has been sent, giving the name
openly. You do not desire this, but you can't
prevent it. My Muse comes to you with this
officium *even though you don't want it.*

VI EPISTULAE EX PONTO 1–3
Ovid Addresses His Friends

OVID HIMSELF ACKNOWLEDGES two significant changes immediately in the prologue of his next collection, its new title and the direct naming of the individuals addressed in its elegies (*P.* 1.1.15–20). Yet he does not discuss others. His statement that its subject matter is the same as that of the *Tristia* is misleading. As we shall see, *P.* 1–3 is quite different from previous collections.

The size of the collection itself is a significant change. Ovid's decision to publish three books in A.D. 13, the fourth year of his exile,[1] marks a major departure from his practice of preceding years. Instead of a single poetic book he now undertakes a much more ambitious project, the publication of three books in a unified collection. We may rightly ask whether the much larger scope of the collection points to a change of poetic purpose.

An even more conspicious change is the much more personal tone in these books. Ovid's decision to write to his friends openly allows their names and personalities to figure prominently. His individual friends, and Ovid's relationship with each of them, cannot be overlooked. These friends take on an additional importance: the poet arranges the thirty elegies of his three books through a carefully developed

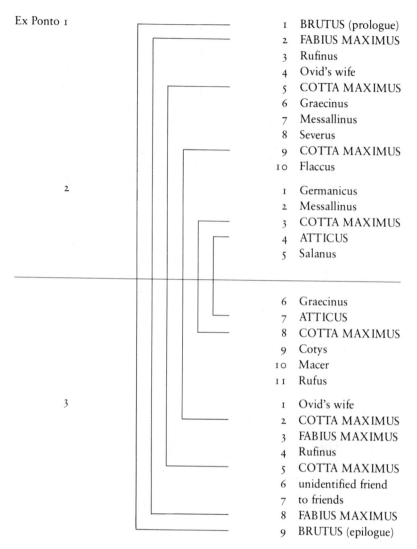

Ex Ponto 1

	1	BRUTUS (prologue)
	2	FABIUS MAXIMUS
	3	Rufinus
	4	Ovid's wife
	5	COTTA MAXIMUS
	6	Graecinus
	7	Messallinus
	8	Severus
	9	COTTA MAXIMUS
	10	Flaccus

2

	1	Germanicus
	2	Messallinus
	3	COTTA MAXIMUS
	4	ATTICUS
	5	Salanus
	6	Graecinus
	7	ATTICUS
	8	COTTA MAXIMUS
	9	Cotys
	10	Macer
	11	Rufus

3

	1	Ovid's wife
	2	COTTA MAXIMUS
	3	FABIUS MAXIMUS
	4	Rufinus
	5	COTTA MAXIMUS
	6	unidentified friend
	7	to friends
	8	FABIUS MAXIMUS
	9	BRUTUS (epilogue)

symmetry of addressees. He declares in his epilogue (*P.* 3.9.53–54) that he is merely sending to his friends letters which he has assembled at random ("utcumque sine ordine") and that the collection has not been specially selected for publication ("opus electum"). We shall return to this statement later, but we know that it is incorrect. The study of Hartmut Froesch has demonstrated that there is nothing haphazard about Ovid's arrangement: he organized the collection according to the addressees of individual elegies, and the resulting symmetrical scheme is too carefully developed to be accidental. [2]

Although Froesch's work has made a valuable contribution to our understanding of *P.* 1–3, there is still need to assess this collection in relation to the *Tristia:* how does it differ in content and purpose from the books which preceded it? Why does Ovid write to his friends openly at this point in his relegation? We must therefore go beyond the symmetrical skeleton of the books to examine their contents. Here the large size of the collection presents a problem; some elegies are more important than others and must receive more detailed discussion.

Ovid's arrangement by addressees also indicates the relative importance of each of his friends within the collection; some are much more prominent than others. Ovid writes to Cotta Maximus most frequently, in six elegies in all, two of which appear in each book. All other individuals, including Ovid's wife, appear much less frequently, and many only once. Because the personalities of Ovid's addressees and his relationship with each are significant in determining the tone and purpose of the books, our discussion will be organized around the friends to whom Ovid writes. While we will not attempt to provide a detailed prosopographical study of the individuals addressed in the books,[3] it will be useful to review their careers and personalities as they appear. We will begin with the prologue and end with the epilogue before turning to a general discussion.

PROLOGUE: TO BRUTUS (*Epistulae ex Ponto* 1.1)

denique Caesareo, quod non desiderat ipse,
    non caret e nostris ullus honore liber.
si dubitas de me, laudes admitte deorum,
    et carmen dempto nomine sume meum.

To sum it up: not one of my books fails to
do honor to Caesar, even though he needs
it not. If you have doubts about me, admit
my praise of the gods, and take my poetry
without mentioning my name.

Because he appears in both prologue and epilogue, Brutus may be Ovid's publisher. Yet his personality is not signficant, and Ovid reveals nothing about him in either poem.[4] Instead this prologue, like earlier ones, is a general address to Ovid's reader.

The poem has many parallels with *Tr.* 3.1.[5] Ovid describes his books as offspring (ll. 21–22 — cf. *Tr.* 3.1.73–74) and like the book in the earlier prologue, presents them as "libellos ... peregrinos" desiring an "hospitium" (l. 3 — cf. *Tr.* 3.1.20). He states that they cannot enter public libraries and think it safer to hide in a private home (ll. 3–6, 9–10 — cf. *Tr.* 3.1.79–80). He again disclaims the *Ars amatoria* (ll. 7–8, 11–14 — cf. *Tr.* 3.1.3–4, 65–66). Earlier Ovid used Roman topography, particularly the oak wreath on Augustus's door, to support a plea for mercy (*Tr.* 3.1.33–52); here he alludes to the free circulation of the writings of Antonius and Brutus to ask that his own books be accepted (ll. 23–26). Both poems treat the emperor's divinity (ll. 29–30, 45–46, 77–78 — cf. *Tr.* 3.1.37–38) and make similar requests: that the new collection be accepted by its readers (ll. 1–22 — cf. *Tr.* 3.1.79–82) and that Ovid receive a new place of exile (ll. 77–80 — cf. *Tr.* 3.1.75–76).

Yet Ovid's presentation of these themes is different here. In contrast to all earlier prologues, he gives no apology for his poetry; indeed, literary matters are not his primary concern. He first introduces his new collection (ll. 1–22), explaining that the books should be welcomed as respectable poetry ("patet castis versibus ille locus," l. 8), then turns to his relationship with Augustus: because his books praise the emperor, they should be admitted (ll. 23–36). Ovid's rhetorical question, "non iter omne patebit?" (l. 35), echoes his earlier statements about the book's reception ("iter," l. 6: "patet," l. 8).

He next extends his declaration of piety by adopting the poetic role of priest: since no one refuses a devotee of Isis or Cybele, Ovid's celebration of greater divinities, the "gentis Iuleae nomina sancta" (l. 46), must be accepted (ll. 37–48). But his particular situation, that of a priest who has offended his god, moves him in the final lines to still another role, that of a repentant sinner expressing remorse for past actions and hopes for another place of exile (ll. 49–80).[6]

The theme of this prologue is therefore a variation on the imperial panegyric seen earlier, particularly in *Tr.* 5.2. But in declaring his loyalty Ovid almost seems to protest too much. His rhetorical questions concerning his books' reception (ll. 31-35, 37–40) and pose of *vates*, complete with religious formulas and sacerdotal imperatives ("vaticinor moneoque. locum date sacra ferenti," l. 47) appear stridently challenging and even incongruous with the emotional expressions of guilt in the final lines. Ovid's comparison of his books' bearing eulogy of Augustus with Aeneas's carrying Anchises (ll. 33–36), while a familiar example of pious devotion (cf. Propertius 4.1.43–44), is also almost too ingenious to be taken seriously. But on the

whole Ovid uses his role as *vates*, not to promote his position, but to
declare his loyalty, ending with the most lengthy and carefully
developed confession of remorse seen so far. Rather than merely
introducing his new collection, Ovid's prologue presents a dramatization of his frame of mind in which he reflects on his situation and
forcefully asserts his good intentions.

COTTA MAXIMUS

Cotta, the adopted son of Ovid's former patron Messalla Corvinus,
appears to have been the poet's best friend at the time of his
relegation.[7] He assumed the name Messallinus at the death of his elder
brother M. Valerius Messalla Messallinus, to whom Ovid writes in *Tr.*
4.4, *P.* 1.7, and *P.* 2.2, and later held the consulship in A.D. 20. Accused
of treason (*laesa maiestas*) in A.D. 32, he was freed through a letter
written in his behalf by Tiberius. Tacitus (*Annales* 4.20.6, 5.3.2, 6.5.1,
6.7.1) portrays him as a notorius *delator*, or informant, eager to gain
the emperor's favor. Pliny the Elder (*Natural History* 10.22.27)
describes Cotta as a gourmand, and Persius (2.72) refers to him as the
"blear-eyed offspring of the great Messalla."
   In contrast to a generally unfavorable historical tradition,[8] Ovid
appears to have thought well of Cotta. He praises his talents in both
rhetoric (*P.* 3.5) and poetry (*P.* 4.16.41–44), declares that he has
known Cotta from the cradle (*P.* 2.3.71–72), and reveals that he was
with him on Elba when he received news of his sentence (*P.* 2.3.83–
90). Cotta appears to have been one of few friends who stood by Ovid
at that time (*P.* 2.3.29–32). That he is addressed in twice as many
elegies in this collection as anyone else is evidence of a close friendship.
We will discuss five poems (the sixth, *P.* 2.8, was treated in Chapter 1).

To Cotta: On His Poetry from Tomis (Epistulae ex Ponto 1.5)

cur ego sollicita poliam mea carmina cura?
   an verear ne non approbet illa Getes?
forsitan audacter faciam, sed glorior Histrum
   ingenio nullum maius habere meo.
hoc, ubi vivendum est, satis est, si consequor arvo
   inter inhumanos esse poeta Getas.
quo mihi diversum fama contendere in orbem?
   quem fortuna dedit, Roma sit ille locus.

Why should I polish my verses with anxious
care? Should I be afraid that a Gete will not like
them? I may be acting rashly, but I can boast that
the Danube has no poetic talent greater than my
own. Here, in the land where I must live, it is
enough if I manage to be a poet among the
savage Getae. What good is it to try to reach a
different world through fame? Let the place
which fortune has given me be my Rome.

Despite his close relationship with Cotta Maximus, Ovid does not
pay much attention to him in this poem: Cotta is addressed in the
opening couplet, but is named only once afterwards (ll. 9–10). The
elegy, an apology for Ovid's new collection, is intended not so much
for Cotta as for the larger Roman literary audience. Ovid even uses the
plural "vos" (all the poets in Rome, Cotta included) in addressing his
readers (ll. 57, 85).

Ovid's apology is familiar but much more bitter than those apologies
in earlier books. He explains that his talent has declined in idleness,
that it is difficult to write, but even more painful to revise and correct
(ll. 1–24). Next he discusses the question of gain from his literary
activities, using conventional imagery of agriculture to illustrate the
ideas of profit and return (ll. 25–56):[9] since poetry allows him to pass
his time in exile and forget his troubles, this alone is sufficient return
("satis est," l. 56).

Ovid concludes with a renunciation of poetic fame (ll. 57–86):
others may strive for renown (the "vos" addressed in l. 57), but he is
satisfied ("satis est," l. 59) with verses easily composed. He intensifies a
boast seen earlier in *Tr.* 5.1.74, "inter Sauromatas ingeniosus eram,"
and declares that he is already the pride of the Danube, that it is
enough for him to be a poet at all where he is ("satis est," l. 65, the
third appearance of the phrase in twelve lines).[10] Ovid goes still further:
he is so distant from Rome that his poor verses ("scriptis mediocribus,"
l. 83) are probably no longer read there. Even if they are, and, more
incredibly, still find favor, this success cannot help him. He is sure that
his reputation died when he himself left.

Ovid's apology, an intensification of those apologies seen earlier in
Tr. 5, seems intended not so much to defend the exile poetry as to
shame readers about the poet's situation. His repetition of "satis est"
and expansion of an earlier boast of being the greatest poet of Scythia,
coupled with the concessive "forsitan audacter faciam," express the
stinging irony of his resignation.

To Cotta: Good Faith and Loyalty (Epistulae ex Ponto 1.9 and 2.3)

funera non potui comitare nec ungere corpus
  aque tuis toto dividor orbe rogis.
qui potuit, quem tu pro numine vivus habebas,
  praestitit officium Maximus omne tibi.

.   .   .   .

qui quoniam extinctis, quae debet, praestat amicis
  et nos extinctis adnumerare potest.

I could not accompany your funeral procession,
Celsus, or anoint your body. I am separated from
your pyre by an entire world. He who could,
Maximus, whom you when alive regarded as a
god, furnished to you every duty which one friend
owes another....Since he pays what he owes to his
dead friends, he can count me too among the
dead.

The first of these two elegies, on the death of a mutual friend Celsus,
is the more forceful and interesting. Celsus, whose identity is
unknown, appears to have been a close friend who remained loyal to
Ovid at the time of his relegation (ll. 9–16).[11] Yet Ovid concentrates
not so much on his dead friend as on Maximus himself. Unlike *P.* 1.5,
which opened with Maximus and then discarded him for a poetic
apology, this elegy is centered from beginning to end on Ovid's
friendship with both men.

Ovid begins with a statement of his grief at Celsus's death (ll. 1–8):
no other news so bitter has come to him in exile. The poet then moves
from the present to memories of past associations (ll. 9–24). He
remembers the good times but most of all the period of his departure
when Celsus stood by him, wept at Ovid's own *funus,* and consoled
him with hopes for a pardon. Ovid now addresses Maximus directly
(ll. 25–40): what Celsus told him most frequently was that Cotta
would work to soften Augustus's anger. Can those words have been
spoken in vain?

In the final lines (ll. 41–56) Ovid returns to the present situation.
He repays the tears which Celsus shed at the time of his relegation and
will honor Celsus in the only way he can, through a poem testifying to
his character. Maximus, he tells Celsus, has provided the required
honors. Since he has furnished the necessary duties to his dead friends,
he can number the poet as well among the dead.

Ovid's appeal is based on two themes developed earlier, those of exile as a living death, and the time of his relegation as his *funus*. Celsus, who stood by Ovid, promised him Maximus's aid and support. Cotta, who attended the funeral, has discharged his obligations to Celsus; yet he should carry out his responsibilities to Ovid as well. Like his friend, Ovid is also dead and expects Maximus's assistance.

P. 2.3, thanking Maximus for support, is a positive treatment of this theme. The poem begins and ends with two six-line addresses praising Cotta (ll. 1–6, 95–100). In the first of two longer sections (ll. 7–48) Ovid elaborates on the rarity of good faith. He then turns to his long association with Cotta (ll. 49–94). When Maximus heard his sentence, his anger was no less than Caesar's; yet after he learned the nature of the poet's *error*, he reassured Ovid that there was hope for a pardon. In contrast to the reproach of P. 1.9, the elegy celebrates Cotta as an exemplary friend. Yet Ovid stresses that past association leads him to hope for continued loyalty. In this way his praise becomes a challenge to his addressee.

To Cotta: Good Faith among Friends (*Epistulae ex Ponto* 3.2)

scilicet hac etiam, qua nulla ferocior ora est,
    nomen amicitiae barbara corda movet.
quid facere Ausonia geniti debetis in urbe,
    cum tangant duros talia facta Getas?
adde quod est animus semper tibi mitis, et altae
    indicium mores nobilitatis habent.

Well, then, even in this land, than which there
is none more uncivilized, the name of friendship moves savage hearts. When such deeds
affect even the cruel Getae, what should you
do, you who were born in the Ausonian city?
And besides, Maximus, you have a tempera-
ment which is always gentle, and your
character gives proof of your high nobility.

In this poem Ovid varies his theme by narrating the Orestes / Pylades legend. In the opening lines (ll. 1–6) he sends greetings to Maximus: others may have deserted him, but his friend is singled out for his loyalty. The poet then explains that he forgives those who

abandoned him, but praises the few who have remained faithful.
Posterity will read of their loyalty (ll. 7–36).

   This promise introduces the major section of the poem, an account
of Orestes and Pylades (ll. 37–102). When Ovid told the Scythians
about his friends' *pietas,* an old man answered him, stating that the
Getae also honor friendship. Through a literary device characteristic of
Callimachus's *Aetia* and his own *Fasti,* the poet retells the Greek legend
in the guise of local tradition ("dixere priores," l. 45; "fama refert,"
l. 51) narrated by an aged Gete; his narrative is similar in style and
tone to many sections of the *Fasti.*[12] After an introductory *ekphrasis* or
descriptive setting, ("est locus in Scythia ...," l. 45) and background
about Thoas and Iphigenia, the old Scythian recounts the legend. He
gives emphasis to a speech by Iphigenia (ll. 77–84) and the
disagreement between the two heroes as to who will die, then moves
quickly to the recognition scene and escape, concluding with the
present renown of the two friends ("nunc quoque nomen habent,"
l. 96—cf. *Fast.* 5.128). Ovid then comments on the applause which the
story received. The moral is obvious: if the Getae honor friendship, he
expects at least as much from fellow Romans.

   Although the Orestes / Pylades legend appeared previously in *Tr.*
4.4.63–82, Ovid varies his presentation of it here. Instead of the much
briefer account in the earlier poem, introduced to illustrate the
savagery of Pontus, he retells the story at greater length, stressing the
mutual loyalty of the two friends. The grim conditions of Tomis appear
only in a concluding rhetorical question (ll. 99–102); he even seems to
present the region and its inhabitants in a favorable light ("hac ego
sum terra, patriae nec paenitet, ortus," l. 47). Ovid's emphasis now is
not on savagery, but on good faith. Like *P.* 1.9, the poem becomes a
challenge to Maximus, urging him to take some action in his behalf
(ll. 103–10).

To Cotta: Communication and Remembrance
(Epistulae ex Ponto 3.5)

namque ego, qui perii iam pridem, Maxime, vobis,
    ingenio nitor non periisse meo.
redde vicem, nec rara tui monimenta laboris
    accipiant nostrae, grata futura, manus.

For I, Maximus, who have long been dead as far
as you in Rome are concerned, strive through my

poetic talent not to be completely dead. Repay me
in turn, and let my hands receive reminders of
your work, and not infrequent ones, which will
bring me joy.

Ovid here combines the motif of mental vision seen earlier in *Tr.* 4.2
with the theme of his poems functioning as his surrogates in Rome (*Tr.*
1.1, 3.1, 5.4).[13] He begins with greetings which he would prefer to
present in person and thanks Maximus for a copy of a speech sent to
him (ll. 1–14). He next expresses a wish to listen to Maximus in
person: happy are those who can hear his voice in Rome (cf. *Tr.*
4.2.65–68, *P.* 2.8.57–58). Since fate has begrudged him this, Ovid
asks Maximus to send additional speeches so that the two may seem to
be more together (ll. 15–36).

The poem ends with questions (ll. 37–58): does Cotta remember
Ovid at recitations, does he talk about the poet as if he were still in
Rome? Ovid declares that he has not forgotten his friend and in his
imagination returns to Rome to enjoy conversations with him.
Although such fantasies give him happiness, they also make the reality
of Pontus much more difficult. Ovid concludes on this sober note. If
his hopes to leave are completely in vain, may Cotta take them from
him.

Like *Tr.* 4.2, this poem introduces happy illusions which end in bitter
reality. In this way Ovid returns to the themes seen earlier in *P.* 1.9 and
3.2. Despite their friendship, continual contact through mental vision,
and communication through exchange of speeches and poems, he asks
whether Maximus will do anything to help him.

FABIUS MAXIMUS

Paullus Fabius Maximus, a former patron of Ovid, is undoubtedly the
most well known man addressed in this collection. An important
member of a famous family, he held high political offices, including the
consulship in 11 B.C., and was a pontifex and member of the *fratres
Arvales*.[14] His wife Marcia, to whom Ovid refers in *P.* 1.2.137–38, was
a cousin of the emperor Augustus. Tacitus (*Annales* 1.5) describes his
death in A.D. 14 as a possible suicide shortly after his trip with
Augustus to visit the exiled Agrippa Postumus. While the historian's
account concerning the trip itself may not be true, it points to Fabius's
influence as a friend of the emperor. Fabius was also sufficiently at ease

with Augustus to joke about the meagerness of the emperor's handouts to friends (Quintilian *Institutes* 6.3.52).

Ovid was not the first poet to address Fabius Maximus in verse; Horace recommended him to Venus as a suitable victim in place of himself in the first poem of *Carmina* 4, at a time when Fabius was beginning a promising political career. P. 1.2.116, "auxilio trepidis quae solet esse reis," may be an echo of Horace *Carmina* 4.1.14, "et pro sollicitis non tacitus reis."[15] Ovid was no doubt conscious of his literary precedent in writing to Fabius. His relationship with his former patron is also quite different from that with Cotta Maximus. Ovid obviously did not enjoy an intimate friendship with Fabius; in contrast to his letters to Cotta, his appeals in the three elegies addressed to Fabius are more respectful and restrained.

To Fabius Maximus: An Appeal (Epistulae ex Ponto 1.2)

suscipe, Romanae facundia, Maxime, linguae,
  difficilis causae mite patrocinium.
est mala, confiteor: sed te bona fiet agente,
  lenia pro misera fac modo verba fuga.
nescit enim Caesar, quamvis, deus omnia norit,
  ultimus hic qua sit condicione locus.

Maximus, who embody the eloquence of the
Roman tongue, undertake the kind patronage
of a difficult case. It's a bad one, I admit, but
it will become good if you plead it. Only speak
some soothing words on behalf of an unhappy
exile. For Caesar does not know, even though
a god knows everything, in what condition
this remote place lies.

Like Horace in *Carmina* 4.1, Ovid describes Fabius as a gifted speaker, and in his appeal to his former patron the poet presents an oration of his own. The elegy, like *Tr.* 2, is organized like a speech. Ovid begins with a formal exordium (ll. 1–12) expressing hopes that Fabius will be receptive, then turns to a long narratio (ll. 13–58) describing conditions in Tomis. He concentrates on the warfare and danger of the region, expanding on the descriptions of *Tr.* 3.10, 4.1, and 5.7. Ovid then turns to the *propositio* of his address (ll. 59–68). All he can hope for is a change of exile; may Fabius undertake his case.

He argues in a long *probatio* (ll. 69–100) that it can be won and with Fabius as advocate it is assured of success.

In his *peroratio* (ll. 101–50) Ovid repeats his request. He explains that he does not demand a comfortable exile, only a less dangerous one ("non petito ut bene sit, sed uti male tutius," l. 103), a request seen earlier at *Tr.* 5.2.77–78 ("sed precor ut possim tutius esse miser"), or, if he dies, the right to be buried in a more secure place. Ovid strengthens this request by appealing to his long association with Maximus's house. Playing on the rhetorical convention of the *miseratio*, in which a speaker appeals for sympathy through references to the family and friends of the accused, he now introduces his wife and her ties with Fabius's household. Indeed, her request is the climax of the poem: may the emperor's anger be softened by Fabius's prayer so that her husband's tomb will be nearer to Italy!

There is little in Ovid's description of Tomis that we have not seen before. In direct contrast to its savagery he stresses Augustus's *clementia:* the emperor would not rejoice in the death of any citizen at the hands of barbarians, much less that of Ovid, whose life he spared (ll. 87–92). Ovid is also careful not to damage Fabius's influence with the emperor (ll. 133–34, 137–40) and describes Augustus as almost certain to be moved by an appeal. He even furnishes arguments in support of his case, urging Fabius to use his eloquence and influence in his behalf. Although the elegy is, like *Tr.* 2 and 5.2, a request to Augustus himself, Ovid makes his appeal through Fabius, stressing the position of his patron.

To Fabius Maximus: An Appearance of Amor
(Epistulae ex Ponto 3.3)

'pone metus igitur: mitescet Caesaris ira
   et veniet votis mollior hora tuis.

. . . .

dum faciles aditus praebet venerabile templum,
   sperandum est nostras posse valere preces.'
dixit, et aut ille est tenues dilapsus in auras,
   coeperunt sensus aut vigilare mei.

"Put away your fears then; Caesar's anger will
be softened, and a kinder hour will come for
your entreaties. ...While the venerable temple
gives us easy access we must hope that our

prayers can prevail." He spoke and either he
disappeared into thin air or my own senses
began to awake.

Here Ovid narrates an elaborate poetic theophany of Amor well
described as "rich in literary and personal associations."[16] His
borrowings from earlier elegies are so evident in this poem that it often
takes on the appearance of a literary pastiche. Yet the result is one of
the most imaginative elegies from Tomis.

Ovid begins with a short address to Maximus (ll. 1–14), then turns
immediately to the theophany (ll. 5–94), which occupies the main
portion of the elegy. The vision is introduced through a fully developed
ekphrasis (ll. 5–12); Amor appears as a sad and unkempt figure.
Ovid's description recalls his earlier depiction of Cupid in mourning at
the death of Tibullus in *Am.* 3.9.7–12. An even closer parallel to this
theophany is Amor's appearance at *Rem. am.*, ll. 555–76, where the
god advises the poet how to forget his love.

Ovid addresses the god, reproaching Amor for the ruin he has
brought upon him (ll. 21–64). His outburst is a medley of themes
presented earlier: he served Amor faithfully in writing elegy, only to be
ruined by his devotion. Yet the god must know that the *Ars amatoria*
has not corrupted anyone. Ovid therefore closes with a prayer that
Amor intercede with his relative Augustus to win him a better place of
exile.

When Amor replies (ll. 65–92), we see that his unkempt, mournful
appearance has symbolic value, producing the effect of a palinode. The
god is no longer haughty and triumphant, and his speech is certainly
the expression of a recantation, at least in part. He agrees that the *Ars*
was harmless, but cannot defend his master's offense. Although Ovid
wishes to call it *error,* it deserved the punishment it received. The god
assures him that Caesar is now ready to relent. Then he suddenly
departs, leaving the poet at the end, as at the beginning (ll. 3–4), in
doubt about what happened. The poem concludes with a second
address to Fabius Maximus (ll. 95–108): in contrast to the ambiguity
of the vision itself, Ovid expresses hopes that his patron will be
favorably disposed to his story.

Ovid deliberately creates a dreamlike, supernatural atmosphere
through his expressions of doubt concerning the reality of his vision
(ll. 3–4, 93–94). In this way his literary theophany gains the
impression of an actual experience, theophany through a dream, to
give greater force to his prayers: the greater the reality of the vision, the

more justified Ovid's hopes. He also gives a sort of divine sanction to his hopes. If Amor assures him that his brother Augustus is ready to relent, shouldn't he be justified in his expectations for a change of exile?

Within the theophany itself, Ovid's defense of the *Ars*, his apology for his *error*, and imperial flattery are nothing new. Yet they gain fresh treatment by being presented in this literary setting. Even more effective is the force of his appeal to Maximus following the elaborate description of his vision. Now that Amor has assured him that the situation is favorable and Ovid himself has demonstrated that he has changed from the cocky, self-assured poet of earlier days, won't his patron take steps in his behalf?

To Fabius Maximus: A Gift from Tomis (Epistulae ex Ponto 3.8)

nil igitur tota Ponti regione sinistri,
   quod mea sedulitas mittere posset, erat.
clausa tamen misi Scythica tibi tela pharetra:
   hoste precor fiant illa cruenta tuo.
hos habet haec calamos, hos haec habet ora libellos.

There was nothing then in the whole region of ill-
omened Tomis that I could send in my concern for
you. Yet I have sent you some arrows enclosed in
their Scythian quiver; may they be stained, I pray,
with the blood of your enemies. Such pens as these,
such books does this region have.

Ovid addresses this letter, the shortest in the collection, only to "Maximus" (l. 22), but its recipient is more likely to be Fabius Maximus than Cotta; his reference to consular purple (ll. 7–8) is more appropriate for Fabius, who held the consulship in 11 B.C., and the flattery of lines 3–4 recalls that of earlier letters to him. Moreover, the symmetrical arrangement of the collection supports identification with Fabius.[17] Ovid adapts here the convention of a gift poem written to accompany a present. He asks what he can send to Fabius: because Pontus lacks objects associated with a civilized life, such as metals, handicrafts, and fruits, the only present he can find is a quiver of Scythian arrows. The double meaning of "calamos" (l. 21), "arrows" as well as "reed pens," reinforces the irony of his final request: may Fabius accept this modest gift, representative of life in Tomis.[18]

In his first poem to Fabius, Ovid commented at length on the physical danger of Tomis and Scythian arrows (*P.* 1.2.13–58); in the second he contrasted the character of his patron with those who would harm the unfortunate, carrying arrowheads dipped in poison (*P.* 3.3.105–6). With this gift of Scythian arrows Ovid reinforces earlier pleas with strongly implied criticism that Fabius has done too little to help him.

TO OVID'S WIFE

In contrast to *Tr.* 5, where Ovid's wife appeared more prominently, only two elegies in this three-book collection are addressed to her. Ovid's decision to write to his friends openly by name may have reduced her importance. Yet she is addressed in the longest poem of the collection (*P.* 3.1) and is mentioned in several other poems (*P.* 1.2.145– 50, 2.11.13–16, 3.7.11–12).

To His Wife: Old Age without You (Epistulae ex Ponto 1.4)

te quoque, quam iuvenem discedens urbe reliqui,
    credibile est nostris insenuisse malis.
o, ego di faciant talem te cernere possim
    caraque mutatis oscula ferre comis.

I can believe that you too, whom I left still
young when I departed from Rome, have grown
old from my misfortunes. Oh may the gods
grant that I can see you, such as you are, and
give kisses to your hair turned gray.

As in *Tr.* 1.6 and 3.3, Ovid reworks elegiac motifs to express his separation from his wife after four years of exile and to give an account of his misfortunes.[19] He begins with a picture of himself in old age (ll. 1–22). His wife would no longer recognize him because of the changes he has undergone, both in physical appearance and mental state. He explains that the years have brought about his decline, but that there is another reason, his mental distress and continual hardships, which he illustrates through a catalog of exempla similar to that of *Tr.* 4.8.17–20 and 5.12.23–28.

In a central section (ll. 23–46) Ovid presents a *syncrisis,* or extended comparison, of himself with Jason, a famous mythological lover; the hero came to this region, but his misfortunes were far less. Unlike Jason, Ovid may never return home unless Augustus relents (ll. 43–44). We may compare the climax of his earlier *syncrisis* of himself with Ulysses (*Tr.* 1.5.81–84). In conclusion Ovid turns to his wife's old age (ll. 47–58): she too may be withered and gray, but he hopes for a reunion so that they may offer incense together to the Caesars and Livia.

To His Wife: A Request for Aid (Epistulae ex Ponto 3.1)

quid facias, quaeris? quaeras hoc scilicet ipsum:
  invenies, vere si reperire voles.
velle parum est: cupias, ut re potiaris, oportet,
  et faciat somnos haec tibi cura breves.
velle reor multos: quis enim mihi tam sit iniquus
  optet ut exilium pace carere meum?
pectore te toto cunctisque incumbere nervis
  et niti pro me nocte dieque decet.
utque iuvent alii, tu debes vincere amicos,
  uxor, et ad partis prima venire tuas.

You ask what you should do? You may indeed
ask this very thing! You will find out if you
really wish to learn. It is not enough to have
good intentions: to gain an end you must set
your heart on it. This is the concern which
should keep you awake. Many, I think, have
good intentions; for who would be so unjust as
to want my exile to lack peace? It is right that
you work with all your heart and strength and
strive in my behalf night and day. Although
others aid me, you, wife, must outdo my friends
and be the first to play your part.

This elegy, Ovid's longest address to his wife in the books from exile and the longest poem of this collection, merits detailed examination. In many ways the elegy is a summary statement of all earlier letters to her. But it also goes farther in its request for assistance than any single poem seen so far in all the books.

Ovid writes as before with elegiac overtones but also in the spirit of *Tr.* 5.2, accusing his wife of being remiss in her support and demanding

that she assist him. The poem is also unusual in its structural
development.[20] Ovid begins with a lament, not to his wife, but to
Tomis (ll. 1–30): will he ever leave, or must he die and be buried there?
With its permission ("pace tua, si pax ulla est tua," l. 7, a particularly
ironic word play), he declares that Pontus is the worst place on earth,
giving a synopsis of its conditions: there is no sign of seasonal changes,
for everything is cold and ice (cf. *Tr.* 3.10, 3.12); no water fit to drink
(cf. *Tr.* 3.3.7, 3.8.23); no trees or birds (cf. *Tr.* 3.10.73–76, 3.12.16);
only bitter absinthe in the countryside (cf. *P.* 3.8.15–16). No wonder,
Ovid concludes, that he desires another place of exile. As a carefully
developed and self-contained poem within a poem, this opening lament
summarizes complaints seen not only in this collection but also in
earlier books of *Tr.* 3–5. It therefore serves as a proem to what
follows.

Only after this introduction does Ovid turn to his wife with a
reproach directly linked to his opening lament. It is a greater wonder
("magis est mirum," l. 31–cf. "non igitur mirum," l. 29) that she can
refrain from tears at his sorrows. Indeed, he expects greater loyalty
from her (ll. 31–42). Ovid now makes much more explicit the theme
of literary glorification seen earlier in *Tr.* 5.14.19–20: because he has
praised her loyalty, she must live up to her image (ll. 43–66). She is as
well known as Bittis, the mistress celebrated by Philetas (ll. 57–58), an
elegiac echo of his first letter to her (*Tr.* 1.6.1–2). Future readers will
ask whether she was worthy of her husband's praise; many will be
envious of her position (cf. *Tr.* 5.14.7–10). She should not seem "lenta"
(l. 66), like an elegiac mistress, to his situation.

Instead Ovid's wife should fulfill the duties of her marriage bond
and "socialis amor" (l.73–cf. *Tr.* 5.14.28): Ovid would be equally
loyal to her if the situation demanded it (ll. 67–74). Moreover,
through her conduct she should demonstrate her devotion to Marcia,
the wife of Fabius Maximus (ll. 75–78). Ovid declares that he deserves
such support (ll. 79–86), then ends his lecture with a *praeteritio*, or
rhetoric omission of details, similar to that of *Tr.* 5.14.43–46: his wife
should not be angry if he reminds her to do what she is already doing
(ll. 87–94).

This explanation that the letter is an exhortation, not a reproach,
provides a transition from impatient scolding to calmer, less emotional
instructions (ll. 95–128): the poem takes on didactic qualities familiar
from love elegy. Ovid now makes explicit his wife's task: she must
approach the empress in his behalf. The poet introduced didactic
themes in his earlier section when he described her mission as not

dangerous, "utque ea non teneas, tuta repulsa tua est" (l. 88); the last half of the line repeats instructions given to the lover at *Ars* 1.346. Now these elements enter into full play. Exempla of wifely loyalty, all seen earlier in *Tr.* 1.6, 5.5, and 5.14, are introduced, not for comparison, but inspiration. Ovid also describes Livia in flattering terms, contrasting imperial virtues with negative exempla (ll. 119–24), as in his earlier request for aid to Fabius Maximus (*P.* 1.2.119–22). He also reintroduces the title "femina princeps" (l. 125) seen earlier in *Tr.* 1.6.25.

Specific instructions follow (ll. 129–66). Ovid's wife should choose a suitable time, and the poet explains why present conditions in Rome favor her appeal. She should not attempt a defense of her husband, but ask only for a change of exile. She should also weep and take Livia's knees, since tears can be persuasive ("interdum lacrimae pondera vocis habent," l. 158), a direct echo of *Her.* 3.4 ("sed tamen et lacrimae pondera vocis habent"). Ovid ends with instructions to choose an auspicious day and offer preliminary sacrifices, then adds his own prayer that Augustus, Tiberius, and Livia look on his wife's tears with a kindly eye ("non duris...vultibus," l. 166). We may compare a similar prayer for imperial favor at *P.* 2.8.44, "accipe non dura supplicis aure preces."

Like his letter to Fabius Maximus, this poem is addressed to an individual whom Ovid hopes to enlist as an advocate. Yet the contrasts between it and *P.* 1.2 are instructive. Because his wife, unlike Fabius, is not a trained speaker, Ovid does not give her specific arguments for the presentation of his case. Instead his instructions recall those of a *praeceptor amoris*, with exempla and aphorisms for inspiration and advice on the use of tears. Even more striking is the difference in tone from that of *P.* 1.2. Ovid writes, not as a respectful client to a former patron, but as a husband indignant that his wife has done nothing for him. His impatience and superior tone bring to a climax themes seen in earlier poems to her; the verbal echoes of previous elegies we have noted are therefore not accidental.

In *Tr.* 1.6 Ovid promised his wife poetic immortality in return for her faithfulness. In *Tr.* 3.3.25–26 as a dying lover he questioned whether she still remembered him. In *Tr.* 4.3 he reworked elegiac conventions to express doubts about her loyalty (4.3.1–26, 49–56). In *Tr.* 5.2 Ovid made a specific request that she appeal to the emperor for him; when she appeared hesitant, he abruptly delivered his own plea to Augustus (5.2.47–78). In *Tr.* 5.14 he reminded her of obligations to him.

Now the dialogue between poet and wife seen in earlier poems is expanded and even more dramatic. Ovid's requests are also more direct and explicit: it is time for his wife to do something. He thinks it disgraceful that she cannot or will not take effective action. While the poet does praise her "probitas" and loyalty (ll. 89–94), qualities commended in earlier letters (*Tr.* 1.6.19, 5.5.45–46, 5.14.22), this elegy cannot be described as laudatory. Ovid in fact is more impatient and demanding than ever before, determined to bully and upset his addressee.

Ovid's reproach goes far beyond the suspicion typical of the elegiac lover seen in earlier poems ("ambiguo spes...mixta metu," *Tr.* 4.3.12). If we wish to take his words at face value, *P.* 3.1, as the summary and climax of all his letters to his wife, presents a disturbing picture of his marriage. In contrast to other addressees within this collection, Ovid's wife seems to have no real personality of her own. We are left with the impression that she is uncaring or ineffectual, that their relationship has been poisoned, and that there is little personal feeling between her and the poet. The elegiac language which appears is now almost an inversion of that which came earlier: Ovid's wife should go without sleep, not in longing for him, but working for his recall (ll. 39–40—cf. *Tr.* 4.3.21–26). Indeed Ovid's appeal is based, not on affection, but objective, legalistic demands, the obligations and duties of the marriage bond, "socialis amor foedusque maritum" (l. 73). Because of her husband's distress, Ovid's wife herself must bear the marriage yoke (ll. 67–68—cf. *Tr.* 5.2.40); if the situation were reversed, he would do the same thing for her (ll. 69–72). Even more important are his wife's ties to Marcia, the wife of Fabius Maximus. She must confirm her devotion to that household by undertaking her husband's cause (ll. 75–78).

Such details reveal the reason Ovid gives this long harangue such prominent position within his collection. Although it is addressed to his wife, *P.* 3.1 is an appeal based mainly on social obligations and conventions.[21] Whatever her personal feelings, Ovid's wife has responsibilities to him which she cannot shirk; her position demands that she assist her husband in some concrete way, exploiting her ties with Fabius Maximus to advance his cause. Ovid's introduction of Marcia not only links this poem to *P.* 1.2, his earlier lengthy request to Fabius but also reinforces the appeals of that elegy. Like his former patron, his wife has obligations to him in exile.

But given Maximus's position and the strictures of the patron-client relationship, Ovid can make only a respectful request for support to him. With his wife no such deference is necessary. We would perhaps

expect a more personal appeal, but Ovid deliberately assumes a
different role, that of an angry husband, to express frustrations after
years of exile and disappointment at lack of support. His letter
therefore becomes a poetic outlet for dramatizing his plight and
expressing such feelings, reinforcing individual requests to friends
elsewhere in the collection.

Ovid's poetic exploitation of his wife may strike us as cold or even
brutal. But through his demands on her he expresses the urgency of his
situation, his desire that someone take action in his behalf. Such
frustrations are presented through this epistle addressed, not to a
patron or friend, but to his wife, an individual who must accept his
reproaches without complaint.

TO MESSALLINUS: A PATRON'S RESPONSIBILITIES
(*Epistulae ex Ponto* 1.7) AND A REQUEST (*Epistulae ex Ponto* 2.2)

M. Valerius Messalla Messallinus, the son of Ovid's former patron
Messalla Corvinus and elder brother of Cotta Maximus, was an
extremely influential member of a distinguished family who pursued a
successful political career. Elected to the college of the *quindecimviri,*
he also held the consulship in 3 B.C. and served under Tiberius during
the Pannonian campaign in A.D. 6–9. In contrast to his warm
friendship with his younger brother Maximus, Ovid's relationship with
Messallinus appears to have been that of client and patron, much more
formal and restrained. He writes only two letters to him and presents a
carefully correct and respectful tone in each.[22]

quo libet in numero me, Messalline, repone,
   sim modo pars vestrae non aliena domus:
et mala Nasonem, quoniam meruisse videtur,
   si non ferre doles, at meruisse dole.

Put me in whatever group of clients you
wish, Messallinus, if only I am not in that
part completely divorced from your household. And as for Ovid's misfortunes, since
he does appear to have deserved them, if you
are not sorry that he suffers them, at least
feel sorry that he has deserved them.

The first of Ovid's letters begins with concerns whether his patron
still considers him a client (ll. 1–16). He next elaborates on these

worries (ll. 17–36): his claims to being part of Messallinus's *clientela* are not false, and his addressee cannot deny that he was Ovid's patron. Moreover, his father and brother have always supported the poet. Association with Ovid has not harmed Cotta Maximus; if the poet is lying, may the whole house be closed to him! This ironic assertion (ll. 35–36) strengthens Ovid's claim on Messallinus's patronage; "mendacem" in line 35 recalls "mentito" at the beginning of the section (l. 19).

Ovid explains that he is guilty only of stupidity and that a pardon is possible (ll. 37–52). In the final lines (ll. 53–70) he returns to his relationship with Messallinus: he has some right to his patron's support.

P. 1.7 is modeled in part on *Tr.* 4.4, also written to Messallinus.[23] In both elegies Ovid links praise of his patron to that of Augustus. In *Tr.* 4.4.13–16 he explained that recognition of Messallinus would not harm his addressee, since even Caesar allows himself to be the subject of his verses. In P. 1.7.21–22 he declares that everyone thinks himself a friend of Caesar and that Messallinus has been a Caesar to him. For this reason his patron cannot refuse his praise. In both elegies Ovid also appeals to the support which he received from Messalla (*Tr.* 4.4.25–34, P. 1.7.27–30), defends himself and his conduct (4.4.35–44, 1.7.39–44), praises Augustus's leniency (4.4.45–48, 1.7.45–46), and requests that Messallinus intercede (4.4.53–54, 1.7.47–48).

Yet the ending of this poem is much different from that of *Tr.* 4.4, which concluded with a mythological illustration of Pontic savagery. We now see far greater emphasis on Ovid's former ties with Messallinus's household, along with persistent requests that his patron not forget or abandon him: the poet insists that Messallinus earn his client's devotion through his own aid and support (ll. 61–62). The result is an elegy much more individual in tone than *Tr.* 4.4, but also more stilted in its language and syntax. Ovid seems to have little to say to Messallinus, and the relationship between client and former patron appears cool.

We may compare P. 2.2, Ovid's second address to Messallinus, to P. 1.2 and 3.1, his appeals for support to Fabius Maximus and to his wife. There are obvious similarities between all three poems: in each we see instructions to seek only a transfer, not a complete pardon (2.2.95–96, 109–10—cf. 1.2.103–12, 3.1.151–52); praise of imperial *clementia* contrasted with negative exempla (2.2.113–16—cf. 1.2.119–26, 3.1.121–28); and Ovid's admission that his case is difficult (2.2.43–44—cf. 1.2.67–70, 3.1.147–48). As a request to a former patron, the

poem is most similar to *P.* 1.2. In both elegies Ovid fears that his
addressee may refuse his request (2.2.5–6, 39–40—cf. 1.2.7–8) and
praises the eloquence and influence of his advocate (2.2.47–50—cf.
1.2.65–68).[24]

But there are also significant differences between this poem and
P. 1.2. Ovid here does not give an extended description of Pontus (cf.
1.2.13–58) and supplies fewer arguments for use in his behalf. He
begins by discussing his *error* and admits that his patron may be angry
at him (ll. 1–38), then requests Messallinus's support and gives
instructions (ll. 39–66): his patron, like his wife, is to choose an
appropriate time (ll. 63–64—cf. 3.1.129–32, 141–42) and is told that
conditions in Rome favor the appeal (ll. 67–94—cf. 3.1.133–38).
Ovid ends (ll. 95–126) with a second request for aid supported by
arguments already seen in *P.* 1.7: his father Messalla would favor him
(ll. 97–98—cf. 1.7.27–28), his brother Cotta desires to help (ll. 99–
100—cf. 1.7.31–34), and Ovid has a claim on his addressee as a client
(ll. 101–2—cf. 1.7.15–16). As in *P.* 1.2, he cites the *clementia* of the
emperor (ll. 119—cf. 1.2.59).

TO RUFINUS: MY TRIUMPH POEM (*Epistulae ex Ponto* 3.4)
AND CONSOLATION (*Epistulae ex Ponto* 1.3)

This Rufinus may be C. Vibius Rufinus, later legate of upper Germany
in A.D. 43. The medical language which appears in *P.* 1.3 is not
evidence that he was a doctor or connected with medicine; medical
imagery often appears as a topos in literary consolations, and Ovid
may have adopted such terms deliberately to answer a recent epistle
from his friend.[25]

nec mihi nota ducum nec sunt mihi nota locorum
    nomina. materiam non habuere manus.
pars quota de tantis rebus, quam fama referre
    aut aliquis nobis scribere posset, erat?
quo magis, o lector, debes ignoscere.

Unknown to me were the names of the generals
and places concerned. My hands could not get
hold of the subject matter for a poem. How great
a part of such momentous events could rumor
repeat or someone write to me? All the more
then, reader, you should forgive me.

The more important of these poems is *P.* 3.4, another apology for the poetry from Tomis directed not so much to Rufinus as to all the poets in Rome: Ovid even presents a general address to them in lines 67–68. Rufinus's personality does not figure prominently, and the poet introduces only once (ll. 7–8) the medical terminology which appears throughout *P.* 1.3.

Ovid first apologizes for a triumph poem which he has sent to Rome (ll. 1–44). He calls attention to his absence as an excuse for its poor quality, then turns to other reasons why the poem should be pardoned. Happy subjects are now foreign to him (ll. 45–50). Since other poems on the triumph have preceded his own, the subject is no longer fresh; the tardiness of his poem is a direct result of his distance from Rome (ll. 51–64).

He next explains (ll. 65–76) that his remarks are not detraction or criticism of poems on the triumph by others. All poets, he declares, have common rites ("communia sacra," l. 67) among themselves; each deserves the loyalty and support of colleagues. Since Ovid became a dead poet when he went into exile, the envy of his rivals should not deny him sympathy.

He then pleads good intentions, citing the "voluntas" which he demonstrated in undertaking the triumph poem (ll. 77–82). In this way he reworks a theme quite familiar in the Augustan poetic apology, that of the modest sacrifice; we may compare Propertius 2.10.5–6 and 23–24.[26] Ovid argues that the subject would have been too much for Virgil (ll. 83–84) and that his elegiac meter was unsuitable for the theme (ll. 85–86). This discussion of metrical difficulties provides a transition to the final section of the elegy, in which he predicts a future triumph over Germany (ll. 87–114).

The ending of the poem introduces a new tone. Earlier in this elegy Ovid used the term "vates" ambiguously to describe himself and his fellow poets (ll. 17, 65, 84): they could be understood as poetic seers, an image seen earlier in *P.* 1.1, or simply as versifiers. Now "vates" reappears with the definite meaning of poet-prophet as Ovid confidently predicts the new triumph which will be celebrated shortly.[27] He emphasizes his vatic authority again and again ("irrita votorum non sunt praesagia vatum," l. 89; "deus est in pectore nostro," l. 93; "praedico vaticinorque," l. 94; "omen...meum," l. 98; "crede, brevique fides aderit," l. 99; "di quorum monitu sumus eventura locuti," l. 113) as he closes with vivid predictions of the future triumph.

Ovid's ending invites us to reexamine the apology which precedes it. An elaborate picture of the triumphal procession, comparable to that of *Tr.* 4.2, it allows him to expand the imperial flattery already introduced in lines 35-36 and to demonstrate his poetic skills. In this way *P.* 3.4 becomes another declaration that even in exile Ovid is still a poet whose works are being read in the capital. The poem closes, not with a self-deprecating apology, but with a proud demonstration of his abilities.

P. 1.3, the other letter to Rufinus, treats a philosophical theme seen earlier in *Tr.* 5.12, the inadequacy of consolation. Ovid begins and ends with two ten-line addresses, first thanking Rufinus for his kindness and interest (ll. 1-10), then cautioning him that efforts at consolation will be in vain (ll. 85-94). The major sections of the poem answer an attempt by Rufinus to console Ovid by means of "praecepta" (all wounds can be healed) and "exempla" (others have borne similar misfortunes); Ovid mentions "praecepta" in the first half (l. 27), "exempla" in the second (l. 61).[28]

Ovid first explains that his wounds are beyond all cure (ll. 11-46), then answers two of his friend's arguments point by point (ll. 47-84): Rufinus may object that Ovid still enjoys life "in...humano...loco" (l. 48), but existence in Tomis is almost worse than no life at all. To the second argument that other men have borne exile bravely, Ovid replies that no one has ever been forced to undergo conditions like his own. Ordinary consolation is therefore impossible.

TO GRAECINUS: REQUESTS FOR SUPPORT
(*Epistulae ex Ponto* 1.6 and 2.6)

C. Pomponius Graecinus is probably to be identified with the Graecinus whom Ovid addressed in *Am.* 2.10. The poet describes him as an old friend now pursuing an active political and military career (*P.* 1.6.10). Graecinus later became suffect consul in A.D. 16, and Ovid writes a congratulatory poem to him on his assumption of the office in *P.* 4.9. In both poems Ovid's association with Graecinus appears distant and formal; the friendship between the two men may have cooled after the poet's relegation.[29]

tecum tunc aberant aegrae solacia mentis,
    magnaque pars animi consiliique mei.
at nunc, quod superest, fer opem, precor, eminus unam,
    adloquioque iuva pectora nostra tuo.

At the time of my relegation along with you were
absent that which solaces a sick mind and a large part

of what gives me courage and good counsel. But now
for the future, bring me this one aid from afar, I pray,
and help cheer my soul with your comforting words.

In P. 1.6 Ovid begins by remembering the time of his relegation
(ll. 1–16): although Graecinus was absent, Ovid knows his character
and is sure that he was distressed. Yet the poet lacked the comfort and
consolation which his presence would have provided. Next he
discusses his case, expressing hopes that his punishment will be
lightened (ll. 17–46). In a lengthy hymn to Hope, Ovid presents an
aretalogy of the goddess based on a well-known elegiac model,
Tibullus 2.6.19–28; we may compare P. 1.6.31 ("haec facit ut vivat
fossor quoque compede vinctus") with Tibullus 2.6.25 ("Spes etiam
valida solatur compede vinctum"). But unlike Tibullus, who begins his
catalog of Hope's blessings with thoughts about his own suicide ("iam
mala finissem leto," 2.6.19), Ovid rearranges his aretalogy to heighten
its impact, moving from general background about Hope (ll. 29–30)
to the exempla of bondsmen (ll. 31–32), shipwrecks (ll. 33–34), the
sick (ll. 35–36), condemned prisoners (ll. 37–38), and suicides (ll.
39–40) before closing with his own attempt to take his life (ll. 41–
42). But the catalog ends on a positive note, the goddess's assurance
that Augustus will relent (ll. 43–46—cf. the conclusion of Tibullus's
hymn, "Spes facilem Nemesim spondet mihi, sed negat illa," 2.6.27),
which introduces a final plea to Graecinus for support (ll. 47–54).

The poet proclaims both at the beginning and end of his elegy that
Graecinus's loyalty is well known; "liquet" at line 50 recalls "liquet" in
line 4. Yet he plays on the demands of an old friendship. Although
Graecinus was not with him at the time of his sentence, he can now do
something to help. Is he more interested in his own career ("qua sinit
officium militiaeque labor," l. 10) or will he support his friend?

P. 2.6, a second letter, is a shorter and more perfunctory treatment of
the same theme. Ovid first replies to his friend's scoldings about his
error (ll. 1–18): it is too late for Graecinus to lecture him, for he is
already shipwrecked (cf. Tr. 1.5.35–36, 1.6.7–8, 5.9.15–20). Then he
shifts his argument, declaring that it will be disgraceful for Graecinus
not to help (ll. 19–38).

TO ATTICUS: MISFORTUNES AND MEMORIES
(*Epistulae ex Ponto* 2.4 and 2.7)

Nothing is known about Atticus, who appears to have been Ovid's
close friend and perhaps a fellow poet (P. 2.4.11–20). He is probably

the same individual whom Ovid addresses at *Am.* 1.9.2 and is perhaps to be identified with the *eques* Curtius Atticus who was a friend of the emperor Tiberius (Tacitus *Annales* 4.58.1, 6.10.2).[30]

iam dolor in morem venit meus, utque caducis
   percussu crebro saxa cavantur aquis,
sic ego continuo Fortunae vulneror ictu,
   vixque habet in nobis iam nova plaga locum.

Grief has now become a habit for me. As rocks
are hollowed out by water which constantly
falls upon them, so I am continually struck by
the steady blows of Fortune. Scarcely is there a
place left on me for a new wound.

In *P.* 2.7 Ovid gives an extended description of misfortunes addressed not so much to Atticus as to a general readership. Ovid's friend is not important, and at the end of the elegy the poet even drops him to address a new group of friends ("vos…pauci," l. 81).

Ovid gives a general account of his hardships in the first half of the poem (ll. 1–46). In contrast to earlier descriptions, we are given almost no factual information about Tomis; instead he illustrates his situation and anxiety through stock comparisons. Then his description becomes more concrete in a series of single couplets (ll. 47–74); each hexameter gives an expression of consolation or some hope that Ovid's condition may improve, which is denied or rejected in the pentameter which follows. Ovid begins with the theme of his literary pursuits and private life (ll. 47–50), then moves on to the circumstances of his relegation (ll. 51–54), his scolding by Augustus at the time of his sentence (ll. 55–56–cf. *Tr.* 2.133–34), his journey to Tomis (ll. 57–60), his lack of companions (ll. 61–62), and conditions in Tomis itself (ll. 63–74). In contrast to the topicality of what appeared earlier, Ovid in couplet after couplet now emphasizes the singularity and unique quality of his plight.

After such extended complaints, the poem concludes on a surprisingly positive note (ll. 75–84): Ovid has not yet lost heart ("omnia deficiunt. animus tamen omnia vincit," l. 75) and still hopes that Caesar's anger will diminish. His loyal friends in Rome are an additional solace (ll. 81–84).

Atticus is more important in *P.* 2.4, a short poem in which Ovid discusses their former friendship and literary activities. He begins by asking whether Atticus still remembers him (ll. 1–6), then shifts to his

own memories of the past introduced through mental vision (ll. 7–30).
He recalls former conversations and Atticus's comments on his poems:
he published only those which his friend had approved and often made
corrections which Atticus recommended. In the final lines (ll. 31–34)
he appeals to Atticus not to betray his trust.

SEVERUS (*Epistulae ex Ponto* 1.8)

Nothing is known about Severus except the information which Ovid
gives in this poem; he is not to be identified with the poet Cornelius
Severus, whom Ovid addresses for the first time in *P.* 4.42.[31] Severus
appears to have been prosperous and to have owned lands in Umbria
as well as a villa in the Alban Hills (1.8.63–68). The poet addresses
him as "iucunde sodalis" (l. 25) and "pars animae…meae" (l. 2).

non meus amissos animus desiderat agros,
    ruraque Paeligno conspicienda solo,
nec quos piniferis positos in collibus hortos
    spectat Flaminiae Clodia iuncta viae.

                    .   .   .   .

pro quibus amissis utinam contingere possit
    hic saltem profugo glaeba colenda mihi!

My spirit does not long for the fields it has
lost and the fine country land on Paelig-
nian soil, nor for the gardens on the pine-
covered hills which the Via Clodia surveys
at its junction with the Flaminia. … In
exchange for these losses, would that it
were my lot at least to till a clod of earth in
exile!

Ovid begins with a warning (ll. 1–24): Severus should not inquire
about his condition, for he can give only a summary of his troubles;
his friend will be more kindly to his verses when he realizes that they
were written on the battlefield. To illustrate the warlike conditions
Ovid turns to a digression about the foundation of the nearby city
Aegisos, describing King Aegisos's defeat of the Getae.

He next returns to his original theme ("unde abii," l. 25), his
unhappiness in exile (ll. 25–48). Warfare is only one hardship added
to his troubles. After four years away from Rome Ovid remembers his

friends and his wife, and in his mind he revisits the beautiful places of
the capital and recalls the pleasures of the country now denied to him.

In place of all these losses he gives wishes for the future (ll. 49–72):
a small plot of ground in exile where he could pasture goats and sheep,
yoke the oxen, and even learn to speak to the animals in Getic. With
his own hands he would guide a plowshare and sow, work the hoe,
and water his plants. But conditions in Tomis put an end to such
georgic fantasies. Ovid is protected from the enemy by only a wall and
closed gate. Severus is more fortunate; does he hope that Augustus will
check his anger and that he can again entertain Ovid? The poet
reminds him that he seeks too much and in a final couplet (ll. 73–74)
expresses his own wish to be exiled in a peaceful place closer to Rome.

The elegy is uneven in its development; the digression on Aegisos
appears out of place with that which follows. Yet the poem is
successful because of its juxtaposition of former happiness with present
reality. Ovid moves from a description of Pontus to a picture of Rome
before reflecting on the pleasures of country life. We are given
memories of gardening in Rome and fantasies of an idyllic happiness,
followed only by the realities of Pontus. Ovid bases his visions on
familiar elegiac motifs: we may compare a similar description of escape
to an idealized country life in *Rem. am.*, lines 169–98, where the poet
advises unhappy lovers to turn to farming.[32] Ovid's picture of himself
as a happy rustic also recalls fantasies in the *Amores:* he imagines
himself as his mistress's ring in *Am.* 2.15.9–26 and becomes a winning
charioteer in the circus in *Am.* 3.2.9–18. But in this poem, as in *Tr.* 3.8
and 4.8, he demonstrates that such escapes are not possible. In this
way his fantasy, although playful in its details, becomes deeply ironic.[33]

FLACCUS (*Epistulae ex Ponto* 1.10)

L. Pomponius Flaccus, like his brother Graecinus, whom Ovid
addresses in *P.* 1.6 and 2.6, pursued a political career and held the
consulship in A.D. 17. Although he writes only one elegy to him, Ovid
mentions him again in *P.* 4.9.75–88, a congratulatory poem to
Graecinus on his consulship. From Suetonius we learn that Flaccus had
a reputation for gluttony and high living (*Tiberius* 42.1); Ovid's
emphasis on poor health and loss of appetite in *P.* 1.10 may therefore
be deliberate.[34] He opens with a description of physical ills in exile
(ll. 1–20), then turns to a psychosomatic account of his poor health
(ll. 21–44), emphasizing his insomnia and lack of complexion. Ovid
states that his deterioration is not the result of excessive eating and

drinking or of love (a direct acknowledgement that he is playing with elegiac themes), but of the bad weather and atmosphere and above all, of "anxietas animi" (l. 36), described earlier in *P.* 1.4.

TO GERMANICUS: THE PANNONIAN TRIUMPH
IN ROME (*Epistulae ex Ponto* 2.1)

There is no need to discuss at length Germanicus's life and career.[35] What is interesting is Ovid's relationship with the prince, who was consul in A.D. 12, shortly before the publication of this collection. There is no evidence that the poet knew Germanicus personally, although he was acquainted with poets and literary figures on his staff, such as Albinovanus Pedo, Salanus, Sextus Pompey, Carus, and Suillius. Although Ovid addresses him here and at the beginning of the *Fasti,* almost all of his letters to individuals connected with Germanicus appear in *P.* 4, not in this collection. Salanus (*P.* 2.5) is the only exception.

quod precor, eveniet: sunt quiddam oracula vatum:
    nam deus optanti prospera signa dedit.
te quoque victorem Tarpeias scandere in arces
    laeta coronatis Roma videbit equis.

What I am praying for will come to pass. The
prophecies of poets are worth something, for the
god has given signs favorable to my prayer. You
too will happy Rome see climbing as victor to the
Tarpeian citadel, your horses crowned with
garlands.

In this elegy Ovid gives an extended description of Tiberius's Pannonian triumph, predicts another triumph for Germanicus, and promises a second poem in honor of that future occasion. We may compare the poem to *Tr.* 4.2 as a second attempt to correct his playful treatment of the triumph theme in the *Ars amatoria* and to gain imperial favor.[36] In contrast to *Tr.* 4.2, however, it is written, not in anticipation of the triumph, but afterwards.

In his introduction (ll. 1–18) Ovid reworks the theme of *Tr.* 4.2, his participation in the general happiness and the subordination of his personal misfortunes to public thanksgiving. But now he extends this idea: since Caesar has given happiness to the whole world, he cannot keep Ovid from rejoicing. Like the weed or "inutilis herba" (l. 15) which benefits from Jupiter's rain, he too shares in public joys. His statement recalls similar thoughts in *Tr.* 4.4.13–16, *P.* 1.1.27–36, and *P.* 1.7.21–22, all of which emphasized the public nature of the principate.

Ovid now addresses Fama, who brought him the news (ll. 19–48). She described the spectators and divine favor shown by the heavens, Tiberius's distribution of gifts and solemn sacrifice, and details of the procession, all similar to those of *Tr.* 4.2. He concludes with the captives, most of whom received mercy; why should he think that Augustus's anger cannot be softened?

Only now does Ovid write to Germanicus directly as he returns to his own situation (ll. 49–68); the many personal pronouns in lines 49–54 (*tui, te, tibi, a te, tuae*) underscore the direct address. Fama told him that the young general was given credit for towns he himself had captured: Ovid proclaims his oracular powers as poet and predicts a long life and successful career for the prince ("oracula vatum," l. 55; "vaticinante," l. 62; "omina…mea," l. 68). Perhaps he will sing of Germanicus's own triumph. If the poet is still alive when Germanicus receives it, the general will declare that both predictions, that of the triumph and the poem celebrating it, have come true.

There are similarities between this poem and *P.* 3.4: both elegies begin with celebration of a present triumph and move on to predictions of a future one.[37] As in *P.* 3.4.87–114, we again see Ovid's emphasis on his role as poetic *vates.* In addition, his description of the triumph demonstrates his literary skill and gives greater force to his promise of a future poem.

Despite these parallels with *P.* 3.4, we can best understand this elegy by comparing it with *Tr.* 4.2. In that poem Ovid's description of the triumph led him to reflections on his separation from Rome and inability to participate in public life. He ended with praise of the imperial house, subordinating private concerns to the *publica causa* (*Tr.* 4.2.73–74). Such sentiments are the starting point of *P.* 2.1. While Ovid stresses his power both as poetic celebrant and *vates,* he introduces these ideas for specific reasons, to flatter Germanicus and to request support. If the poet can describe a triumph this well in exile, he will do even better in the future if he leaves Tomis. Far from being an "inutilis herba," Ovid as master poet can bring glory to his subjects. Germanicus's favor will therefore not be without return.

SALANUS

Little is known about Cassius Salanus, a rhetorician and tutor of Germanicus. He is mentioned once by Pliny the Elder (*Natural History*

34.18.47). He is, however, the only member of Germanicus's staff who appears as an addressee in this collection.[38]

To Salanus: Poetic Ties (Epistulae ex Ponto 2.5)

huic tu cum placeas et vertice sidera tangas
    scripta tamen profugi vatis habenda putas.
scilicet ingeniis aliqua est concordia iunctis,
    et servat studii foedera quisque sui.

            .   .   .   .

tu quoque Pieridum studio, studiose, teneris,
    ingenioque faves, ingeniose, meo.

Even though you find favor with Germanicus and touch the stars with your fame,
you still think that the writings of an exiled
poet are worth reading. Certainly kindred
spirits enjoy some sort of bond, and each
one observes the ties of his own pursuit....
You too, lover of study, are held by a love
for the Muses, and as a man of talent you
show favor to my own talent.

This letter presents another apology for the books from Tomis as well as a tribute to Salanus's pupil Germanicus. In the first half (ll. 1–36) Ovid stresses the direct relation between the quality of his poetry and the circumstances of its composition. His statements about warlike conditions in Scythia are direct and explicit: there is no place on earth which less enjoys the *pax Augusta* (ll. 17–18). Yet Salanus reads and praises his verses, bad as they are. Ovid explains in an elaborate *recusatio,* or polite disclaimer, that he can write on only meager subjects; he attempted a work of greater scope in honor of Tiberius's triumph ("tantae...molis opus," l. 28), but it was beyond his capabilities.[39]

Then Ovid praises Salanus's own ability (ll. 37–76). Since his friend has guided Germanicus to the heights of success, Ovid is all the more pleased that Salanus still considers his poetry worth reading. He next turns to a theoretical discussion of their common bond. Both poet and rhetorician are worshipers of the liberal arts; his own verses gain strength from eloquence, while he can add poetic brilliance to a speech. Such ideas are little more than generalities,[40] but Ovid introduces them for an immediate, practical purpose: Salanus must consider himself the poet's ally.

Through its praise of Salanus, the elegy becomes a second tribute, after *P.* 2.1, to Germanicus. As his teacher brings glory to Germanicus through rhetoric, Ovid too can glorify the prince through his poetry. He bases his appeal for Salanus's support on an idea treated in earlier poems, the bonds between "consortes studii" (*Tr.* 5.3.47), whether they are fellow poets (*Tr.* 3.7.11, 4.7.3–4; *P.* 3.4.67) or, as in this case, engaged in related literary pursuits.

COTYS (*Epistulae ex Ponto* 2.9)

Cotys was established as client king of Thrace along with his uncle Rhescuporis in A.D. 12 (Tacitus *Annales* 2.64).[41] Since his succession was roughly contemporary with the publication of this collection, *P.* 2.9 may well have been written to him to celebrate the event. Cotys is the only person to whom Ovid writes who is not in Rome. The elegy may have been sent separately, then revised for inclusion in this collection.

Ovid's subject is that of poetic ties, treated earlier in *P.* 2.5. He first discusses the general obligations which kings have toward suppliants (ll. 1–38): Cotys's conduct should bring credit both to his position and his ancestry. Next Ovid presents a more individual appeal, describing Cotys's education and literary interests and appealing to common ties (ll. 39–80). As in his earlier poem to Salanus, he cites the "foedus" (l. 63—cf. *P.* 2.5.60) which links them as worshipers of the liberal arts ("cultor, l. 64—cf. 2.5.66), apologizes for the *Ars amatoria*, praises Augustus, and closes with the wish that he may live safely under Cotys's protection. In contrast to other epistles, Ovid does not specifically request Cotys's assistance in returning to Rome; there was probably little that a client king could do for him.

MACER (*Epistulae ex Ponto* 2.10)

Pompeius Macer was an old friend and also a poet in his own right; Ovid addresses him in *Am.* 2.18. The son of the historian Theophanes of Mytilene, he was appointed head of the Palatine Library by Augustus and must have enjoyed some reputation in Roman literary circles.[42] Ovid, however, writes to him in *P.* 2.10 as an equal, a fellow poet, and long-time friend.

This letter links an extended account of past associations with the present reality of exile. Ovid first reminds Macer of their long friendship, his family ties with the poet's wife, and common literary interests, then introduces the theme of mental vision: when the poet remembers these things, he seems to see Macer before him (ll. 1–20).

Ovid now describes past experiences (ll. 21–42), recounting a year-long grand tour made together with Macer. He remembers their long conversations en route and the dangers at sea. These past associations then lead to thoughts about the present (ll. 43–52). Since his friend is present when the poet's imagination summons him, Macer has even visited Pontus without knowing it. Ovid closes with a clever twist of this idea: may Macer repay him and bring him back to the capital by keeping him in mind as well! The letter ends with concerns about whether Ovid is remembered. Ovid also writes to Macer as a fellow poet who shares "communia sacra" (l. 17) with him. This is his third such appeal to literary ties within the collection.

RUFUS (*Epistulae ex Ponto* 2.11)

Nothing is known about Rufus, the uncle of Ovid's wife, except the information which Ovid presents in *P.* 2.11.[43] The poet first describes Rufus's support at the time he left Rome (ll. 1–12), then turns from past assistance to the present time (ll. 13–28), discussing in particular his encouragement of Ovid's wife: like a racehorse spurred by applause, she emulates her uncle and under his influence does much for her husband. These details about his wife give Ovid's letter a more personal tone. He describes her as an individual who, while decent ("probitate," l. 17) and able to take action on her own, is more effective under proper guidance and supervision. This description reinforces the picture presented of her in *P.* 3.1 and elsewhere.

TO AN UNNAMED FRIEND (*Epistulae ex Ponto* 3.6)

hactenus admonitus memori concede poetae
    ponat ut in chartis nomina cara suis.
turpe erit ambobus, longo mihi proximus usu
    si nulla libri parte legere mei.

After this warning allow a mindful poet to
name those dear to him in his pages. It will
be disgraceful for both of us if you, my

intimate from long association, will be read
in no part of my book.

This poem was mentioned in Chapter 1 but should be examined
further. Although Ovid describes his addressee as "proximus usu"
(l. 53 —cf. *Tr.* 3.5.9, 3.6.19), he gives no clues concerning his identity.
The friend, like earlier enemies, is probably a lay figure representing
others whom the poet has not named. The elegy reminds us of the
Tristia, where no addressees were named except Ovid's wife and Perilla
(*Tr.* 3.7). The opening couplet with its playful admission that the name
almost slipped out presents echoes of *Tr.* 4.5.9–10.[44]

Ovid first returns to a theme introduced in his prologue to the
collection, assuring the friend that association with himself is not
dangerous (ll. 1–22 —cf. "quod metuas non est," *P.* 1.1.23). We may
also compare his statement that those blasted by Jupiter's thunderbolt
often revive (ll. 17–18) to that of *Tr.* 4.9.13–14, which shows some
similarity of theme: in the earlier elegy Ovid threatened to expose an
enemy to notoriety; here he wishes to glorify a friend who does not
want recognition.

Ovid next discusses the establishment of the cult of Justitia Augusta
in Rome (ll. 23–38), then asks the friend why he persists in his fears
(ll. 39–60), introducing negative exempla, as in *P.* 1.2.119–120,
2.2.113–114, and 3.1.119–24, to illustrate the emperor's *clementia.*
The friend should therefore allow his name to appear. Yet Ovid
declares that he will not be more open in his devotion ("officiosus," l.
56 —cf. "officio," l. 4) than the friend permits.

The poem is more than imperial panegyric. By not naming his friend,
Ovid also provides a significant variation on his good faith and loyalty
theme. Since the addressee persists in his reluctance to be named, Ovid
ends the elegy on a teasing, ironical note: he gives his friend permission
to love him secretly. Unlike other recipients of letters, he will not be
forced to accept the poet's tribute. The understatement is certainly
deliberate: Ovid uses this unnamed friend to address others who have
not been named in the collection, asking that they continue in their
friendship and not be ashamed of association with him.

A GENERAL APPEAL (*Epistulae ex Ponto* 3.7)

torqueor en gravius, repetitaque forma locorum
    exilium renovat triste recensque facit.
est tamen utilius, studium cessare meorum

quam, quas admorint, non valuisse preces.
magna quidem res est, quam non audetis, amici:
   sed si quis peteret, qui dare vellet, erat.

Look, I am tortured all the more, and repeating
a description of my place of exile only renews it
and makes it fresh. Yet it is better that my
friends be remiss in their interest for me than
the prayers that they have made in my behalf
not have any effect. It is a difficult thing which
you dare not try, my friends; but if someone
were to ask it, there is one who would be
willing to grant it.

Following the address to the unnamed friend we find a second
general appeal, perhaps the single most important elegy in this
collection, addressed to all of Ovid's friends in Rome. Described as a
poem which speaks "directly...to the emotions,"[45] it presents so many
verbal echoes of earlier requests that we must view it as a summation
of the three books, intended to reinforce individual letters.

The poem is divided into two halves, each ending with Ovid's
declaration that he is now resolved to die in Tomis; "fortiter Euxinis
inmoriemur aquis" (l. 40) echoes "venimus in Geticos fines; moriamur
in illis" (l. 19). Ovid begins with an admission: his many requests for
support, delivered again and again, have left him at a loss for words
("verba mihi desunt" l. 1) and have also bored his readers. He
announces his intentions to end his fruitless labor, which he compares
to rowing upstream (an image perhaps borrowed from Virgil at
Georgics 1.201–3), and asks forgiveness of his friends for having had
empty hopes in them. His next statement is even more bitter: he will no
longer trouble his wife, who is a good woman, but timid and
ineffective, a declaration which recalls his reproaches to her in *P.* 3.1.

In lines 21–40 Ovid again discusses his change of heart, this time
beginning in more theoretical terms: it is better to abandon empty
hopes. He illustrates his situation through familiar exempla of wounds
and shipwreck, then follows with rhetorical questions: Why did he
even think he could leave Pontus and enjoy a better place of exile?
Were these vain hopes also a part of his fate? "Speravi" (l. 31) is a
direct echo, in the same metrical position, of an earlier line in which
Ovid gave more explicit expression of hopes that friends would aid
him ("quod bene de vobis speravi, ignoscite, amici," l. 9). Yet, he

declares, although his request is great, if someone would speak for him, someone would grant it. As in the first half of the poem, Ovid ends with another statement of resolution, this time even more bitter than before: he will die bravely in Pontus if Caesar's wrath has not denied him this right.

The last lines of the poem are deliberately shocking, as the climax of a series of apologies, expressions of despair and resignation, and announcements that this elegy is Ovid's swan song, the last time he will bother his friends (ll. 1–8, 35–36). Yet his sarcasm in the final couplet, while seemingly aimed at Augustus, is actually directed elsewhere, to the friends addressed in the poem.

Ovid's bitter statement of resignation is, in effect, one last appeal: if someone were loyal enough to ask for a change of exile, Augustus would be willing to grant it. We may compare a similar statement to Messallinus at *Tr.* 4.4.53–54:

quantaque in Augusto clementia, si quis ab illo
  hoc peteret pro me, forsitan ille daret.

Augustus's *clementia* is such that if someone
were to seek this for me, perhaps he would
grant it.

In both poems Ovid links his appeal for a spokesman to praise of the emperor's *clementia*. Now, however, after an extended discussion of imperial *clementia* and *iustitia* in the preceding elegy, his statement in *P.* 3.7.37–38 is stronger, unqualified by "*forsitan*": Augustus *will* relent, but *someone* must ask him. As he brings his collection to a conclusion, Ovid presents himself as having reached the point of deepest despair because his friends cannot or will not take action. This bitter resignation makes this poem, his last direct appeal, the most forceful of all.

EPILOGUE: TO BRUTUS (*Epistulae ex Ponto* 3.9)

nec liber ut fieret, sed uti sua cuique daretur
  littera, propositum curaque nostra fuit.
postmodo collectas utcumque sine ordine iunxi:
  hoc opus electum ne mihi forte putes.
da veniam scriptis, quorum non gloria nobis
  causa, sed utilitas officiumque fuit.

Not that a book be composed but that to each
be delivered his own letter has been my purpose
and intent. Afterwards I put them together
without any order, so that you may not by
chance think that this is a specially selected
work. Pardon what I have written; poetic fame
was not its cause, but my own self-interest and
a sense of duty.

Unlike the prologue, which discussed the collection only briefly and
treated Ovid's relationship with Augustus at greater length, this
epilogue is entirely concerned with the problem of writing in exile and
an apology for these books. As in the prologue, Brutus is not
important, and the elegy is directed to a general readership.

Ovid first anticipates the most obvious criticism, that of repetition
and monotony (ll. 1–12), discussed earlier in *P.* 3.7.1–8. He
acknowledges this shortcoming but declares it one among many. He
also reworks the topos of literary works as the writer's offspring (cf. *P.*
1.1.21–22) by introducing the exemplum of Thersites: although Agrius
might call his son attractive, Ovid is well aware that his books have "a
face only a father could love."[46]

Ovid then answers another objection (ll. 13–32): why doesn't he
revise or correct his poems? Again we see the explanation of *P.* 1.5.15–
20 and *Tr.* 5.1.71–72: revision is more painful than composition itself.
He returns to the problem of monotony in the final lines (ll. 33–56),
declaring it excusable: his subject matter merely reflects his circumstances and physical state. Ovid also introduces another defense
against this criticism. Should he have written to only one friend,
instead of many individuals, to avoid repetition? Such artistic
standards were not worth the price, and his reputation meant less to
him than his own welfare. Ovid's purpose was, not to create a poetic
book, but to send letters, assembled at random, to friends at Rome.
"Utilitas" and "officium" have motivated this collection.

THE COLLECTION AS A WHOLE

The epilogue is an appropriate starting point for a general examination
of these thirty poems. Despite Ovid's statement that the books were
assembled "sine ordine," study of their arrangement has shown that
there is nothing haphazard about their presentation. Like individual
books of the *Tristia,* this collection is artistically arranged. Ovid's plan

is a modification of that used in *Tr.* 5, where he distributed letters in such a way that each of four elegies to his wife was separated by two other poems addressed to unknown friends.

We see a similar arrangement in *P.* 1–3. Cotta Maximus, the poet's most intimate friend, has assumed the position held by Ovid's wife in the arrangement of the earlier book. Poems addressed to him form the core of Ovid's structural pattern. Because he organizes a three-book collection of thirty poems instead of a single *libellus,* the scope of his undertaking is much more ambitious. Ovid's symmetrical scheme is also more complicated because it is based on specific individuals addressed by name. Some recipients become more important than others through the placement of their letters, content and length of the elegies, and the number of times they appear. Yet in organizing this collection Ovid follows the principle of arrangement which he used the previous year.

In addition to its structural plan, Ovid's collection shows other evidence that it is not a random grouping of poems. As in earlier books, we see a constant effort to avoid monotony through variation of theme whenever possible. Within *P.* 1, Ovid's complaints are varied from poem to poem: in *P.* 1.2, written to Fabius Maximus, he stresses hostilities and threats of warfare, in 1.3, to Rufinus, the harsh climate and landscape, in 1.4, to his wife, his separation from her, in 1.5, to Cotta, the difficulty of writing. In the next five elegies we see similar *variatio*: in *P.* 1.6, to Graecinus, Ovid discusses his *error*; in 1.7, to Messallinus, he stresses the responsibility of a patron; in 1.8, to Severus, he presents fantasies of escape; in 1.9, a second elegy to Cotta, he much more grimly plays on the obligations of friendship; and in 1.10 to Flaccus he discusses physical and spiritual ills.

P. 2 likewise shows concern with *variatio*. The book begins with the spirited triumph poem in which Germanicus figures prominently. *P.* 2.2, a second poem to Messallinus, returns to the theme of *P.* 1.7, responsibilities in a patron-client relationship. *P.* 2.3 praises Cotta's loyalty, and 2.4, to Atticus, treats memories of a past friendship. *P.* 2.5, to Salanus, allows Ovid a second opportunity to praise Germanicus. In contrast, *P.* 2.6, a second letter to Graecinus, is a shorter treatment of the good faith theme. In 2.7, Atticus is not important, and Ovid concentrates on a lengthy complaint about Tomis. *P.* 2.8, which follows immediately, is a prayer to the imperial family; 2.9, to Cotys, stresses the *communia sacra* of poets, a theme treated earlier in 2.5; and 2.10, to Macer, concerns the presence of friends through mental vision. The book ends with a short address to Rufus, uncle of Ovid's wife.

Poems within the collection also appear deliberately arranged to introduce and heighten the effect of those that follow. *P.* 2.11, Ovid's letter to his wife's uncle, serves as an introduction to 3.1, his direct address to his wife at the beginning of the next book; after addressing Rufus, the poet writes to his wife with the implication that she, like her uncle, should support him.[47] The order of poems within book 3 is even more carefully developed. *P.* 3.1, Ovid's request to his wife to approach Livia, is the longest elegy of the collection; its opening lament on conditions in Pontus provides a summary of what has come before as well as a proem to the third book itself. Ovid's scolding about his wife's reluctance to take action is the most forceful request for aid we have seen and careful preparation for the appeals which follow: in the first elegy of the book Ovid presents himself impatient and frustrated in his requests for support. *P.* 3.2, to Cotta, emphasizes the responsibilities of friendship through a retelling of the Orestes / Pylades legend, and 3.3 presents a poetic recantation by Ovid in a literary epiphany of a repentant Amor. *P.* 3.4, which treats another triumph poem, permits Ovid to proclaim loyalties to the imperial house, and 3.5, to Cotta, gives a last challenge to his friend not to forget the poet.

The final poems of the books are also arranged in a deliberate sequence, perhaps the most subtle of all. *P.* 3.6, the letter to the unnamed friend, introduces 3.7, an address to all of Ovid's friends. These two general appeals appear at the end of the collection, after we have read some twenty-five letters to individuals. Because of its position, *P.* 3.7 itself becomes a final request, a last attempt by Ovid to strengthen the impact of earlier appeals. The poet presents himself in utmost despair to reinforce his pleas for the active support of his addressees. His bitterness is heightened even more by the irony of *P.* 3.8, which gives a final description of Pontus and strongly implied criticism of a patron who should take action in his behalf. Certainly this arrangement was carefully chosen and not haphazard.

We must therefore reject Ovid's statement that the three books are a simple group of letters written individually and collected at random. Such an explanation is more than merely an example of literary modesty common among Augustan poets and particularly suitable for Ovid's presentation of his work from exile.[48] Instead his purpose is to appeal for sympathy and to enhance the impact of his books. By announcing that this collection is only a group of "letters" written to individual friends, Ovid appeals to his readers directly, without the complications of a literary pose. Because of his situation in Tomis, he no longer pretends to be a poet, but presents himself simply as a man in need writing to his friends.

We must also examine Ovid's explanation of why he published the collection: to what extent are his motives of "utilitas" and "officium," "self-interest" and "a sense of duty," the real reasons for these books?

"Utilitas" has two possible interpretations applicable to Ovid's situation. The most obvious is one furnished by the poet himself. As he explains in *P.* 3.9.13–32, he writes in Tomis to forget his troubles. Versification has become a type of medicine for him, a means of removing himself from the grim conditions of exile. We may compare *Tr.* 4.1.37–38, where he was even more explicit:

forsitan hoc studium possit furor esse videri,
    sed quiddam furor hic utilitatis habet.

Perhaps this literary interest may seem to be
madness, but this madness has a certain
benefit for me.

In *P.* 3.9, however, Ovid joins "utilitas" with "officium" as his motive for writing, and there is more to his meaning than the opportunity to forget his troubles. To determine the full significance of the word we must first explore the meaning of *officium.* The poems of this collection are an expression of *officium* to friends in Rome, a duty which Ovid, as a poet in exile, can properly render to them. He explains that he has assembled the elegies, not to produce a book, but to provide a letter to each of his friends (ll. 51–52). Such is his *officium* to them; unlike a man of political influence or wealth, he cannot help them materially, but can express his gratitude by praise in his verses.

Officium also appeared in Ovid's earlier books. We may recall *Tr.* 3.4.63–66, where he explained that fear prevented him from giving open recognition to friends in his verses ("sed timor officium cautus compescit"). In this collection, he describes his elegy on the death of Celsus as an act of *officium* to his friend, a substitute for obligations which he could not fulfill in person; Maximus, who was present, rendered "officium...omne" to Celsus (*P.* 1.9.43–50). In his prologue Ovid announces that his dutiful Muse ("officiosa...Musa") will give recognition to all his friends, even those who do not wish it or who find it bothersome (*P.* 1.1.19–20). Ovid also plays on the idea of

rendering tribute through poetry in *P.* 2.6.31–32 and 3.4.51–52 and
77–78. We may compare *P.* 3.6.3–4 and 55–56, where the poet's
officium would have brought a complaint from the unnamed friend.

Ovid's reference to *officium* as a duty owed to a friend is closely
connected to a second, more important meaning of *utilitas*, "one's own
advantage or benefit." *Officium* is nothing more than a tangible
example of the advantages of friendship. Thus for Ovid *utilitas* is
much more than simply a means of distraction through versification. It
is also for him a concrete benefit to be gained by enlisting the active
support of friends and associates in Rome. Likewise *officium* has more
than one meaning. It not only describes the service which Ovid
performs for friends in gratitude, but, more important, also implies a
service owed in return. The poet has therefore extended his theme seen
earlier in *Tr.* 5.14: because he gives his wife and friends immortal praise
in his verses, they must repay this service by doing something for
him—by pleading his case before Augustus. In poem after poem within
the collection, Ovid appeals for a spokesman or intermediary, a friend
who will champion his cause. Friendship, as he points out frequently,
implies responsibilities and obligations on both sides. As much as he
wants to honor his friends and demonstrate his gratitude for their
loyalty,[49] he also reminds them that they must work actively to improve
his situation.

This reminder takes many forms, allowing Ovid a significant *variatio*
in appeals to different addressees. At times it is a formal request to an
old patron supported by appeals to a long association and family ties
(*P.* 1.2 to Fabius Maximus) or a reminder of noblesse oblige (1.7 to
Messallinus). Ovid also appeals to an earlier intimacy (1.6 and 2.6 to
Graecinus, 2.4 to Atticus) or to the *communia sacra* of poets (2.5, 2.9,
2.10, 3.4). Most varied in their presentation are the letters to Cotta
Maximus. At times Ovid praises Cotta's loyalty (2.3, 3.2.1–35);
elsewhere he sternly reminds him of his obligations to a friend in exile
(1.9; 3.5). In two other poems Cotta is addressed only in the opening
lines, after which Ovid turns to other subjects (1.5, 2.8). In these
elegies the poet seems to introduce his friend only to maintain his
overall symmetrical arrangement by addressee.

At times Ovid's request for continued support receives less emphasis,
such as in the triumph poem dedicated to Germanicus (2.1), his two
apologies for his Pannonian triumph poem (2.5, 3.4), and his epistle to
Cotys (2.9). Yet in contrast to earlier books of the *Tristia* where we saw
a variety of subjects, this theme is present, or at least implied, in every
piece. Very few elegies treat the subject of poetics so prominent earlier.

P. 1.5 and 3.9 are the only extended apologies for the poetry in the collection, and throughout the three books Ovid shows himself most concerned with obtaining the support and assistance of his friends, now more than at any earlier time in his exile. While he attempts to vary his presentation of these thirty poems through their subject matter, emphasis, and tone, the elegies have a striking similarity of theme.

The differences from earlier books of the *Tristia* are therefore obvious. Yet we must view this collection as an extension of Ovid's strategy in *Tr.* 5, published one year earlier. In that book he turned from chiefly descriptive poems on his experiences and feelings in exile, as in *Tristia* 1–4, to what he called *publica carmina,* more direct appeals for help in the form of poetic epistles; he also expressed hopes for at least a new place of exile if a complete pardon were impossible. Concomitant with this change in purpose, Ovid presented himself in *Tr.* 5 as no longer a poet by Roman standards but simply a correspondent in verse. This role too is maintained in his new collection: Ovid declares that he has not attempted to create a poetic book ("liber"), but merely sends letters to individual friends (*P.* 3.9.51–52). Because external circumstances have reduced him to this much lower function, his appeals to the *communia sacra* of poets become more pathetic. If this phrase were Ovid's own invention, a variation of the commonplace of poetry as sacred,[50] his sarcastic references to himself as a "vates" throughout the collection (*P.* 1.1.47, 2.1.55–68, 2.5.58, 2.9.65, 3.4.89–114) underscore the extent of his decline from the higher calling of his earlier career.

In contrast to *Tr.* 5, in which friends were not named and his wife was addressed most frequently, Ovid now decided to write openly to particular individuals. The role of his wife appears reduced but is still of key importance. Although she is addressed in only two poems, the second is the longest of the collection and Ovid's most forceful request for aid. In it he not only brings to a climax earlier lectures to her but also uses his reproaches to underscore other appeals in the collection. Ovid's harangue to her is therefore a poetic vehicle for expressing his frustration at lack of support. But the poet seems to have placed greater hopes for success in other friends, mainly the two sons of Messalla Corvinus and his former patron Fabius Maximus, with whose family his wife was connected. The prominence of the poems addressed to these men certainly seems deliberate: letters to Fabius Maximus appear directly after the prologue and before the epilogue, and *P.* 3.1 to Ovid's wife cites her ties with Marcia, Maximus's wife (3.1.77–78—cf. 1.2.136–50).

In this fourth year of exile Ovid no longer hesitates to associate the names of such men with his own. He writes to them directly, reminding them much more forcefully of obligations to him. The three books are a collection of open letters which give much greater impact to his requests for help; the friends to whom Ovid writes are reminded of their responsibilities and duties before the Roman literary public. Ovid's attempt to win their support cannot be described as a form of poetic blackmail; he can do nothing to force his friends to help him and indeed is completely dependent on their good will. Yet he does remind them, before all of his readers in Rome, that they must not forget their obligations to him.

The personalities of Ovid's addressees and his individual relationships with them give the collection a highly effective *variatio* of tone. At the time of publication most of the men appearing within the book were important and influential figures. Ovid's readers in the capital would have been much more alert than we are to changes of presentation within the individual elegies. They would also have been struck by his skillful reinforcement of individual appeals through other letters in the collection.

The size of the collection shows that it was the single most ambitious project which Ovid undertook in exile. While the poet did not necessarily write all thirty elegies within the same twelve-month period, he published them in a unified collection which reveals clearly his aims, to present a general appeal articulated through a series of individual letters.[51] For several reasons explored earlier in Chapter 1, Ovid thought that conditions in A.D. 12−13 were favorable for obtaining imperial clemency. References to contemporary events such as the Pannonian triumph and the establishment of the cult of Justitia Augusta underscore his appeals. Far from being a random grouping of poems, *P.* 1−3 is a collection published for a specific and compelling cause, to gain spokesmen in Rome. The contrast with earlier books from Tomis which we found in *Tr.* 5 has now become even more dramatic. Although he publishes *publica carmina* intended for a general audience, Ovid uses his books for an immediate, personal reason, functioning no longer as a poet of exile as much as a poetic apologist for himself. The fact that he was unsuccessful in his attempt in no way detracts from the artistry which these books display. In their singularity of purpose and presentation they are a poetic collection unique in ancient literature.

VII EPISTULAE EX PONTO 4 A Final Book

Many things distinguish *P.* 4 from *P.* 1–3 and individual books of the *Tristia*. First, it is much longer than any of the previous single books. With sixteen elegies of 880 verses, it has a length 100 lines greater than each book of *P.* 1–3 and is much longer than any book of the *Tristia*. In addition, its poems are addressed to a group of friends quite different from that of *P.* 1–3. Only two of its addressees, Brutus (4.6) and Graecinus (4.9), appeared in the earlier collection, and all of its other elegies are written to individuals whom we see for the first time. In contrast to previous collections, there is no poem to Ovid's wife.

But the most striking difference between *P.* 4 and the books which precede it is the chronological span of its elegies. Each book of the *Tristia* gave clear reference to its year of composition, and *P.* 1–3 also showed a chronological unity pointing to publication in A.D. 12–13. The poems of this book represent a longer period, from sometime in A.D. 13 to A.D. 15. *P.* 4.4 and 4.5 describe the future consulship of Sextus Pompey in A.D. 14; Ovid speaks of the year as the "proximus annus" (4.4.18) and alludes to Augustus as still alive (4.5.23–28). These earlier elegies must have been written in A.D. 13, perhaps at

approximately the same time as *P.* 1–3. The latest poem in the book, *P.*
4.9, is to be dated to A.D. 15, since Ovid congratulates Graecinus on
his future consulship the following year. Other references to Ovid's
sixth summer and winter in exile (4.10.1, 4.13.40) indicate that at least
two poems were written in the summer and winter of A.D. 14–15.[1]

This wide chronological span and Saint Jerome's notice that Ovid
died at Tomis in A.D. 17 (*Ab Abraham* 2033) have led almost all
scholars to consider *P.* 4 a posthumous book, not assembled and
published by the poet himself, but arranged from elegies written before
his death.[2] A brief review of its sixteen poems will confirm their
judgment. Our examination of them will be more concise than of those
of previous collections: many of the poems are short, and in almost all
of them Ovid treats familiar themes, expressions of gratitude and
requests for support. Our purpose is therefore to determine what is
new in this final book, how Ovid uses or reworks themes seen earlier,
and what significance *P.* 4 has within the larger block of exile poetry.
As in the preceding chapter, our discussion will be organized around
the individuals addressed in Ovid's poems.

SEXTUS POMPEY

Pompey, a member of an illustrious family and holder of high political
offices, appears to have been closely connected with Germanicus (*P.*
4.5.25–26).[3] As consul in A.D. 14, the year of Augustus's death, he
broke his leg while carrying the emperor's body to Rome (Cassius Dio
56.45.2) and was among the first to swear allegiance to Tiberius
(Tacitus *Annales* 1.7). He became proconsul of Asia in A.D. 27, where
he was accompanied by the writer Valerius Maximus. In *P.* 4.5.31–36
Ovid thanks Pompey for securing him a safe journey by land from
Tempyra to Tomis in A.D. 9; it is probable that he was prefect of
Macedonia at that time.

To Pompey: On His Consulship (Epistulae ex Ponto 4.4, 4.5) and Gratitude (4.1, 4.15)

ecce domo patriaque carens oculisque meorum,
    naufragus in Getici litoris actus aquas,
qua tamen inveni vultum diffundere causa
    possim, fortunae nec meminisse meae.

Look why I, deprived of my home, my
country, and the sight of my loved ones, a

shipwreck driven to the Getic shore, have still
found a reason to gladden my face and forget
my fortune.

To celebrate Pompey's installation as consul, Ovid in *P.* 4.4 presents
an elaborate poetic fiction, an epiphany of Fama bringing him the
happy news (ll. 1–22); as he was walking alone on the shore (a
dramatization of his condition, that of a shipwreck in exile), the divine
messenger appeared out of the sky, a disembodied voice which the poet
could not see ("nec erat corpus, quod cernere possem," l. 13). Ovid's
vision takes on greater reality as he imagines the occasion in Rome and
presents a spirited account of Pompey's installation (ll. 23–42), similar
to earlier triumph descriptions in *Tr.* 4.2, *P.* 2.1, and *P.* 3.4. The poet's
claim that he seems to view the proceedings ("cernere iam videor,"
l. 27) becomes even more positive ("cerno," l. 31) as he presents a
mental vision account of the ceremony.[4]

Then, as in *Tr.* 4.2, Ovid returns in the concluding lines (ll. 43–50)
from the world of imagination to reality. Again we see the verb *cerno*,
as the poet states that he will not be seen in the throng honoring
Sextus (non ego cernar," l. 43); instead he will participate only in his
imagination, "qua possum mente videbo" (l. 45, a direct echo of *Tr.*
4.2.57).

In *P.* 4.5, another congratulatory poem, Ovid gives instructions to a
personified letter which will greet Pompey as the poet's representative
in Rome. As in *Tr.* 1.1 and 3.7, we first see detailed instructions about
the journey and the destination, here Pompey's house (ll. 1–14). Ovid
explains that his poem will not be able to see the consul immediately,
since Pompey will be busy with official duties or with the imperial
family (ll. 15–26); his reference to his "turba rerum" (l. 27) recalls
similar instructions to his wife on approaching the busy Livia at *P.*
3.1.144. Finally he anticipates the consul's receipt of the letter and
gives it a specific message to carry (ll. 27–46), Ovid's expressions of
gratitude for past support.

P. 4.1 reworks the theme of poetic *officium*. Ovid declares that he is
ashamed not to have given earlier recognition to Pompey, then states
confidently that he will continue to receive his friend's support and
protection: he is not the least of Pompey's possessions. Although the
first poem in the book, this elegy is unlike any of Ovid's earlier
prologues. He makes no mention of a book, and although he compares
himself, as Pompey's possession, with acknowledged masterpieces of
antiquity (ll. 29–34), he is not concerned with poetics.

P. 4.15, the fourth epistle in this group, is highly derivative of earlier elegies. Ovid opens with praise of his addressee (ll. 1–22), introduced by questions whether the reader remembers him in Rome. We may compare *Tr.* 1.1.17–18 and 3.10.1–4. He also expands on the theme introduced in *P.* 4.1.27–36: he belongs to Pompey as one of his possessions. Next Ovid requests that Sextus continue to intercede with the gods in his behalf (ll. 23–42) and apologizes for constantly presenting the same requests (cf. *P.* 3.7.1–4), explaining that oars help a ship under a favorable wind (ll. 27–28—cf. *P.* 2.6.37–38).

TO TUTICANUS: A PLAYFUL APOLOGY (*Epistulae ex Ponto* 4.12)

Little is known about Tuticanus, who appears to have been the poet's contemporary and a Roman of senatorial rank. He seems to have had literary interests and was the author of a *Phaeacis,* which Ovid mentions at *P.* 4.16.27.[5]

ast ego non alium prius hoc dignarer honore:
    est aliquis nostrum si modo carmen honor.
lex pedis officio fortunaque nominis obstat,
    quaque meos adeas est via nulla modos.

For my part I would consider no one else
more worthy of this honor, if only my poetry
implies some honor. It is the metrical law
and the bad luck of your name which block
my act of homage, and there is no way by
which you can enter my rhythms.

Ovid first explains (ll. 1–22) that the name Tuticanus ($-u-u$) can be inserted into elegy only by violent means: by dividing the name between lines (ll. 7–8) or by giving false quantities to its antepenult (ll. 9–10), the first syllable (ll. 11–12), or the second (ll. 13–14).[6] After having already forced, despite these objections, the name into a pentameter and hexameter (ll. 10–11), Ovid playfully rejects such *vitia* but declares that he will give delayed homage to his friend.

He next gives the reason for such recognition (ll. 23–38), his early literary associations with Tuticanus in which each criticized the other's writings. Ovid's statement that he corrected Tuticanus's poems, "saepe tibi admonitu facta litura meo est" (l. 26) is a direct echo of *P.* 2.4.18 ("non semel admonitu facta litura tuo est"), which described Atticus's criticism of his poetry. He also praises his friend's literary endeavors, presents a series of *adynata,* or impossible phenomena, to illustrate his forgetting Tuticanus, and closes (ll. 39–50) with a short request that his friend pray to the *princeps* in his behalf. Ovid does not specify the prayer, appealing to Tuticanus's greater wisdom. He thus extends the literary relationship introduced earlier: Tuticanus will know better what to ask. Yet Ovid's request is not urgent, and with its metrical play the poem is more a recollection of past friendship than a plea for help.

To Tuticanus: My Exile (Epistulae ex Ponto 4.14)

quam grata est igitur Latonae Delia tellus,
    erranti tutum quae dedit una locum,
tam mihi cara Tomis, patria quae sede fugatis
    tempus ad hoc nobis hospita fida manet.
di modo fecissent, placidae spem posset habere
    pacis, et a gelido longius axe foret.

As dear therefore as the Delian shore is to
Latona, which alone gave her a safe place
in her wandering, so dear is Tomis to me,
since she to this time remains a faithful
host for me exiled from my native land.
Would that the gods had only brought it
about that she could hope for calm peace
and be farther away from the frozen pole!

In contrast to *P.* 4.12, Tuticanus figures only in the first couplet of this poem. In the opening lines Ovid presents familiar complaints (ll. 1–14), then discusses at great length (ll. 15–44) the reactions of the local populace to such complaints, defending himself and pleading good intentions. Ovid's statements about the adverse effects of his poetry ("plectar et incauto semper ab ingenio," l. 18; "tela adhuc demens, quae nocuere, sequor," l. 20; "ad veteres scopulos iterum devertar," l. 21) recall earlier apologies for continuing to write in *Tr.* 2.2, 4.1.35–36, and 5.7.33–36. He insists that he has criticized only the land and climate, not its inhabitants, and that some "malus interpres" is slandering him among the Getae. Again this defense reminds us of earlier protests against enemies in *Tr.* 3.11, 4.9, and 5.8; Ovid's statement of personal innocence (ll. 43–44) is similar to that at *Tr.* 2.563–66.

In the last section (ll. 45–62) Ovid praises the loyalty and generosity of the local population, which has proved its Greek origins through its treatment of him (a direct retraction of earlier complaints at *Tr.* 3.9.1–4 and 5.7.51–52): he has received immunity from taxes and the honor of a public crown. Tomis, he concludes, has been a faithful host. It is questionable whether we should accept such details as autobiographical evidence of an adjustment to Tomis, or rather as protreptic exempla, intended to challenge Tuticanus and other Roman readers to prove their greater humanity through support.[7] Unlike Ovid's earlier account of the Orestes / Pylades myth, in which even the savage Getae approved of loyalty among friends (*P.* 3.2.101–2), or his description of the local reaction to his Getic poem (*P.* 4.13.35–38), to be discussed below), the poet makes no open request for aid in this elegy.

CORNELIUS SEVERUS (*Epistulae ex Ponto* 4.2)

Cornelius Severus enjoyed a considerable reputation as a poet.[8] Seneca (*Suasoriae* 6.26) states that no one described the death of Cicero as well as he did; Quintilian describes him as a better versifier than poet ("versificator quam poeta melior") but concedes that he might have become an epic poet second only to Virgil if he had written his whole poem on the Sicilian War as well as he had its first book (*Institutes* 10.1.89). He is not to be confused with the Severus to whom Ovid wrote in *P.* 1.8.

In *P.* 4.2 Ovid discusses writing in exile, first complimenting Severus on his poetic gifts and stating that he has sent him many an "officiosa epistula" in prose (ll. 1–14); at the end of the elegy (ll. 47–50) he turns to his friend with a request for Severus's own poems. The main body of the poem, an explanation for not having written (ll. 15–46), gives a familiar apology for the books from exile.

BRUTUS (*Epistulae ex Ponto* 4.6)

This Brutus is probably the same man addressed in the prologue and epilogue of *P.* 1–3. In *P.* 4.6 Ovid supplies additional details about him: Brutus appears to have been his close friend (ll. 23–24, 39–42), who pursued a successful legal career (ll. 27–30).

This elegy treats subjects already seen many times (a review of past misfortunes, praise of a loyal friend, and gratitude for continued support), but it is interesting for additional details: the death of Ovid's former patron Fabius Maximus (ll. 9–12) and the death of Augustus (ll. 15–16), both of which date the elegy to A.D. 15. Ovid also refers to a poem he has written on the deification of the emperor (ll. 17–18). This work, to which he alludes again at *P.* 4.9.131–32, may be the composition in Getic described in *P.* 4.13.17–42. But this identification is not certain; Ovid does not state here that his deification poem was in Getic.

VESTALIS (*Epistulae ex Ponto* 4.7)

Vestalis was a Roman centurion, or *primipilaris* (ll. 4.7.15, 49), who participated in Vitellius's campaign against Aegisos in A.D. 12, distinguishing himself by bravery in the attack. He later held an administrative office or extraordinary commission in Pontus.[9] Ovid had alluded to the capture of Aegisos, a recent event in the region, at *P.* 1.8.11–24. Although he discusses it here in more detail, the poet does not appear to have been a close friend of Vestalis, makes no reference to past associations, and presents no real request for support.

Ovid's subject is Vestalis's familiarity with Tomis (ll. 1–14): the legate can bear witness to phenomena like frozen wine, the frozen sea, and poisoned arrows. He then discusses the honors recently won by his addressee and gives an extended account of his bravery (ll. 15–54), ending with an announcement that he wishes to pay tribute to Vestalis's deeds. The "testata...tua...facta" of the last couplet (ll. 53–54) directly recalls Ovid's opening address. As Vestalis can bear witness to the conditions of exile in Tomis ("testis eris," l. 4), Ovid in turn has testified to his bravery.

TO SUILLIUS (AND GERMANICUS): POETIC TIES
(*Epistulae ex Ponto* 4.8)

Suillius Rufus, the son-in-law of Ovid's wife (*P.* 4.8.11–12), was also a member of Germanicus's staff. He served as *quaestor* to Germanicus in A.D. 14–16, was exiled under Tiberius in A.D. 24, but was recalled by Caligula and became a notorious informant under Claudius. An enemy of Seneca, he was banished again in A.D. 58 (Tacitus *Annales* 4.31, 13.43).[10] Like *P.* 2.5, addressed to Salanus, another member of Germanicus's staff, this elegy is a poem intended for Germanicus himself.

non potes officium vatis contemnere vates:
    iudicio pretium res habet ista tuo.

quod nisi te nomen tantum ad maiora vocasset,
  gloria Pieridum summa futurus eras.
sed dare materiam nobis quam carmina maius.

As a poet you cannot scorn the tribute of a
fellow poet: literary activity has a value in your
judgment. If so great a name had not called
you to loftier things, you were destined to
become the highest glory of the Muses. But it
is more important to furnish us themes for
poetry than poems themselves.

Ovid's opening address to Suillius (ll. 1–26) treats the bonds of the
family relationship. He asks that the young man not reject him, defends
his background and personal reputation, and ends with a request that
Suillius intercede with Germanicus.

The central section of the elegy (ll. 27–88), a long appeal to
Germanicus himself, is divided into three sections. In the first (ll. 27–
42) Ovid reworks the familiar theme of the humble offering: he cannot
build Germanicus a marble temple (perhaps an echo of Virgil's promise
to Augustus at *Georgics* 3.13–15) but offers to repay the general in the
one way he can, in verse. He next appeals to Germanicus as a ruler
(ll. 43–66), stressing, as in *P.* 2.1 and 2.5, the fame which poetry gives
to men of action.

These general appeals are followed by a more individual request to
Germanicus as poet and patron of the liberal arts (ll. 67–88): because
he and Ovid worship "communia sacra" (l. 81–cf. *P.* 2.5.60, 2.9.64,
2.10.17, 3.4.67), Germanicus should help him to leave Pontus; Ovid
can then celebrate the general's acts with as little delay as possible. The
elegy ends with another address to Suillius (ll. 89–90). Ovid bases his
requests on his relationships with the addressees, both family ties (in
the case of Suillius) and the more important spiritual ties he shares
with Germanicus. Although the elegy presents themes already seen in *P.*
1–3, it is much more direct than earlier appeals to members of
Germanicus's staff.

TO GRAECINUS: ON HIS CONSULSHIP
(*Epistulae ex Ponto* 4.9)

C. Pomponius Graecinus is the same friend addressed in *P.* 1.6 and 2.6
and brother of Pomponius Flaccus to whom Ovid wrote in *P.* 1.10. In

contrast to earlier epistles, Ovid now presents a much more lively tone
in writing to Graecinus. Instead of lectures on the responsibilities of
friendship, Ovid praises both Graecinus and his brother to secure their
support.

ut, quoniam sine me tanges Capitolia consul
    et fiam turbae pars ego nulla tuae,
in domini subeat partes et praestet amici
    officium iusso littera nostra die.

Since as consul you will reach the Capitolium without me and I will become no
part of your retinue, let my letter take its
master's place and furnish the tribute of a
friend on the appointed day.

This elegy transfers the themes of *P.* 4.4 and 4.5, on the consulship
of Sextus Pompey, to the consulship of Graecinus. We again see
expressions of congratulation linked to mental vision as Ovid
introduces the elegy as his surrogate in Rome for the occasion (ll. 1–
8). Next follows a long and spirited account of Graecinus's installation
(ll. 9–56), which ends with a request that the new consul appeal to
Tiberius in Ovid's behalf. Ovid also introduces a second reason for joy
(ll. 57–74): Graecinus's brother Flaccus will succeed him in office.

Ovid strengthens his request for spokesman by reminding Flaccus of
his own experience in Pontus (ll. 75–124): Graecinus's brother can
testify both to local conditions and the poet's good reputation in Tomis
and to his piety towards the imperial family. Expanding on the earlier
picture of his patriotism in *P.* 2.8, he describes his household shrine
with images of Tiberius, Livia, Drusus, and Germanicus, then
concludes (ll. 125–34) with hopes that the emperor will learn of his
loyalty. Certainly Augustus, now a god, hears the poet's prayers; may
he be moved by the recent poem Ovid has written on his deification.

This poem is more ambitious than earlier elegies to Graecinus;
perhaps Ovid felt that an appeal to the newly appointed consul would
be fruitful. As in earlier triumph poems where he treated festive events
in the capital, Ovid stresses his loyalty and patriotism in an attempt to
win support. The result is an overlong but carefully developed appeal.

TO ALBINOVANUS PEDO: LIFE IN EXILE
(*Epistulae ex Ponto* 4.10)

This individual, whom Ovid addresses as an old friend and literary
colleague (*P.* 4.10.3, 71–72), served as Germanicus's commander of

cavalry in A.D. 15 (Tacitus *Annales* 1.60) and celebrated his campaigns
in an epic poem.[11] In contrast to other elegies addressed to friends
associated with Germanicus, Ovid never mentions the prince in this
poem.

qui veniunt istinc, vix vos ea credere dicunt.
   quam miser est, qui fert asperiora fide!
crede tamen: nec te causas nescire sinemus,
   horrida Sarmaticum cur mare duret hiems.

Those who come from Rome say that you
scarcely believe these things. How wretched
is he who endures things too grim for belief!
Yet take my word for it: I'll not let you be
ignorant of the reason why the harsh winter
freezes the Sarmatian sea.

   Ovid begins with a playful description of his troubles (ll. 1–36),
presenting a *syncrisis* of himself with Ulysses which emphasizes points
of comparison less obvious than those seen in *Tr.* 1.5.57–84: the
legendary hero had pleasant interludes ("placidae...morae," l. 12)
during his wanderings, such as visiting Calypso and Aeolus and
listening to the Sirens. The poet instead endures continual misfortunes
and things scarcely believable.

   To win credibility Ovid next gives a lengthy explanation of why the
Black Sea freezes (ll. 37–70). Although he discusses its low salt
content, an actual phenomenon noted both in antiquity and modern
times,[12] Ovid's purpose is hardly scientific. Instead we are given a
statement of Pontus's geographical position (ll. 39–44), a catalog of
fifteen rivers which flow into the sea (ll. 45–60), a brief explanation
how the fresh water floats on top and freezes (ll. 61–64), and the now
familiar statement that such descriptions allow the poet to forget his
troubles (ll. 65–70).

   The elegy shows obvious parallels of detail to those details in Ovid's
extended treatment of the Pontic winter in *Tr.* 3.10; we may compare *P.*
4.10.57–58 and *Tr.* 3.10.27–30; 4.10.33–34 and 3.10.39–40; and the
hic / istinc antithesis of 4.10.31–35 and 3.10.1 and 71. But there are
even more significant differences. Because Ovid presents himself as
writing in summer ("aestas," l. 4.10.1), not winter, his description of
the Scythian cold lacks the immediacy of his earlier account, which
culminated in a grim picture of warfare and destruction (*Tr.* 3.10.51–
66). The poet is now more concerned with describing the color and

freshwater content of the Black Sea as a phenomenon interesting in itself (ll. 59–64); the Pontic winter has been left far behind at the end of his catalog of rivers. The poem is therefore not primarily a description of misfortunes or an appeal for aid. Although Ovid returns to Pedo in the final lines (ll. 71–84) with a request for continued support, his lively mood, both in his treatment of Ulysses and his account of the Black Sea, shows that this is poetic play intended to amuse his addressee as well as other readers.

JUNIUS GALLIO (*Epistulae ex Ponto* 4.11)

A famous rhetorician, Gallio was a friend of the elder Seneca and an author of a book on rhetoric.[13] He appears to have been quite friendly with Messalla Corvinus, and Ovid writes to him as an intimate friend in *P.* 4.11, a consolation poem on the death of his wife. Ovid first announces his intent to console Gallio (ll. 1–10), then declares that his distance from Rome makes any attempt useless (ll. 11–20). He even suspects that Gallio's grief has already ended ("iam pridem suspicor" — cf. *P.* 3.4.54, "iam pridem populi suspicor ore legi," a similar complaint about the tardiness of his triumph poem). The elegy ends with hopes that Gallio may already be happily remarried (ll. 21–22). The closing wish is not gratuitous; through it Ovid points out that his absence delays the *officium* which he owes to his friends and that life in the capital is going on without him. Ovid's consolation therefore becomes a statement on his exile: the contacts normally maintained between friends are impossible for him.

TO CARUS: A GETIC POET (*Epistulae ex Ponto* 4.13)

Carus was a poet friend who also served on Germanicus's staff as tutor to his children. He seems to have written a poem on Hercules (*P.* 4.13.11–12, 4.16.7–8) and is perhaps to be identified with the addressee of *Tr.* 3.5.[14] As in *P.* 4.2, written to fellow poet Cornelius Severus, Ovid returns to the theme of poetics.

a, pudet, et Getico scripsi sermone libellum,
    structaque sunt nostris barbara verba modis:
et placui (gratare mihi) coepique poetae
    inter inhumanos nomen habere Getas.
materiam quaeris? laudes: de Caesare dixi.

O, I am ashamed! I have also written a book in
the Getic language and set barbarous words to
our measures. I even found favor (congratulate
me!), and I have begun to enjoy a reputation as
poet among the savage Getae. You ask my
subject matter? You would approve: I sang about
Caesar.

Ovid introduces an apology for his poems by comparing them to the
works of his addressee (ll. 1–16): Carus's poetry can be recognized by
its good qualities, Ovid's by its ugliness and shortcomings. The
exemplum of Thersites (l. 15) seen earlier at *P.* 3.9.9–10 illustrates the
comparison.

Now Ovid departs from what we have seen in earlier discussions of
poetics. Instead of familiar arguments about the difficulty of writing
and absence of a literary audience, he presents himself as almost a
Getic poet ("paene poeta Getes," l. 18) and discusses his first literary
efforts in the language (ll. 17–42). As a logical extension of statements
in earlier books that he was learning Getic to communicate with the
inhabitants (*Tr.* 5.7.55–58, 5.12.58; *P.* 3.2.40), he has now become a
Getic poet. Ovid treats this accomplishment, like his poetic reputation
itself in Scythia, with deliberate irony.[15] The echoes of *P.* 1.5.63–66 in
the passage quoted above are especially striking:

forsitan audacter faciam, sed glorior Histrum
   ingenio nullum maius habere meo,
hoc, ubi vivendum est, satis est, si consequor arvo,
   inter inhumanos esse poeta Getas.

Perhaps I'm acting boldly, but I boast that the
Danube has no poetic talent greater than my own.
Here, where I must live, it is enough if I manage
to be a poet among the savage Getae.

Ovid states that his first Getic poem celebrated the deified Augustus
and members of the imperial family (ll. 23–32). Whether or not we
wish to accept his account as factual,[16] Ovid describes his first *recitatio*
before a Getic audience (ll. 33–38). The natives reacted favorably ("et
caput et plenas omnes movere pharetras," l. 35), and a Getic
spokesman ("aliquis," l. 37) remarked that the poet should be restored
for his praise of the emperor. Ovid's development of the scene is similar
to that in *P.* 3.2.37–100, where he retold the Orestes / Pylades myth

through the mouth of an aged Gete to report the populace's approval of loyalty among friends; the elaborate fiction reinforced his appeal to the *officia* of friendship. In like manner here ("longum Getico murmur in ore fuit," l. 36) Ovid's Getae support his request for a pardon.

From this picture of a Getic *recitatio* Ovid moves abruptly to the reality of his situation (ll. 39–42): after six years in Tomis, poetry has only contributed to his unhappiness. The last section of the poem (ll. 43–50) is a direct request to Carus for assistance. Because of Carus's position on Germanicus's staff, Ovid's parenthetical praise of the prince and his family is certainly deliberate.

This elegy has been much discussed as evidence about Ovid's literary undertakings in Getic.[17] But its primary significance lies, not in autobiographical or linguistic interest, but as Ovid's final apology for his poetry from exile. As a culmination to earlier apologies where he decried conditions of composition, the weakening of his poetic *ingenium*, and the barbarization of his style, he now presents himself as "paene poeta Getes," no longer to be considered a Latin poet to be judged by Rome's civilized standards.[18] Yet the irony of this presentation is tempered by the humor of the *recitatio*: Ovid cannot resist playing with the incongruities of a poetic reading in the midst of barbarism.

Because Ovid's *recitatio* also emphasizes the conditions of his exile, P. 4.13 is more than a final poetic apology. His transformation into a Getic poet and his choice of an imperial theme as his first endeavor in that language reinforce his appeal to Carus for support. While Ovid presents his artistic deterioration and the end of his career as a Latin poet with bitter sarcasm, the *materia* of his poem and Getic reaction strengthen his requests for assistance.

TO A FAITHLESS FRIEND (*Epistulae ex Ponto* 4.3)

This elegy reminds us of similar *querelae* in *Tr.* 1.8 and 5.6. Because Ovid appeals to a long association and years of intimacy (ll. 11–18), he may well have a particular individual in mind. Yet his complaint, with appeals to a former friendship (ll. 1–30) and a lecture on the mutability of Fortune (ll. 31–58), presents nothing new. Ovid's only variation appears in the opening lines (ll. 1–4), where he refuses to name the friend lest he gain glory through such recognition. We may contrast *Tr.* 4.9, where the poet threatened to expose an enemy to notoriety.

TO ENVY: POETIC FAME (*Epistulae ex Ponto* 4.16)

Invide, quid laceras Nasonis carmina rapti?
   non solet ingeniis summa nocere dies,
famaque post cineres maior venit. et mihi nomen
   tum quoque, cum vivis adnumerarer, erat.

Envious one, why do you gnaw on my poems
now that I have been carried off? It is not
customary that one's poetic talents are harmed
by his final day. A greater reputation comes after
one is ashes. And I also had renown even then,
when I was numbered among the living.

This elegy, which reworks themes seen in previous discussions of
poetics, is formally modeled on one earlier poetic apology, *Am.* 1.15,
where Ovid answered the criticism of Livor and triumphantly praised
his life dedicated to poetry:

quid mihi, Livor edax, ignavos obicis annos
   ingeniique vocas carmen inertis opus,
non me more patrum, dum strenua sustinet aetas
   praemia militiae pulverulenta sequi.   [*Am.* 1.15.1–4]

Why, biting Envy, do you charge me with lazy
years and call poetry the work of an idle talent,
that I do not, while my hearty youth allows me,
pursue according to custom the dusty rewards of
military service.

He then presented a catalog of poets whose fame would never die (*Am.*
1.15.9–30) and claimed poetic immortality for himself as well (ll. 31–
42).

   Ovid certainly had this earlier prologue in mind when he planned *P.*
4.16; the structural plans of both poems are too similar to be
accidental. Ovid begins with a question to Livor (ll. 1–4), presents a
catalog of poets (ll. 5–46), and ends with reflections about himself
(ll. 47–52). Yet in his final lines the similarity between the two poems
ends. Ovid concludes this elegy on a bitter, not triumphant, note.

   For his theme Ovid expands a boast seen earlier in his poetic
autobiography:

nec, qui detractat praesentia, Livor iniquo
   ullum de nostris dente momordit opus.
nam tulerint magnos cum saecula nostra poetas
   non fuit ingenio fama maligna meo.   [*Tr.* 4.10.123–26]

Nor has Envy, which attacks its contemporaries, gnawed with unjust tooth any work of
mine. For although my generation has brought
forth mighty poets, fame has not been stingy to
my talent.

He therefore begins *P.* 4.16 on a note of confidence reminiscent of the
opening lines of *Am.* 1.15, reworking the theme of death-in-exile
("Nasonis...rapti, cineres") to give greater force to his subject, the
immortality of poets and their fame after death. He even adds to his
boast, declaring that he had no small reputation before his exile.[19]
   Ovid next turns to the catalog of his contemporaries (ll. 5–46)
discussed at length in our introduction. Here he expands one line of his
poetic autobiography (*Tr.* 4.10.125, quoted above) where he invited his
reader to supply names such as Horace or Virgil for the "magnos...
poetas"; instead of these giants of Augustan poetry, he now lists thirty-
nine contemporaries, a new generation of writers active in Rome at the
beginning of the first century, none of which is Ovid's equal. The
contrast with *Am.* 1.15.9–30, which presented a catalog of illustrious
writers, both Greek and Latin, ranging from Homer to Cornelius
Gallus, is even more striking, hinting at a change in mood. Ovid's
review of his contemporaries closes on a note of exaggerated humility:
among such fellow poets he is proud that his Muse won glory (ll. 45–
46).
   For this reason, he concludes (ll. 47–52), Envy should not attack
him. We return from the long catalog to another direct address to Livor
like that of the opening lines. But Ovid's mood has changed. Instead of
a proud statement on immortality we find only bitter complaint. He
makes more specific the death to which he alluded in the first line
("rapti," l. 1); it is the living death of exile ("summotum patria," l. 47).
There is also a second, more specific reference to "cineres," no longer
the ashes of poets who enjoy immortality (l. 3), but the remains of
Ovid himself which Livor seeks to disturb ("neu cineres sparge,
cruente, meos," l. 48). Ovid declares that he has now lost everything
except his life; this, however, only gives him consciousness and an

opportunity to experience greater misfortune. The final couplet is even
more grim.

quid iuvat extinctos ferrum demittere in artus?
    non habet in nobis iam nova plaga locum.   [ll. 51–52]

What pleasure does it give to send your sword
into limbs already dead? There is no place in
me now for a new wound.

Ovid's last line is modeled on an earlier one, "vixque habet in nobis
iam nova plaga locum" (P. 2.7.42—cf. Tr. 5.6.34). Now, however, the
poet's despair appears total and his bitterness much more complete.
Instead of ending this discussion of poetic fame on a triumphant note,
as in Am. 1.15, Tr. 3.7, and Tr. 4.10, Ovid undercuts any faith in poetic
immortality (cf. the last line of Am. 1.15: "parsque mei multa superstes
erit"). Indeed he acknowledges that such defiance of physical reality is
no longer tenable.[20] In striking contrast to his earlier confidence and
self-glorification, he even seems to indicate that a poetic calling such as
his has been a worthless pursuit.

Ovid's intent may have been to shock readers with this desperate and
bitter conclusion. Yet the gloom of his final lines, unparalleled in all
earlier treatments of poetics, may also be evidence that P. 4.16 is an
unfinished poem, begun shortly before his death but never completely
revised. Although its ending is disturbing, the elegy, as a discussion of
poetic fame, is not an unsuitable poem to close the book in which it
appears.

THE BOOK AS A WHOLE

The question whether P. 4.16 is a finished poem leads us to ask the
same thing about the book itself. In comparison to individual books of
the Tristia and P. 1–3, if we are to consider P. 4 a collection arranged
and published by Ovid himself, we see in it a definite regression in plan
and poetic arrangement. Its subject matter is generally the same as that
of P. 1–3: the elegies present expressions of thanks for past support or
requests for aid and assistance in the future. Only P. 4.4 and 4.16 do
not contain some request for aid, either expressly stated or implied.

As already noted, the individuals to whom Ovid writes are largely
different from those addressed earlier. There are four elegies to Sextus
Pompey, who did not appear in P. 1–3, and many poems to individuals
connected with Germanicus or members of his staff: Sextus Pompey

himself; Suillius, the son-in-law of Ovid's wife who served as Germanicus's *quaestor*; Albinovanus Pedo, his commander of cavalry; and Carus, tutor to his children. Although Ovid had praised Germanicus in P. 2.5 and had even addressed him directly in P. 2.1, the seven letters written to individuals in his circle make him much more prominent than in the earlier collection.

Moreover, there are no poems addressed to Cotta Maximus and Messallinus, who figured prominently in P. 1–3. Fabius Maximus, to whom Ovid had previously written three elegies, died in A.D. 14, but the sons of Messalla Corvinus, who were still alive and influential, are conspicuously absent. Only at P. 4.16.41–44 does Ovid refer to Cotta, where he is cited not as a loyal friend, but one of thirty-nine contemporary poets. Brutus and Graecinus do appear again (4.6, 4.9), and Flaccus, to whom Ovid had written P. 1.10, is praised both in 4.7, the poem to Vestalis, and 4.9, the elegy on Graecinus's consulship. The book, however, is directed to a different group of addressees, men associated with Germanicus. Ovid's requests for support are also less demanding than in P. 1–3; there is no general appeal to all his friends in Rome, as in P. 3.7, and the book is much less urgent in tone.

P. 4 is not completely formless in appearance, and there is some evidence of an arrangement within it. The longest of the poems, P. 4.9, which Ovid perhaps intended to be the most important, occupies a position near its center, and P. 4.16 is not unsuitable for the final position. Yet there is no prologue or deliberate arrangement by addressee, as in P. 1–3, and little attempt to offset individual elegies with the same addressee or poetic theme. P. 4.4 and 4.5, both addressed to Sextus Pompey, treat the theme of his consulship. P. 4.6 to Brutus ends with a series of *adynata,* like the elegy to Brutus which precedes it. P. 4.12 and 4.14, the two poems to Tuticanus, are offset by the elegy to Carus on the *Geticus libellus,* but both P. 4.13 and 4.14 treat the same subject, Ovid's relationship with the local population. The book, more than any of the other collections written in exile, has the character of a poetic miscellany instead of a unified collection.

This absence of a structural arrangement as well as the wide chronological span of the book's elegies indicate that Ovid himself did not prepare it for publication in A.D. 15–16. Since the book is posthumous, composed of poems on hand or a selection of the best poems on hand after Ovid's death, there is perhaps no real significance for the large number of elegies addressed to individuals connected with Germanicus. It is interesting, however, that Ovid did not write to these

individuals in *P.* 1– 3, but directed his appeals to Fabius Maximus and
the sons of Messalla Corvinus.

Ovid may have ceased writing to Cotta Maximus and his brother
because of disillusionment after his previous collection had been
unsuccessful. Following the death of Augustus and succession of
Tiberius, he may have decided that appeals to Germanicus through
members of his staff would be more fruitful. We should note that he
dedicated the first book of the *Fasti* to Germanicus when he undertook
revision of the poem after the death of Augustus.[21] Ovid may have even
begun another collection like *P.* 1– 3 addressed to the circle of
Germanicus but then abandoned the attempt. His literary executors
may then have published the elegies on hand as a poetic book after his
death in A.D. 17. The book, however, does not appear to be one
published by Ovid himself.

Because *P.* 4 is not a poetic collection like the others, it is most
interesting for our study because of the contrast which it presents with
earlier books. In individual books of the *Tristia* and *P.* 1– 3 we found
poetic collections organized and developed around specific themes. If
Ovid had lived to finish it, *P.* 4 might well have become a full-fledged
appeal to Germanicus. Ovid could have included additional flattery of
the imperial family along the lines of *P.* 2.8 and perhaps would have
further exploited the *poeta Getes* theme, as in *P.* 4.13, to emphasize his
deterioration and separation from his earlier life and career.

Yet this sort of speculation is idle. *P.* 4 as a collection is unfinished
and incomplete. After our study of earlier collections, it is in some
ways disappointing to end a survey of Ovid's books from exile with *P.*
4. Despite the quality and interest of many of its individual elegies, the
artistry and organization of earlier collections are missing here. Yet our
recognition of what Ovid did not live to finish reveals more clearly
what he did achieve in earlier books.

cur scribam docui. cur mittam, quaeritis, isto?

*I've told you why I keep writing; do you ask why I
send the books to Rome?*

VIII CONCLUSION

ALTHOUGH OUR DIACHRONIC review has not attempted a
comprehensive examination of all aspects of the exile poetry, it has
demonstrated the development and changes in Ovid's individual
collections. Yet some general observations are in order. When Ovid left
Rome for exile, he did not expect to remain there for the rest of his life
and therefore had no general plan for a corpus of poetry. Instead, as we
have seen, the exile poetry can be said to have evolved as Ovid wrote
and published collections as separate units, each organized and planned
by itself. Except for *Tr.* 2, which is one continuous poem, Ovid chose
as his medium the Augustan *Gedichtbuch* of collected elegies, a
literary form which at the time of his relegation was standard fare in
poetic circles. His format of poetic books was therefore nothing new to
his Roman readers; what was different was their content.

Ovid also seems to have had no set plan or design for his collections.
There are some obvious similarities between individual books: like
most Augustan *libelli*, each book of the *Tristia* as well as *Ex Ponto* 1–
3 has a formal prologue and epilogue; in *Tr.* 5 Ovid replaces a standard
epilogue with a letter to his wife, but this final poem, like earlier
epilogues, treats his position as poet. Yet as a group the collections are

not organized on a standard pattern. The structural arrangement of elegies within a particular collection is also generally loose; Ovid is more interested in developing his books around particular poetic themes than in maintaining a strict symmetry of poems or a rigid structural pattern within them. Each collection is therefore an entity separate in itself. Although familiar complaints about Tomis appear from book to book, the subjects to which Ovid gives greatest emphasis are different in each.

We noted some structural parallels in *Tr.* 3 and 4, books written during the first years in Tomis. After *Tr.* 1, in which Ovid had a greater variety of themes at his disposal, the journey into exile most prominent among them, he turned to a somewhat different arrangement in the collections of the following years. Unlike *Tr.* 1, which has an organization primarily thematic, *Tr.* 3 and 4 are similar in their general plans: within each collection, letters to individuals in the first half of the book are balanced by more general, descriptive elegies in the second half.

Each of these two books is also developed around a principal theme: *Tr.* 3, the contrast between Tomis and Rome, the poet's present misery as opposed to his happy past; and *Tr.* 4, Ovid's old age in exile, a subject which also allows him to contrast his earlier career, that of a youthful writer of amatory verse, with his present role, that of a poet of exile. Both of these collections therefore play on the before and after aspects of the relegation to win sympathy. But in *Tr.* 4 Ovid's contrast moves from what were external aspects of exilic life in the earlier book to the changes brought about by Tomis in himself. His poetic autobiography which closes the second of the two books is most effective when we remember that throughout *Tr.* 4 he plays on the differences between his elegiac youth and the hardships of his present old age, a dichotomy reinforced by his contrast of his earliest elegiac productions with his more recent books from exile. Despite its shorter length, *Tr.* 4 brings to further development the themes of *Tr.* 3.

Some differences between books are the direct result of Ovid's year-by-year composition and publication. We have noted throughout our study the poet's echoes of lines or phrases which appeared in books published in earlier years. Although he reuses themes, lines, and poetic tags from book to book, this self-quotation is a phenomenon characteristically Ovidian, no more frequent than his use of verbal reminiscences of his earlier verses in his preexilic writings.[1] The individual collections from Tomis must therefore be read as separate works, illustrating the development which Ovid's poetry underwent in his final years.

Our purpose has been to approach the *Tristia* and *Epistulae ex Ponto,* not as autobiographical data on the last years of Ovid's life, but as his literary response to exile. The poet's use of literary conventions and models to present his situation, which we have noted throughout this study, should alert us to the dangers and limitations of a strictly biographical interpretation of the elegies. Yet these poems are also human documents presenting Ovid in exile to his Roman readers, and as we have seen, individual books show distinct changes in tone and mood. Ovid begins in *Tr.* 1 and 2 with a playful exploitation of his status and situation as a relegate; his poetic journey into exile permits him to assume a Ulysses role, and his apology in the second book demonstrates that he does not think the charges against him are all that serious.

This confidence ends in *Tr.* 3, where Ovid develops a poetic book not about his journey, but exile itself. The poet now discards his Ulysses role; his tone is much more sober and serious as he attempts to convey the grimness of his condition to win sympathy. His earnestness is even more pronounced in *Tr.* 4, where Ovid gives greater emphasis to his role as a poet in exile; his autobiography concludes the book with a summary statement about a life and career devoted, both before and after his relegation, to poetry.

Then in *Tr.* 5 we see a second change, marked not only by differences in organization and arrangement but also by a shift in poetic strategy. In this book Ovid now assumes a new role: he announces that his books of *publica carmina* are not to be compared to his earlier, preexilic works. Moreover, his elegies now concern themselves not so much with a presentation of exile as direct appeals for support. In this collection and the books which follow, Ovid functions primarily as a poetic spokesman for himself. Instead of poems describing exile intended for a general readership, Ovid has turned to elegiac letters arranged in book format by addressee. He may have chosen this format of literary epistles as an expression of *sermo absentis,* one means of maintaining contact with friends and former associates in Rome.[2]

Ovid's reassessment of his poetic role is even more pronounced in *P.* 1–3, where he writes letters to his addressees openly by name. In contrast to earlier books, this collection contains relatively few descriptive elegies. Instead Ovid presents now familiar complaints about exile in open letters directed to specific individuals. His pleas for support gain greater force through his identification of their recipients: through appeals to former patrons and friends and demands to his wife, Ovid seeks to dramatize the urgency of his situation. *P.* 1–3 is therefore a collection of personal apologetics in poetic form. *P.* 4 might have become a second collection with a similar format and purpose if Ovid had lived to complete it.

Ovid's books from Tomis were a literary pursuit separate from his private prose correspondence (*P.* 4.2.3–6). In publishing them Ovid was writing for a literary public; he describes his verse as *publica carmina,* poems intended for everyone. Although the experience of exile at Tomis, as he presents it, offered only a limited *materia* for poetic books, Ovid kept on writing. His new books, beginning with *Tr.* 1, were a significant departure from those produced by earlier Augustan poets and unparalleled even in all of ancient literature. He undertook a poetic experiment of this scope and continued with it year after year, perhaps because the idea itself challenged him, but certainly because of his preeminence in the literary circles of the capital. His popularity in Rome assured him a ready audience to which he could display his talents in a new and strikingly different way. Ovid's readers no doubt looked forward to the publication of individual collections as they appeared.

The changes we have noted in Ovid's books may have surprised or disappointed his readers. Yet they appear deliberate: after three years in Tomis, Ovid turned from poetic presentation of himself in exile to more individual appeals for assistance. The innovations in *Tr.* 5 may reflect a growing awareness that his break from Rome was more complete and that return to his former life and poetic activity was no longer possible.[3] But they are probably best recognized as strategic, introduced to heighten the impact of his literary epistles in winning spokesmen. In his later books Ovid has decided to direct his talents to an immediate goal, that of obtaining another place of relegation, either from Augustus or his successor Tiberius. Personal aims have become more important than any poetic message about exile itself; instead they are now the theme of Ovid's collections.

As a result Ovid ends his literary career as a letter writer in verse seeking sympathy and support. As we noted in Chapter 1, he abandons his pose of artistic and spiritual independence, becoming in later books a panegyricist eager to gain imperial favor. Linked to this new role, and indeed his justification for it, are Ovid's constant complaints about the decline of his poetic skills. In later collections he presents himself as forgetting his Latin, allowing barbarisms into his verses, and as a consequence becoming practically a Getic poet, or a writer who by Roman standards is no poet at all. In a later elegy to a fellow poet, Cornelius Severus, he explains that versification, while a distraction from misfortunes, has now become for him a meaningless exercise and the Muses nothing more than "solacia frigida" (P. 4.2.45). In this same poem Ovid states that his artistic deterioration was pardonable, even inevitable, under such conditions:

si quis in hac ipsum terra posuisset Homerum,
   esset, crede mihi, factus et ille Getes   [P. 4.2.21–22]

If someone had put Homer himself in this
land, he too, believe me, would have become
a Gete.

Such complaints of course make more pathetic his presentation of his situation and strengthen his appeals for assistance. The urgency of his plight which brought about his decline has taken precedence over any artistic considerations.

Ovid knew that his books would command a wide readership and enjoy instant popularity; no doubt he thought he could prod his friends and wife through naming them directly in P. 1–3 so that they would be moved to take action for him. Perhaps they did, but to no avail. Readers today, however, are less enthusiastic about the books from Tomis. Even its more sympathetic critics complain that the corpus is "all too homogeneous" and that a selection of its poems based on interest and real literary merit would include "barely a third" of Ovid's 5,412 lines from exile.[4] Moreover, it has been asserted that "there is no need to exaggerate the merits of the exile poetry" and that it would be "unreasonable" to maintain that all of Ovid's exilic elegies are equally good, "or even that they are all good."[5]

Such observations are not to be dismissed or ignored. Even the most enthusiastic apologist for Ovid's exile poetry cannot be blind to its defects. A writer who seeks to dramatize his plight through constant complaints about his artistic deterioration has abandoned the highest aims of his poetic calling. While from a technical standpoint Ovid's exilic poetry is little different from his earlier verse,[6] his books from exile can scarcely be regarded as his greatest literary achievement. Moreover, it must be conceded that his standing as one of the leading Latin poets would certainly be secure without them.

Yet these collections do not undermine or diminish Ovid's reputation in Latin literature; because we recognize their limitations, we must not for the same reason overlook the poet's achievement. In exile Ovid developed an essentially new genre of poetry, which should be assessed on its own terms, not in comparison with his earlier elegiac works. In addition, his exilic corpus of 5,412 lines is impressive for its size alone. These books reflect the literary output of Rome's leading poet for almost a decade. Even if one were to agree with some critics that a substantial portion of his work from Tomis, perhaps as much as two-thirds, lacks literary merit, a sizable block of very good poetry remains.

Ovid's decision to keep writing in exile, year after year, is in itself significant.[7] His purpose was not so much to achieve poetic immortality as to return to the capital or win an amelioration of his sentence. In pursuit of this goal he used the best weapons he had, his poetic imagination and skill. In many ways, given the position he had already earned in Rome's literary circles, Ovid had nothing to lose by continuing to send poetic books to the capital. His collections from Tomis were therefore directly influenced by their environment, not so much, as he asserts frequently, by the conditions under which they were written as by the literary world in Rome for which they were produced. Like the *Heroides, Ars amatoria,* and *Metamorphoses,* written for a highly sophisticated and literate audience, they show us the preeminent poet of his day experimenting with literary forms and conventions to produce something new and persuasive. In later books, as part of his poetic strategy, Ovid redefined his role as an elegist in an attempt to dramatize his situation and win support. In this endeavor his books were a failure: Ovid was to die in exile, never to return to Rome. Yet because he believed his efforts would have a better chance of success if they were presented through a medium in which he excelled, his collections from Tomis remain an example of literary virtuosity, one never again attempted on such a scale by any ancient poet and never really paralleled in later Western literature.

Because Ovid's poems were written for poetic collections, they must be read as they were published, as a series of books produced annually over an eight-year period of composition. Within the books, some elegies, clearly more important than others, will repay further, more detailed examination. But if we approach Ovid's poetic books as books, we see that all of his poems gain in this way. No single elegy, no matter how good or bad, can be considered complete in itself; each must also be read as part of a larger whole, the collection in which it appears. Ovid's *variatio* within individual books answers in large part the criticisms of monotony brought against the exile poetry as a whole.

These poetic collections are therefore to be viewed as a literary attempt by Ovid to exploit his situation for goals both artistic and personal—an attempt that might end that situation. For Ovid himself, the artistic goals were fulfilled more than the personal. Although he died in exile, he left a poetic corpus well worth studying as Augustan poetic books. The best of what Ovid wrote from Tomis remains very good indeed. As an essential document of Augustan literary art, his books from exile merit more than one reading.

NOTES

ABBREVIATIONS IN THE NOTES

Atti
Atti del convegno internazionale ovidiano, Sulmona, maggio 1958, 2 vols. (Rome: Istituto di Studi Romani, 1959).

Barsby
John Barsby, Ovid, Greece and Rome. New Surveys in the Classics, no. 12 (Oxford: Oxford University Press, Clarendon Press, 1978).

Benedum
Jost Benedum, Studien zur Dichtkunst des späten Ovid, (Diss., Giessen, 1967).

Dickinson
R. J. Dickinson, "The Tristia: Poetry in Exile," in Ovid, ed. J. W. Binns (London: Routledge and Kegan Paul, 1973), pp. 154–90.

Fränkel
Hermann Fränkel, Ovid: A Poet between Two Worlds, Sather Classical Lectures, no. 18 (Berkeley and Los Angeles: University of California Press, 1945).

Frécaut
Jean-Marc Frécaut, L'Esprit et l'humour chez Ovide (Grenoble: Presses Universitaires de Grenoble, 1972).

Froesch, Dichter
Hartmut Froesch, Ovid als Dichter des Exils, Abhandlungen zur Kunst-, Musik- und Literaturwissenschaft, no. 218 (Bonn: Bouvier Verlag Herbert Grundmann, 1976).

Froesch, Epistulae
Hermann Hartmut Froesch, Ovids Epistulae ex Ponto I–III als Gedichtsammlung (Diss., Bonn, 1967).

Galinsky, *Met.*   G. Karl Galinsky, *Ovid's Metamorphoses: An Introduction to*
                          the Basic Aspects (Berkeley and Los Angeles: University of
                          California Press, 1975).
Galinsky, "Triumph"   G. Karl Galinsky, "The Triumph Theme in the Augustan
                          Elegy," *Wiener Studien* 82 (1969): 75–107.
Herrmann   Karl Herrmann, *De Ovidii Tristium Libris V* (Diss., Leipzig,
                          1924).
Kenney   E. J. Kenney, "The Poetry of Ovid's Exile," *Proceedings of the*
                          Cambridge Philosophical Society, n.s. 11 (1965): 37–49.
Luck   Georg Luck, ed. and comm., *P. Ovidius Naso: Tristia*, 2 vols.
                          (Heidelberg: Carl Winter Universitätsverlag, 1967–77).
Nagle   Betty Rose Nagle, *The Poetics of Exile: Program and Polemic*
                          in the "Tristia" and "Epistulae ex Ponto" of Ovid, Collection
                          Latomus no. 170 (Brussels: Latomus, Revue d'Études Latines,
                          1980).
Ovidiana   N. I. Herescu et al., *Ovidiana: Recherches sur Ovide, publiées*
                          à l'occasion du bimillénaire de la naissance du poète, (Paris:
                          Les Belles Lettres, 1958).
PW   A. Pauly, G. Wissowa, and W. Kroll, eds., *Real-Encyclopädie*
                          der klassischen Altertumswissenschaft.
Rahn   Helmut Rahn, "Ovids elegische Epistel," *Antike und*
                          Abendland 7 (1958): 105–20.
Syme   Ronald Syme, *History in Ovid* (Oxford: Oxford University
                          Press, Clarendon Press, 1978).
Thomsen   Mary Helen Thomsen Davisson, "Detachment and
                          Manipulation in the Exile Poems of Ovid" (Ph.D. diss.,
                          University of California, Berkeley, 1979).
Wheeler   A. L. Wheeler, ed. and trans., *Ovid: Tristia, Ex Ponto*
                          (Cambridge, Mass.: Harvard University Press, 1924).
Wiedemann   Thomas Wiedemann, "The Political Background to Ovid's
                          Tristia 2," *Classical Quarterly* 25 (1975): 264–71.
Wilamowitz   Ulrich von Wilamowitz-Moellendorff, "Lesefrüchte (Auszug),"
                          Hermes 61 (1926): 298–302.
Wilkinson   L. P. Wilkinson, *Ovid Recalled* (Cambridge: Cambridge
                          University Press, 1955).
Williams   Gordon Williams, *Change and Decline: Roman Literature in*
                          the Early Empire, Sather Classical Lectures, no. 45 (Berkeley
                          and Los Angeles: University of California Press, 1978).

INTRODUCTION

1. Nagle, p. 5.
2. A. G. Lee, "An Appreciation of *Tristia* III, viii," *Greece and Rome* 18 (1949): 113–
20; Yves Bouynot, *La Poésie d'Ovide dans les oeuvres de l'exil* (Diss., Paris,
1957); Kenney; Frécaut; Froesch, *Dichter*; Barsby; Luck; Syme; Nagle (cited as
B. R. Fredericks), "*Tristia* 4.10: Poet's Autobiography and Poetic Autobiography,"
Transactions of the American Philological Association 106 (1976): 139–54;
Thomsen.

3. Nagle, p. 173.

4. Herrmann. His conclusions are summarized by Edgar Martini, *Einleitung zu Ovid* (Darmstadt: Wissenschaftliche Buchgesellschaft, 1970), p. 52.

5. Froesch, *Epistulae*; Dickinson.

6. See John C. Thibault, *The Mystery of Ovid's Exile* (Berkeley and Los Angeles: University of California Press, 1964).

7. For the chronology, see Wilamowitz, 299–301.

8. For *coercitio*, see A. H. M. Jones, *Studies in Roman Government and Law* (Oxford: Basil Blackwell, 1960), p. 14; for *amicitiam renuntiare* see Robert Samuel Rogers, "The Emperor's Displeasure and Ovid," *Transactions of the American Philological Association* 97 (1966): 373–78.

9. For the date, see Syme, p. 122.

10. For a survey of Ovid's career, see Scevola Mariotti, "La carriera poetica di Ovidio," *Belfagor* 12 (1957): 609–35; and E. J. Kenney, *Oxford Classical Dictionary,* 2d ed., s.v. "Ovid."

11. See Froesch, *Dichter,* pp. 117–18, 176 n.243–44.

12. Nagle, p. 20; Thomsen, p. 48.

13. For a detailed discussion, see Nagle, pp. 19–70, with summary on pp. 69–70.

14. S. G. Owen, ed., *P. Ovidi Nasonis Tristium Libri Quinque, Ibis, Ex Ponto Libri Quattuor, Halieutica Fragmenta* (Oxford: Oxford University Press, Clarendon Press, 1915); L. R. Lind, trans., *Ovid, Tristia* (Athens: University of Georgia Press, 1975); Wheeler.

CHAPTER I

1. For the *Heroides,* see Howard Jacobson, *Ovid's Heroides* (Princeton, N.J.: Princeton University Press, 1974), pp. 7, 354; for the *Ars,* A. S. Hollis, "The *Ars Amatoria* and *Remedia Amoris,*" in *Ovid,* ed. J. W. Binns (London: Routledge and Kegan Paul, 1973), pp. 84–115; for the *Metamorphoses,* Brooks Otis, *Ovid as an Epic Poet,* 2d ed., (Cambridge: Cambridge University Press, 1970), pp. 351, 368.

2. Galinsky, *Met.,* pp. 210–61; Williams, pp. 52–99; William M. Clarke, "Ovid: A Review Article," *Classical Journal* 72 (1977): 322–23.

3. For a survey, see Kenneth Scott, "Emperor Worship in Ovid," *Transactions of the American Philological Association* 61 (1930): 43–69.

4. See R. Marache, "La Révolte d'Ovide exilé contre Auguste," *Ovidiana,* pp. 412–19 (hereafter cited as Marache, *Ovidiana*); N. I. Herescu, "Le Sens de l'épitaphe ovidienne," *Ovidiana,* pp. 420–42; N. I. Herescu, "Ovide, le Gétique (*Pont. IV,* 13, 18: *paene poeta Getes*)," *Atti* 1:55–80 (hereafter cited as Herescu, *Atti*); Yves Bouynot, "Misère et grandeur de l'exil," *Atti* 1:249–68; Walter Marg, "Zur Behandlung des Augustus in den *Tristien,*" *Atti* 2:345–54 (hereafter cited as Marg, *Atti*); Froesch, *Dichter,* pp. 20–21, 97–98; Barsby, pp. 42–43; Syme, pp. 222–25; Nagle, pp. 153–55, 173; Thomsen, pp. 11–16.

5. Ovid's flattery was long ago criticized by Gaston Boissier, *L'Opposition sous les Césars* (Paris: Hachette, 1875), pp. 163–65; his independence in more modern times praised by Luck, 2:6; Barbsy, p. 43; and Syme, pp. 226–29.

6. Williams, p. 97.

7. Williams, p. 97, discusses at length this development, a point made earlier in his *Tradition and Originality in Roman Poetry* (Oxford: Oxford University Press,

Clarendon Press, 1969), p. 88. See also George Kennedy, *The Art of Rhetoric in the Roman World* (Princeton, N.J.: Princeton University Press, 1972), pp. 403–5.

8. An observation made by Barsby, pp. 42–43; Syme, p. 225, and most directly by N. V. Voulikh, "La Révolte d'Ovide contre Auguste," *Les Études Classiques* 36 (1968): 381–82 (hereafter cited as Voulikh, "Révolte"), but without detailed discussion.

9. On the topicality of the Augustus / Jupiter equation, see Stefan Weinstock, *Divus Julius* (Oxford: Oxford University Press, Clarendon Press, 1971), pp. 300–305. For parallels in Ovid's earlier works, see Kenneth Scott, "Emperor Worship in Ovid," *Transactions of the American Philological Association* 61 (1930): 52–53; and Williams, pp. 61–96.

10. For the Ulysses role, see Rahn, pp. 115–19. Cf. Nagle, p. 67 n.112, who without explanation labels "mitissima Caesaris ira" an "ironic oxymoron."

11. Luck, 2:118. Walter Wimmel, *Kallimachos in Rom, Hermes,* supplement no. 16 (Wiesbaden: Franz Steiner Verlag, 1960), p. 331, calls *Tr.* 2 "a dark pendant" to Horace's letter. Nagle, pp. 36–37, discusses other Horatian echoes.

12. For the structure, see S. G. Owen, ed., *P. Ovidi Nasonis Tristium Liber Secundus* (Oxford: Oxford University Press, Clarendon Press, 1924), pp. 48–54. For other discussions, see Wilkinson, pp. 302–11; Luck, 2:93–160, Dickinson, pp. 171–74; and Wiedemann, pp. 264–71.

13. Luck, 2:117, compares Cicero *Natura deorum* 2.167: "magna di curant, parva neglegunt."

14. Another reworking of a topos, the gods' freedom to punish in their own time. See Luck, 2:98. R. Marache, *Ovidiana,* p. 147, cites 2.39–40 as a threat to the emperor, but takes no account of Ovid's remark "id facis" in 2.41.

15. Barsby, p. 43. Wiedemann, pp. 269–70, accepts Ovid's topos about divine responsibilities (ll. 215–38) at face value, but argues that his allusions in lines 225–34 are intended to embarrass the emperor. In suggesting that "quod mallem" (l. 239) implies that Augustus has not spent sufficient time in judging Ovid's case, he overlooks the poet's reference to the "pondus rerum" weighing on the emperor in lines 237–38, a phrase which echoes the "non...tam leve...onus" of lines 221–22.

16. R. Marache, *Ovidiana,* p. 416, labels Ovid's reference to gaming (ll. 471–82) "an open attack" on Augustus, who enjoyed the pastime (Suetonius *Divus Augustus* 71). For Kenneth Scott, "Another of Ovid's Errors," *Classical Journal* 26 (1930–31): 293–96, it is rather an Ovidian faux pas. Both authors misread the passage. In his catalogue of *artes* objectionable to some (ll. 471–92), Ovid's lines on gaming deliberately echo his earlier treatment of the subject at *Ars* 2.205–8 and 3.353–66. His intent is not to embarrass the emperor, who, according to Suetonius (loc. cit.), would not have minded anyway: "aleae rumorem nullo modo expavit." Indeed, this is Ovid's point at 2.472: unlike our ancestors, we live in a relaxed and enlightened age.

17. Wilkinson, p. 312. Cf. Wiedemann, p. 270 n.1: Ovid reused his earlier work because he lacked research facilities in Tomis.

18. Wiedemann, p. 271; Nagle, p. 37.

19. Kenney, p. 39; Wilamowitz, pp. 298–99.

20. R. Marache, *Ovidiana,* p. 413; Barsby, p. 43; Syme, p. 227; cf. Luck, 2:6: "a grand testimony to the spiritual freedom of the artist."

21. Ovid's boast at *Met.* 15.871 that his poem will withstand Jupiter's wrath is not, pace Marg, *Atti* 2:353–54, a polemical reference to the emperor. See Galinsky, *Met.*, pp. 254–55; and Syme, p. 225 n.1.

22. Seneca *Suasoriae* 7.1. I owe the parallel to Voulikh, "Révolte," pp. 378–79.

23. N. V. Voulikh, "Ovide et Auguste," *Vestnik Drevnei Istorii* 103 (1968): 151–60, cited by Wiedemann, p. 264.

24. For the chronology, see Luck, 2:238; and Syme, p. 45.

25. See Galinsky, "Triumph," pp. 102–3.

26. Cf. *P.* 2.1.17–18, describing Ovid's joy at the Pannonian triumph: "gaudia Caesareae mentis... / sunt mea: privati nil habet illa domus."

27. Galinsky, "Triumph," 104–7. Cf. Williams, pp. 77–79, who finds in *Ars* 1.177–222 an "unmistakable" tone of panegyric.

28. Kenney, p. 44; Nagle, pp. 153–54; Thomsen, p. 208.

29. So correctly, Marg, *Atti,* 2:350–51, on the public nature of Ovid's challenge. But it does not follow that the poem must be ironic.

30. An element of conventional panegyric; see R. G. M. Nisbet and Margaret Hubbard, *A Commentary on Horace's Odes* (Oxford: Oxford University Press, Clarendon Press, 1970) on Horace *Carmina* 1.2.45; and Nagle, p. 126 n.26.

31. Wheeler, p. 355 n.1. We may compare cameos representing the emperor and his family described by G. M. A. Richter, *Engraved Gems of the Romans* (London: Phaidon, 1971), pp. 99–107. Cf. Syme, p. 127: "silver statuettes."

32. Cf. a similar presentation in *Tr.* 1.2.107–8, also introduced by "fallor an": Ovid interprets the end of his storm as evidence of divine favor. Cf. Thomsen, pp. 105–6, who reads the poem as a challenge to the emperor's divinity.

33. Benedum, pp. 121–24, followed by Thomsen, pp. 158–60, interprets the poem as critical of the emperor: the friend's fears belie Ovid's statements about imperial *clementia.* But this reading cannot be reconciled with Ovid's decision to write to other friends openly throughout *P.* 1–3 or his plea for a new place of exile in *P.* 3.6.37–38.

34. See Peter Garnsey, *Social Status and Legal Privilege in the Roman Empire* (Oxford: Oxford University Press, Clarendon Press, 1970), p. 112 n.5.

35. For the date, see Syme, p. 40.

36. Syme, pp. 40–41.

37. Syme, pp. 128, 156.

38. Cf. Herescu, *Atti,* 1:55–80, who reads Ovid's references to the Getic poem as ironic, but overlooks his appeal for a change of exile in *P.* 4.13.43–50.

39. Wiedemann, pp. 268, 271.

CHAPTER II

1. E. K. Rand, *Ovid and His Influence* (Boston: Marshall Jones, 1925), p. 95; Kenney: 39; Wilamowitz, pp. 298–99.

2. The details in *Tr.* 2.187–206 (the seven mouths of the Danube, the tribes which inhabit the other side of the river, the extreme cold of the region) could well be based on information obtained from a geographical handbook. It is also noteworthy that among the Scythian tribes which Ovid names in this passage, the

Ciziges, Colchi, Teretae, and Bastarnae are mentioned only here in the exile poetry. Syme, pp. 37–38, observes that *Tr.* 2 predates the *clades Variana* of autumn A.D. 9.

3. Herrmann, pp. 13–38; Wilamowitz, p. 298; Dickinson, pp. 161–70; Froesch, *Dichter,* pp. 22–44.

4. Rahn, pp. 105–120.

5. Rahn, pp. 106–9. Rahn's conclusions about Horace's influence are qualified by Nagle, p. 35 n.33. For Ovid's use of literary models, see Luck, 2:11–12; and Thomsen, pp. 70–72.

6. Frécaut, p. 311 n.44. Cf. *Am.* 1.1.4, 3.1.8.

7. For a discussion of its structural plan, see H. O. Kröner, "Aufbau und Ziel der Elegie Ovids *Tristia* I, 2," *Emerita* 28 (1970): 163–97; and "Elegisches Unwetter," *Poetica* 3 (1970): 392–93.

8. Dickinson, pp. 162–63, calls it "a symbol of the danger and uncertainty of Ovid's fate." Nagle, p. 148, labels the storm of *Tr.* 1.11 "an image of Augustus."

9. The most striking parallels between this storm and Ovid's "Compleat Storm" (I owe the phrase to Galinsky, *Met.,* p. 145) are as follows: 1.2.19–22—cf. *Met.* 11.503–4 (the mountains of waves and their valleys deep as the underworld, an image inspired by *Aeneid* 3.564–65); 1.2.31–32—cf. *Met.* 11.492–93 (the helplessness of the pilot); 1.2.47–50—cf. *Met* 11.508–9, 529–30 (the storm compared to a siege); 1.2.34, 106—cf. *Met.* 11.569 (verbal echo of "obruit unda").

10. Cf. Wilamowitz, p. 299, arguing that *Tr.* 1.4 is an "accurate" account of a real storm, composed after Ovid was again on dry land.

11. Kenney, p. 47 n.1; and *Classical Review* 20 (1970): 340. Froesch, *Dichter,* pp. 26–27, discusses dramatic elements in the poem.

12. Nagle, pp. 23–24.

13. Nagle, p. 44.

14. Luck, 2:42, compares Tibullus 1.3.19–20 and *Met.* 10.452.

15. The name is linked with the Ulysses role which Ovid assumes in the collection; at *Tr.* 1.2.10 and 1.5.76 he describes the goddess as protectress of the hero. Nagle, p. 166, also suggests Minerva's association with poetry as a reason for the name.

16. Wilamowitz, p. 301.

17. Nagle, p. 42, suggests that the imitation is pathetic in intent, since the two ships travel in opposite directions.

18. Nagle, pp. 40–41, compares Catullus's treatment of the demands of *amicitia* in his poetry.

19. Several manuscripts begin a new elegy at line 45, probably because of the abrupt transition. Yet the poem makes good sense in its progression, and there is no need to divide it. See Luck, 2:50.

20. Rahn, pp. 115–19.

21. Luck, 2:68–74. Nagle, p. 40, compares Catullus 30, a reproach to the faithless Alfenus.

22. F. W. Lenz, "A Disputed Question, Ovid, *Tristia* I, 9," *Latomus* 28 (1969): 583–87.

23. In his discussion of the poem (to which I owe much) Kenney, p. 41, suggests that Ovid's praise of Livia (ll. 23–28) is an addition to the original elegy. Yet the balanced structure of the poem argues against it being a later insertion. Cf. Dickinson, pp. 169–70.

24. For other enemy poems, cf. *Tr.* 3.11, 4.9, 5.8, and the *Ibis.* "Nescioquis" (l. 13), as Wilkinson, p. 347, observes, implies that Ovid's enemy is a nobody, not that the poet did not know who he was.

25. Fränkel, pp. 243–44 n.4, calls attention to Ovid's play on "tabulas" (l. 8), which are both the boards of his shipwreck (an image used frequently to describe the relegation) and his account books, representing the property which the enemy is attempting to seize.

26. Nagle, pp. 51–52, cites *Am.* 1.3.25–26 as a parallel.

27. See Albert Grisart, "La Publication des Metamorphoses: une source du récit d'Ovide, (*Tristes* I, 7.11–40)," *Atti* 2:125–56; Brooks Otis, *Ovid as an Epic Poet*, 2d ed. (Cambridge: Cambridge University Press, 1970), pp. 89–90 n.1; and Thomsen, pp. 72–74.

28. The verbal echoes are numerous: *Tr.* 1.11.15 ("custos Atlantidos ursae")—cf. 1.4.1 ("custos Erymanthidos ursae"); 1.11.19—cf. 1.4.9 ("stridunt…rudentes"); 1.11.21–22—cf. 1.2.31–32, 1.4.11–12 (the helplessness of the pilot); 1.11.23—cf. 1.2.23 ("quocumque aspicio, nihil est, nisi…").

29. Nagle, pp. 147–50.

30. Kenney, p. 42.

31. For other analyses of the collection cf. Herrmann, pp. 13–38 (a strict symmetrical arrangement of elegies framing 1.6, the central poem); Froesch, *Dichter,* p. 24 (a series of three groups of three poems each, 1.2–1.4, 1.5–1.7, 1.8–1.10); and Dickinson, p. 161 (division of the book into four main themes, each given roughly equal space: "Prologue / Epilogue," "Travel and Storm," "Friendship," and "The remainder"). Their arguments are not convincing: *Tr.* 1.5 and 1.7 are both written to friends, but have little else in common.

CHAPTER III

1. For the chronology, see Wilamowitz, pp. 301–2; Syme, p. 38.

2. Luck, 2:161–230; Wilamowitz, pp. 301–2; Dickinson, pp. 174–79; Herrmann, pp. 38–47; Yves Bouynot, *Ovide, livre III des Tristes, étude rythmique et stylistique* (Diss., Paris, 1957), hereafter cited as Bouynot, "*Tr.* 3."

3. Cf. Suetonius *Divus Augustus* 7.

4. Nagle, p. 85.

5. Scevola Mariotti, "La carriera poetica di Ovidio," *Belfagor* 12 (1957): 175–76. J. H. Bishop, "Palatine Apollo," *Classical Quarterly,* n.s. 6 (1956): 189, cites *Aeneid* 8.306–69 as Ovid's model.

6. Giuseppe Lugli, "Commento topografico all' elegia I del III libro dei *Tristia*," *Atti* 2:379–403.

7. Cf. *Ars* 1.74, where the poet lists these porticoes, among others, as a suitable place for an assignation: "Belides et stricto stat ferus ense pater."

8. R. Marache, "La Révolte d'Ovide exilé contre Auguste," *Ovidiana,* p. 417, argues that Ovid's reference to Libertas's refusing access to his book is a comment on the despotic nature of Augustan rule, but takes no account of the poet's pleas for a pardon within the elegy. Ovid ends with the Atrium Libertatis, not to make a point about liberty (or the lack of it) in Rome, but to bring his itinerary full circle to its starting point near the *fora* of Caesar and Augustus. On the location, see

Ferdinando Castagnoli, "Atrium Libertatis," *Rendiconti della reale accademia dei Lincei*, ser. 8, 1 (1946): 276–91.

9. Walther Kraus, "Ovidius Naso," *PW* 18, no. 2 (1942): 1919; Fränkel, p. 114; Syme, p. 229. Cf. Luck, 2:170–71. On book-banning in Rome and the operation of the libraries, see Anthony J. Marshall, "Literary Resources and Creative Writing in Rome," *Phoenix* 30 (1976): 261–63. Syme, pp. 212–13, 229, observes that the prosecutions of Labienus and Cassius Severus, both condemned by the Roman senate for their writings, were different.

10. Nagle, pp. 47–49; Luck, 2:176–82.

11. Nicolae Lascu, "L'epitaffio di Ovidio: epigrafia e poesia," *Studi classici in onore di Quintino Cataudella* (Catania: Facoltà di Lettere e Filosofia, 1972), 3:331–38.

12. Cf. N. I. Herescu, "Le sens de l'épitaphe ovidienne," *Ovidiana*, pp. 420–42, who reads the epitaph as Ovid's protest against his arbitrary condemnation and a tombstone attack on Augustus.

13. The metaphor is no doubt proverbial. See Nagle, pp. 35, 92, 169 n.1.

14. See, for example, Luck, 2:184–85. Cf. Herrmann, pp. 46–47; and Bouynot, "*Tr.* 3," pp. 216–17, who consider it a single poem.

15. Cf. Walter Marg, "Zur Behandlung des Augustus in den *Tristien*," *Atti*, 2:350: Ovid does not name friends to set in greater relief the conflict between himself and Augustus.

16. Wheeler, p. xvii, 505. Marg, "Zur Behandlung des Augustus in den *Tristien*," p.350 n.2, suggests that Perilla's name is a pseudonym, chosen because of its association with Perillus, the inventor of the bull of Phalaris who perished by his own art (cf. *Tr.* 3.11.39–54). Yet the name is not significant and appears only twice (ll. 1, 29) within the poem. Dickinson, pp. 176–77, treats its structural plan, and Nagle, pp. 150–52, gives an excellent analysis.

17. See A. G. Lee, "An Appreciation of Ovid, *Tristia* III, viii," *Greece and Rome* 18 (1949): 113–20. Luck, 2:205, compares Ovid's rejection of mythological daydreams at *Am.* 3.6.13–18. See also Walter Nicolai, "Phantasie und Wirklichkeit bei Ovid," *Antike und Abendland* 16 (1973): 108–9.

18. Bouynot, "*Tr.* 3," p. 269.

19. Bouynot, "*Tr.* 3," pp. 276–78.

20. This farfetched explanation also appears in Apollodorus *Bibliotheca* 1.9.24. Another ancient etymology links the name with Tomos, a legendary founder of the city who is represented on local currency. Modern linguists explains *Tomis* as a Thracian word meaning "swelling" or "promontory," related to the Sanskrit *tumra-s* ("obese") and Latin *tumulus*. The city is situated on a promontory on the Black Sea—cf. *Tr.* 5.10.17. See also Radu Vulpe, "Ovidio nella città dell' esilio," *Studi Ovidiani* (Rome: Istituto di Studi Romani, 1959), pp. 44–45.

21. Fränkel, pp. 125–26.

22. See Harry B. Evans, "Winter and Warfare in Ovid's Tomis (*Tr.* 3.10)," *Classical Journal* 70, no. 3 (1975): 1–9.

23. Kenney, pp. 42–43, compares Catullus 46 and Horace *Carmina* 1.4, 4.7, 4.12. See also Nagle, p. 42 n.47, for specific echoes.

24. Francis Cairns, *Generic Composition in Greek and Latin Poetry* (Edinburgh: Edinburgh University Press, 1972), pp. 135–37, labels the poem an "inverse genethliacon."

25. So Paul van de Woestyne, "Un Ami d'Ovide, C. Julius Hyginus," *Musée Belge* 33

(1929): 31–45. The elegy does not give us enough information to support a positive identification. Cf. Luck, 2:227.

26. Bouynot, "*Tr.* 3," p. 171, cites parallels of "fatalité"; Luck, 2:161, "das Schicksalmotiv."

27. Luck, 2:161.

28. The elegy may also be compared to *Tr.* 3.9 in its presentation of mythological narrative. In explaining the names of Tomis, Ovid retells the Medea legend in compressed elegiac style; in 3.11 he illustrates the enemy's cruelty by comparing him to Perillus.

29. For other analyses of the book, cf. Herrmann, pp. 38–47, to which I am in part indebted; Dickinson, pp. 174–75; and Luck, 2:161, 170. Division of *Tr.* 3.4 into two poems, which Dickinson and Luck support, would not greatly change the structural plan. Yet the elegy should be considered a single poem. While its division would produce a total of fifteen elegies, multiples of five, while common in Augustan poetic books (Dickinson, p. 190 n.46), are not canonical. *Tr.* 1 itself contains eleven poems.

30. Cf. Nagle, p. 47 n.71, who finds it "curious" that Ovid in *Tr.* 3.3 does not emphasize "Odyssean" elements of Tibullus 1.3; and Rahn, pp. 115–18, who gives the impression that the Ulysses role continues unchanged throughout the books. Ovid does compare himself to Ulysses at *Tr.* 5.5.3–4 and his wife to Penelope at 5.5.51–52 and 5.14.35–36. But the motif is not developed as in *Tr.* 1. In his longest citation of Ulysses in later books (*P.* 4.10.9–30), the poet directly rejects the comparison by emphasizing the "*placidae morae*" (l. 12) enjoyed by the mythological hero. Other references adduced by Rahn and Nagle (*Tr.* 4.1.31–32; 4.10.1–3, 101–12) do not develop the motif as it appeared in *Tr.* 1.

CHAPTER IV

1. For the chronology, see *Tr.* 4.6.19–20, 4.7.1–2.

2. Luck, 2:1, 231; Dickinson, p. 180; Herrmann, p. 56.

3. Luck, 2:231–76; Theodore Jacob De Jonge, comm., *Publii Ovidii Nasonis Tristium Liber IV* (Groningen: De Waal, 1951), hereafter cited as "De Jonge."

4. Nagle, pp. 155–59, gives a careful analysis of the poem.

5. Luck, 2:232–33.

6. Cf. *Tr.* 4.1.1–2 and 3.14.27–28, 51–52 (pleading circumstances of composition to justify shortcomings); 4.1.55–56 and 3.14.31 ("tot adversis" describing the extent of the poet's misfortunes); 4.1.67–68 and 3.14.23–24 (former popularity); 4.1.69–70 and 3.14.41–42 (the lack of protection); 4.1.89–90 and 3.14.39–40 (the lack of an audience); 4.1.103–4 and 3.14.51–52 (a plea for the reader's *venia*).

7. See Keith Preston, "An Author in Exile," *Classical Journal* 13 (1917–18): 413; and Nagle, p. 158.

8. Nagle, pp. 49–50; Luck, 2:244–45.

9. De Jonge, p. 122; Luck, 2:249; Syme, p. 122.

10. De Jonge, p. 142, suggests that he is Cotta Maximus, the younger son of Messalla Corvinus and brother of Messallinus. Cf. Luck, 2:253.

11. Luck, 2:256.

12. Kenney, p. 44; Luck, 2:259–60; Nagle, pp. 154–55.

13. "Dissolvantur" (l. 18) recalls "solvitur" in *Tr.* 4.6.36.

14. Nagle,pp. 152, 154.

15. Cf. Nagle, pp. 154-55, who reads the poem as an attempt to undercut Augustus.

16. Most valuable is the analysis of B. R. Nagle (cited as B. R. Fredericks), "*Tristia* 4.10: Poet's Autobiography and Poetic Autobiography," *Transactions of the American Philological Association* 106 (1976): 139-54, to which I am much indebted. Cf. also Luck, 2:265-76; Frécaut, pp. 332-36; Vittore d'Agostino, "L'elegia autobiografica di Ovidio (*Tristia* IV, 10)," in *Hommages à Marcel Renard,* Collection Latomus, no. 101 (Brussels: Latomus, Revue d'Études Latines, 1969) 1:292-302; and Ettore Paratore, "L'elegia autobiografica di Ovidio (*Tristia* 4, 10)," *Ovidiana,* pp. 353-78.

17. Cf. Luck, 2:266.

18. Fränkel, p. 235 n.26.

19. Luck, 2.231.

20. For other analyses, cf. Herrmann, pp. 56-57; and Dickinson, pp. 179-80.

CHAPTER V

1. Jacob Theodore Bakker, comm., *Publii Ovidii Nasonis Tristium Liber V Commentario Exegetico Instructus* (Amsterdam: H. J. Paris, 1946).

2. Nagle, pp. 117-19.

3. Luck, 2:280.

4. Nagle, p. 82.

5. Nagle, pp. 111-14. Luck, 2:305-7, following Heinsius and one manuscript, begins a new elegy at line 25; all other manuscripts give a complete elegy of sixty-eight lines. There is a distinct break at line 25, but the transition is not difficult: in keeping with his epistolary format, Ovid answers the friend's questions about Tomis (ll. 11-24) before turning to news from Rome.

6. Fränkel, pp. 157-59; Wilkinson, pp. 363-65; but cf. Nagle, pp. 133-40.

7. Mary Thomsen Davisson, "*Omnia Naturae Praepostera Legibus Ibunt:* Adunata in Ovid's Exile Poems," *Classical Journal* 76 (1980): 124-28, discusses Ovid's play on such paradoxes. Ovid's emphasis on the unreal quality of his relegation also supports Luck's conjecture "insanum" for the "in me aliquid" of the manuscripts at ll. 41-42. See Friedrich Hauben, "*Adnuo* and *Abnuo* in Ovid *Tristia* 5.10.41-42," *American Journal of Philology* 96 (1975): 61-63.

8. For a catalog of such consolations see Cicero *Tusculan Disputations* 5.106-9, discussed by Thomsen, pp. 246-49. Nagle, p. 100, discusses Ovid's rejection of philosophical consolation, but does not cite this elegy. For a different view, cf. Luck 2:5-6: Ovid decides to live a meaningful life through his poetry.

9. Luck, 2:295; Thomsen, p. 191.

10. Luck, 2.324-25. For other epistolary elements in the poem, see Mary Thomsen Davisson, "The Functions of Openings in Ovid's Exile Epistles," *Classical Bulletin* 58 (1981): 17-22.

11. Syme, p. 77: "a man of rank." Luck, 2:284, acknowledges the ambiguity but accepts Ovid's wife as the addressee because of lines 39-40.

12. The major break in the poem is after line 46: Ovid addresses Augustus for the first time at line 47, with the words "arbiter imperii." The interjection "en" in line 45 must be addressed to Ovid's wife; it is much too abrupt to begin a direct appeal

for imperial mercy and is in strong contrast to the rhetorical periods of the couplets which follow. Cf. Dickinson, pp. 183–84, who posits another elegy "2b" at line 45 and considers lines 45–46 an "introduction" to the appeal.

13. Luck, 2:298.

14. These poems are *Tr.* 1.5, 1.7 (which is mainly about the *Metamorphoses*), and 1.9; 3.4, 3.5, and 3.6; 4.4, 4.5, and 4.7. Ovid addresses friends in *Tr.* 4.8.51, but the elegy is primarily a meditation on his old age.

15. These poems are *Tr.* 1.2, 1.3, 1.4, 1.10, and 1.11; 3.8, 3.9, 3.10, and 3.12; 4.2, 4.6, and 4.8.

16. Herrmann, p. 62. His structural diagram is reproduced by Edgar Martini, *Einleitung zu Ovid* (Darmstadt: Wissenschaftliche Buchgesellschaft, 1970), p. 52, and followed by Luck, 2:277, with modifications (fifteen elegies instead of fourteen). For another analysis, cf. Dickinson, pp. 183–84.

CHAPTER VI

1. For the chronology, see *P.* 1.2.25–26 and Syme, p. 42. The books describe events of A.D. 12–13 and, in particular, the Pannonian triumph held on 23 October A.D. 12. See also Anton Scholte, comm., *Publii Ovidii Nasonis Ex Ponto Liber Primus Commentario Exegetico Instructus* (Amersfoort: G. J. van Amerongen, 1933), p. xxiii (hereafter cited as Scholte.)

2. Froesch, *Epistulae,* pp. 127–44.

3. For detailed discussion, see Syme, cited throughout this chapter. Froesch, *Epistulae,* pp. 90–105, also gives a review of prosopographical scholarship on the addressees.

4. Syme, p. 80. Cf. *P.* 4.6, addressed to a Brutus, probably the same man, who pursued a legal career (4.6.27–30).

5. See Scholte, pp. 25–50; Nagle, p. 86; and Luck 2:162–72.

6. See Raffaele Pettazzoni, "Confessions of Sins and the Classics," *Harvard Theological Review* 30 (1937): 1–14; and Nagle, pp. 142–43.

7. For his career, see Syme, pp. 117–31.

8. Cotta's reputation is also improved by a funerary inscription of a freedman who praises his patron's generosity (*Corpus inscriptionum Latinarum,* xiv:2298 [= Dessau, *Inscriptiones Latinae Selectae,* 1949]).

9. Ulrich Knoche, review of Schulte, *Gnomon* 11 (1935): 248.

10. Nagle, pp. 135–37. The phrase is an echo of an earlier apology, *Tr.* 5.7.68.

11. Syme, p. 90, and Scholte, pp. 165–66, suggest that he is Albinovanus Celsus, to whom Horace writes in *Epistles* 1.8.

12. Fränkel, p. 250 n.6. Ulrich Staffhorst, *Publius Ovidius Naso Epistulae ex Ponto III 1–3 (Kommentar)* (Diss., Würzburg, 1965), pp. 68–111 (hereafter cited as "Staffhorst") gives many parallels.

13. Nagle, pp. 91–92.

14. For a review of his career, see Syme, pp. 135–55.

15. Kenney, pp. 47–48. But the phrase is conventional. See Syme, p. 142.

16. Kenney, p. 44, who provides an analysis of the poem. See also Staffhorst, pp. 112–52; Carl Ganzenmüller, "Aus Ovids Werkstatt," *Philologus* 70 (1911): 419–22; and Nagle, p. 124 n.24.

17. Froesch, *Epistulae,* p. 209 n.328; Staffhorst, p. 113 n.1. Cf. Syme, pp. 127–28, who prefers Cotta Maximus.

18. Nagle, pp. 58–59, suggests that this ambiguity may have inspired the poem.

19. For detailed discussion, see Benedum, pp. 8–63.

20. See Staffhorst, pp. 1–64, for a detailed commentary; Thomsen, pp. 113–44; and Nagle, pp. 44–46, 53–54.

21. Cf. Francesca Lechi, "La palinodia del poeta elegiaco: i carmi ovidiani dell' esilio," *Atene e Roma* 23 (1978): 20–21.

22. For his career, see Syme, pp. 117–25; Froesch, *Epistulae,* pp. 92–93.

23. Scholte, p. 143; Luck, 2:249–51. Wheeler, P. 304, notes that Ovid bases his appeal on the requirements of noblesse oblige.

24. Nagle, pp. 44–46 n.63.

25. Syme, pp. 83–87. On the medical language, see F. Wilhelm, "Zu Ovid: *Ex Ponto* I, 3," *Philologus* 81 (1925): 155–56; and Scholte, p. 92.

26. Nagle, p. 125.

27. Nagle, pp. 144–45. Cf. Thomsen, pp. 203–4.

28. Anacleto Cazzaniga, *Elementi retorici nella composizione delle Lettere dal Ponto di Ovidio* (Varese: Seminario Arcivescovile Vegegono, 1937), pp. 27–29.

29. Syme, pp. 74–75; Froesch, *Epistulae,* p. 101; Thomsen, pp. 204–5.

30. Syme, p. 72; Froesch, *Epistulae,* pp. 102–3, 217 n.386. For detailed discussion of *P.* 2.4 and 2.7, see Thomsen, pp. 222–63.

31. Syme, p. 81; Froesch, *Epistulae,* p. 103, 179 n.104.

32. Frécaut, p. 339. For praise of agriculture as an Augustan topos, see Thomsen, p. 236.

33. Robinson Ellis (cited by Scholte, p. 161) describes lines 49–60 as "the most pleasing of the whole collection." For similarities between erotic fantasies in Ovid's earlier works and those of the exile poetry, see Walter Nicolai, "Phantasie und Wirklichkeit bei Ovid," *Antike und Abendland* 19 (1973): 107–16.

34. Syme, p. 74; Froesch, *Epistulae,* p. 102, 216 n.384.

35. See Syme, pp. 87–89; and W. Kroll, "Julius (Germanicus)" (138), *PW* 10 (1919): 435–64.

36. Galinsky, "Triumph": 103–4.

37. Nagle, p. 144.

38. Syme, p. 88; Froesch, *Epistulae,* p. 194, 217 n.389.

39. Ovid's reminiscence of *Aeneid* 1.33, "tantae molis erat..." is unmistakable. Wheeler, p. 343 n.1, suggests that this poem is *P.* 2.1, but it may well be literary fiction.

40. George Kennedy, *The Art of Rhetoric in the Roman World* (Princeton, N.J.: Princeton University Press, 1972), pp. 418–19, discusses this passage briefly.

41. Syme, p. 81; Kahrstedt, "Kotys" (8), *PW* 11 (1922): 1554.

42. Syme, pp. 73–74. Jacques Schwartz, "Pompeius Macer et la jeunesse d'Ovide," *Revue de Philologie* 25 (1951): 192–93, argues that Macer was the father of Ovid's second wife, but the exact relationship cannot be determined. See Froesch, *Epistulae,* p. 218 n.394.

43. Syme, pp. 78–79.

44. Benedum, p. 71. He gives a detailed analysis of the poem, pp. 65–127. Cf. also Thomsen, pp. 158–60, 186.

45. Kenney, p. 49. Cf. Salvatore d'Elia, *Ovidio* (Naples: Istituto Editoriale del Mezzogiorno, 1959), pp. 416–17.

46. Nagle, pp. 86–87.

47. For this reason the transposition of *P.* 2.11 to a position following *P.* 3.4 proposed by Froesch, *Epistulae,* pp. 136–39, is not convincing. Although moving the poem would produce a perfect symmetry for the collection (each Cotta Maximus poem offset from the next by three intervening elegies), the effect of the juxtaposition of *P.* 2.11 and 3.1 would be lost. Cf. Barsby, p. 47 n.15. On the programmatic function of *P.* 3.1, see Thomsen, pp. 114, 122–23.

48. Froesch, *Epistulae,* pp. 157–62.

49. Froesch, *Epistulae,* pp. 44–46, 108, 128, and *Dichter,* pp. 13–14, accepts Ovid's desire to praise his friends as his main purpose in publishing the collection.

50. Nagle, p. 145.

51. See Harry B. Evans, "Ovid's Apology for *Ex Ponto* 1–3," *Hermes* 104 (1976): 103–12.

CHAPTER VII

1. For the chronology, see Wheeler, pp. xxxiv–xxxv; Syme, pp. 46–47; and Froesch, *Epistulae,* pp. 53, 181–82 n.107–10.

2. Edgar Martini, *Einleitung zu Ovid* (Darmstadt: Wissenschaftliche Buchgesellschaft, 1970), p. 54; Martin Schanz and Carl Hosius, *Geschichte der römischen Literatur* (Munich, 1935), 2:247; Luck, 2:277; Froesch, *Epistulae,* pp. 53–54; and Barsby, p. 47 n.15; but cf. Syme, p. 156 n.3. We have no evidence that Jerome's date is in error. Ovid's reference at *Fast.* 1.223–26 to Tiberius's restoration of a temple of Janus in A.D. 18 does not contradict the date; the poet could well have known about the temple before that year. See Wheeler, p. xxxvii; Fränkel, pp. 162–63, 253–55; and Froesch, *Epistulae,* pp. 181–82 n.111.

3. For his career, see Syme, pp. 157–62.

4. Nagle, p. 98.

5. Syme, p. 81.

6. Wheeler, p. 470, gives yet another means of inserting the name into elegy, reading all first three syllables as long. Ovid does not include this possibility, perhaps because its metrical violence would detract from the playful tone of his poem.

7. Fränkel, pp. 158–59; and Wilkinson, pp. 364–65, interpret them as autobiographical; Nagle, p. 167, and Thomsen, p. 212, consider them a rhetorical challenge to Roman readers.

8. See Syme, pp. 80–81; Otto Skutsch, "Cornelius" (369), *PW* 4 (1901): 1509–10; Willy Morel, ed., *Fragmenta Poetarum Romanorum* (Stuttgart: Teubner, 1963), pp. 116–19, for fragments of his works.

9. Syme, pp. 82–83.

10. Syme, pp. 89–90.

11. Syme, pp. 88–89. See Morel, *Fragmenta,* pp. 115–16, for twenty-three extant hexameters on the North Sea storm in A.D. 16.

12. Aristotle *Problemata* 23.6; Polybius 4.42; and Chr. Danoff, "Pontos Euxeinos," *PW,* supp. 9 (1962): 930–32. John J. Gahan, "Ovid: The Poet in Winter," *Classical Journal* 73 (1978): 200–202 takes no account of this fact. For detailed discussion of the poem, see Thomsen, pp. 263–96.

13. Syme, p. 80; Gerth, "Junius Gallio" (77), *PW* 10 (1919): 1035–39.

14. Luck, 2:184. Cf. Syme, p. 81 n.5.

15. Nagle, pp. 133–40.
16. Fränkel, p. 158, 250 n.5, seems to accept the poem as real; Wilkinson, pp. 363–64; and Syme, p. 225, consider it literary fiction. Nagle, p. 138 n.42, considers the question irrelevant to understanding the poem.
17. See Dino Adamesteanu, "Sopra il *Geticum libellum* (*Pont.* IV. 13)," *Ovidiana*, pp. 391–95; Eugene Lozovan, "Ovide et le bilinguisme," *Ovidiana*, pp. 386–403; and N. I. Herescu, "*Poeta Getes*," *Ovidiana*, pp. 404–5.
18. Nagle, pp. 133–40.
19. Cf. Nagle, pp. 163–65, who reads *P.* 4.16.1–4 as a "complaint" and interprets the entire elegy as "apotropaic," to avert the influence of Livor. Yet Ovid's opening, as well as his catalog of poets, is confident in tone; only in the concluding lines does a note of bitterness appear.
20. Nagle, p. 165.
21. For this rededication, see Franz Bömer, ed., *P. Ovidius Naso Die Fasten* (Heidelberg: Carl Winter Universitätsverlag, 1957) 1:17–18.

CHAPTER VIII

1. Cf. Carl Ganzenmüller, "Aus Ovids Werkstatt," *Philologus* 70 (1911): 247–311, 397–437.
2. Nagle, p. 161; Luck, 2:324–25.
3. Nagle, pp. 161–62.
4. Wilkinson, pp. 359–60. Cf. Dickinson, p. 186, who attempts to answer the charge of homogeneity by arguing that it is deliberate: Ovid seeks to convey the monotony of Tomis through the monotony of his poetry.
5. On exaggeration, see Barsby, p. 46; on uneven quality, see Nagle, p. 174.
6. See Georg Luck, "Notes on the Language and Text of Ovid's *Tristia*," *Harvard Studies in Classical Philology* 65 (1961): 243–61.
7. Syme, p. 227, commends the poet for his "industry, tenacity and style."

INDEX